Blank Forms   08
TRANSMISSIONS FROM THE PLEROMA

Wacoan Wins National Contest

Eleven-year-old Jerry Hunt, son of Mr. and Mrs. C. E. Hunt of 3620 Trice Avenue, was awarded first - rating gold medal in the recent National P i a n o Recording Festival, sponsored by the National Guild of Piano Teachers.

The first-rating award has been won by only two other Wacoans, John Mack Ousley of 301 North Fortieth Street and Betty Bob Dave of 3024 Alexander Avenue.

Jerry had been taking piano only three years when he made the recording for the annual contest. A mild - mannered, soft-spoken lad, Jerry touches the keyboard with sensitive fingers. Sometimes, he tries his hand at his own compositions.

"I just hear them in my mind," Jerry said. "I don't whistle them or hum them or anything. I just find them on the piano.

"Sometimes I will go to a movie and the music will remind me of something."

Jerry's other love is science. When he's not playing the piano, he is often pouring over biology or botany books or experimenting with his chemistry set. Jerry hopes to study both science and music when he grows up.

Jaycees to Hear About Salk, Polio

Dr. N. M. Atkins, director of the city-county health unit, and Dr. George Millington, orthopedic surgeon, will talk to Junior Chamber of Commerce at noon Thurs-

"Wacoan Wins National Contest," *Waco Times-Herald*, May 4, 1955.

INTRODUCTION
Lawrence Kumpf

Transmissions from the Pleroma is the first retrospective exhibition dedicated to the work of the maverick Texas composer Jerry Hunt (1943–1993). This book of the same title—a catalog of sorts—is one in an ongoing series of publications, records, and performance projects by Blank Forms exploring Hunt's life and work. Outside of Dallas, the city he lived in or near for his entire life, Hunt was mostly known for his frenetic and oblique approach to performance. His practice gained national and international attention in the '80s at venues like New York's Experimental Intermedia, the Kitchen, and Roulette, and Eindhoven's Het Apollohuis, as well as at festivals such as New Music America, which annually showcased and commissioned work from regional composers in different cities across the US and Canada from 1979 until 1990. While Hunt was an extremely active musician and talented self-promoter from the time he was a teenager, his conscious choice to live and work in Texas—first in Dallas and then, just as he was gaining national recognition, in a remote location outside the town of Canton—would contribute to his obscurity and his mystery. Despite having cracked into the new music circuit in the '80s, Hunt performed in public only a handful of times each year. The frequency of these appearances increased gradually until his premature death, a few days shy of his fiftieth birthday, put an end to a practice that seemed to be almost entirely dependent upon Hunt's presence as the performer. Hunt anticipated his death and took measures for the posthumous presentation of his performances in video renditions, some of which were completed and posthumously distributed as *Four Video Translations* (1994), a commercially available VHS; some have yet to be released, and still others were planned but never made. Hunt, though, was destined to relative obscurity. Like Maryanne Amacher and Ralston Farina, Hunt occupied a place in the mind of devotees who had seen him perform, achieving a legendary status despite making work that resisted documentation by design or intention. The second half of the '90s saw a number of posthumous "collaborations" with Hunt utilizing fragments of his audio and video. *Song Drapes*, a CD produced by John Zorn's Tzadik label in 1999, combined a series of Hunt's "precomposed accompaniments to unspecified text," meant to be utilized by vocalists in performance, with new singing by Hunt's collaborator Karen Finley, his friend Shelley Hirsch, and Mike Patton of the alternative rock band Faith No More. A video work titled *Telephone Calls to the Dead* (1994) by the new media ensemble 77 Hz premiered at New York's Experimental Intermedia as part of a Hunt memorial there, and Hirsch's *For Jerry* (1999) was performed at the Whitney Museum of American Art and at the Hebbel-Theater in Berlin; both utilized video produced by Hunt during his lifetime.

Perhaps the most important contributor to Hunt's legacy has been Michael Schell, a member of 77 Hz, who made the Jerry Hunt Home Page website. The site collects a number of interviews and texts on Hunt as well as a list of works based on notes that Hunt himself compiled shortly before his death; while incomplete it serves as a guidebook to terrain that would otherwise be difficult to navigate. Though the relationship between Hunt's late compositions and scoring is unclear, he certainly produced elaborately notated, though incredibly opaque, scores for much of his work throughout the '60s and '70s. Because Hunt saw each performance as completely unique, disregarding fidelity and repeatability, his scores served as sketches or guides for a multitude of possible paths that might be layered and folded onto one another, at times literally, through the use of playback and sampling of previous iterations. While most of his scores have been lost, we have managed to collect a handful of them during our research for this project. David Rosenboom's essay in this volume, "Drop Line . . . I Know I Don't Know," unpacks some performance strategies he used to approach early Hunt scores found in the David Tudor collection at the Getty Research Institute. In 2004, The Barton Workshop, an ensemble led by James Fulkerson, Hunt's longtime collaborator and primary interpreter during his lifetime, produced *Phalba* (Tzadik), an album of four Hunt scores. While Hunt worked with a number of instrumentalists in his lifetime, including Joseph Celli, Jane Henry, and Lois Svard, his two-decade-long relationship with Fulkerson was the most sustained and significant.

Transmissions from the Pleroma would not have been possible without the dedicated work of Hunt's friends and collaborators, who have kept his memory alive. All of the effort that has gone into this exhibition and publication has built on their care and dedication. Rod Stasick has maintained the Hunt archives for the past three decades in conjunction with Hunt's partner Stephen Housewright. Housewright's memoir, *Partners*, self-published in 1995 and re-released by Blank Forms Editions last December, provides an intimate portrait of Hunt and the time the two of them spent together following their meeting in an eighth grade music class. This project would not have been possible without *Partners* and Housewright's assiduous work organizing and sharing an abundance of materials with us, including an incredible, recently discovered stash of photographs and ephemera from the 1950s and '60s contained in Hunt's mother's scrapbooks.

I want to extend my sincere gratitude to my collaborator in this project, Tyler Maxin, for his incredible contributions to this initiative. We would like to thank Shelley Hirsch for her constant encouragement and for consistently championing Jerry Hunt's work. I also want to thank Ilan Volkov, who introduced me to Hunt's practice. In writing our essay for this volume, Tyler and I conducted a number of interviews with Hunt's friends and collaborators, including BL Lacerta (Robert Price, David Anderson, Maurice Hood, and Les Gay), Guy De Bièvre, Maria Blondeel, Sally Bowden, David Dowe, Werner Durand, Karen Finley, James Fulkerson, Gordon Hoffman, Phil Hughes, Robert Michael Keefe, Philip Krumm, Annea Lockwood, Alvin Lucier, David Rosenboom, Joel Ryan, Michael Schell, Ron Snider, Barton Weiss, Rodney Waschka II, and Jerry Willingham. We also received information and support from Stephen Beck, Joseph Celli, George Cisneros, Nora Day, Paul DeMarinis, Joseph Franklin, Jane Henry, Gene De Lisa, Scott Macaulay, Victor

Masayesva Jr., Jack Massing, Gordon Monahan, Paul Morris, Phill Niblock, Matthias Osterwold, Stephen C. Ruppenthal, Bob Ray Sanders, Werner Schroeder, Hilary Srere, Mark Srere, Shawn Sterling, Pat Strange, Lois Svard, Ed Tannenbaum, David Weinstein, Larry White, and Laurel Wyckoff. Jerry Hunt's longtime friend and collaborator Ron Snider passed away during the making of this book, but we are extremely grateful to have had the opportunity to interview him at the onset of our research. We received valuable materials from Annalise Welte and Nancy Perloff at the Getty Research Institute in Los Angeles; Jon Dieringer at Electronic Arts Intermix (EAI) in New York; Jonathan Hiam at the New York Public Library for the Performing Arts; Hartmut Jörg at ZKM | Center for Art and Media in Karlsruhe, Germany; Katie Salzmann at Texas State University in San Marcos, Texas; Chloe Gerson at Brandeis University in Waltham, Massachusetts; Mary Manning at the University of Houston; and Chris Bohling at the University of Kansas in Lawrence. We would also like to thank Lucy Flint, Heather Holmes, and Dana Kopel for their insightful edits to the texts in this publication, and our interns Parker Allen, Clarice Lee, Camila Santos Escamez, and Guy Weltchek for their indispensable assistance across these interrelated projects.

This volume is the result of many years of research and conversation, bringing together a mix of primary sources with new reflections on Hunt's practice. It is preceded by the publication of Housewright's memoir, *Partners*; a vinyl reissue of Hunt's final album, *Ground: Five Mechanic Convention Streams*; and the release of the boxed set *Irida Records: Hybrid Musics from Texas and Beyond, 1979–1986*, which includes a substantial booklet featuring new essays on Hunt's compositions and his efforts as the proprietor of an independent music label. Taken together, these records, books, concerts, exhibition, and ongoing efforts to place Hunt's archive in a public collection comprise a multipronged approach to considering Hunt's work and supporting his legacy.

Lawrence Kumpf
New York, Winter 2021

TRANSMISSIONS FROM THE PLEROMA
Lawrence Kumpf and Tyler Maxin

Hunt with students and an instructor, 1960. The handwritten dedication reads, FOR JERRY, AFTER A VERY GOOD CONCERT, MAY 15 '60, FROM PAUL VAN KATWIJK. Photographer unknown.

Jerry Hunt was a beguiling presence in North American composition until his untimely death in 1993. At a moment when rigorous electronic music was frequently relegated to insular academic departments and downtown urban art scenes, Hunt was anomalous: a college dropout with a largely autodidactic feel for the musical avant-garde, he spent the majority of his career living in a converted barn in rural Texas, about an hour outside of Dallas. Traveling cross-country (and later throughout Western Europe), Hunt became something of a fixture on the 1980s circuit of new music festivals and conferences.

A typical Hunt performance would foreground the composer himself. Hunt, strikingly gangly and sporting a dramatic comb-over and suit, would illuminate himself with loose light bulbs, gesticulate wildly, make guttural noises, babble, and enter prolonged trancelike episodes. He would interact with an arsenal of prearranged objects—wooden wands, chimes, bells, and found knick-knacks—handling each with ceremonial gravity. Even the marmite suitcase he traveled with would frequently wind up a part of the act as a percussive instrument. Hunt's motions would trigger an array of clever, self-designed technical configurations: sensors adapted from phonograph cartridges and infrared burglar alarms would allow him to control dense walls of electronic sound or initiate samples from afar. Listeners were often perplexed by the relationship between Hunt's gesticulations and the sounds he conjured, an effect the composer honed through translations and delays. Later, he would employ microchips swiped from computer chess modules and optical discs for increasingly sophisticated processes.

Audiences were often unsure what to think of Hunt's spectacles. Much was made of his interest in the occult, a boyhood fascination that persistently informed his compositional framework. Despite having discarded any serious mystical practice by his early twenties, Hunt based his electronic setups on John Dee's Enochian Tablets, and references to Rosicrucian magic are found scattered throughout his work. Commenters would frequently compare Hunt's performance style to that of a shaman, televangelist, or a colorful variation thereof. Gordon Monahan, for instance, referred to him as a "weirdo psycho-religious Texorcist."[1] In some ways, Hunt courted this mystique. His composer biographies and program notes were written in notoriously oblique language that melded technical and spiritual jargon, conceptualizing his pieces as self-contained "transactional systems." But in other ways, the composer felt perennially misunderstood: "The critics [are] baffled yet moved, describing what Jerry did and [their] own reaction to it, but [are] unable to say how the piece worked or what, exactly, it was about or why it impressed him so," Hunt's life partner, Stephen Housewright, has recounted. "Of course, favorable criticism pleased him, but he often told me even that failed to convey what it was he thought he was doing."[2]

Hunt's flair for embellishment and humor, oscillating between registers of self-mythologizing and self-deprecation, belies the depth of his work. A student of American experimentalism, Hunt spent the better part of his teens absorbing the innovations of John Cage and his disciples, exhausting local score libraries and soliciting compositions by mail. By his mid-twenties, Hunt had grown skeptical of Cage's pedantic teachings and rejected the composer's music while retaining an admiration for his social philosophy. Hunt's later outsider status allowed him a bemused ambivalence toward the whole enterprise of musical conceptualism. "You don't go to a concert hall to hear sounds," he would tell William Duckworth curtly in an unpublished interview conducted in preparation for the book *Talking Music* (1995)—withheld perhaps due to Hunt's contrarianism. "The idea of music as sound is a funny notion that a lot of ideas about music in the last forty years have gotten tricked up on." In another interview, he was even more frank:

> I think many of the problems of art from about 1960 belong to what I call "The Cow Tail-Up" syndrome. If you watch the cow when it urinates, it lifts its tail and there is this stream of hot urine that comes out. After a while it's over and the tail comes down. It seems to me that most current art is of this kind. Tail comes up; there's a flow. Everyone watches the flow, estimates the quantity and the look of the flow. The tail goes down: that was a piece. And in a little while another one comes up and it urinates in a different color, a different quantity. The only thing that characterizes it is its continuity and the fact that you can perceive it as it is happening. You showed up and you left. It seems to me that people like Phil Glass and Robert Wilson don't solve this problem at all. Pina Bausch doesn't either.[3]

Hunt had come of age at a time in which new paradigms— post-Cagean music, Fluxus, intermedia, and recent technologies— had opened up vast possibilities for composition. But for Hunt, this came with its own set of limitations. His confounding theatrics, more than simply barnstorming incantations, were part of an effort

14

A

Recital of Improvisational Compositions

by

Jerry Hunt & Phil Hughes

July 21, 1961   Oak Cliff Society of Fine Arts Auditorium

8:15 P. M.   401 North Rosemont

I

Selbsttödtung.................Hunt

Jerry Hunt, Piano

Spiritus Niger.................Hunt

Lashtal.......................Hunt

Jerry Hunt, Piano
Don Hall, Percussion
Phil Hughes, Contrabass

Enochian Calls XI--XVI..........Hunt

Jerry Hunt, Piano

INTERMISSION

II

Fragments I....................Hughes

Fragments II...................Hughes

Jerry Hunt, Piano

III

Incidental Music to
"Leda (or The Glory of Blessed Darkness)"
by Pierre Louys..........Hughes

Jerry Hunt, Piano
Phil Hughes, Reader

Spoken commentary on the compositions and on improvisation in the arts will be

given by Mr. Hughes and Mr. Hunt.

to transcend the emerging norms of what would come to be known as "new music" in search of novel modes of expression. His attempts would take him variously into video, dance, sound installation, and performance art, and jut into explorations of cybernetics, religious experience, narrative, and the grain of American life. Echoing the sentiments of Cage as well as the self-determinism of occultist Aleister Crowley, Hunt wrested a personal, self-contained compositional language from the elements available to him, explaining, "Like a lot of Americans I think what we have to do is self-invention, I'll just invent myself as a composer and I'll use music in this way as this mechanism for inquiry of various kinds—sometimes turned in on yourself, which I think is a tendency in American art, to just spend your entire life figuring yourself out, as if the world cares."[4]

*　　*　　*

Jerry Edward Hunt was by all available accounts a precocious child. He was born in Waco, Texas, on November 30, 1943, to Clarence Edward "Mike" Hunt, a regional sales manager for an evaporated-milk company, and Johnnie Imogene "Jean" Hunt, an executive secretary for a petroleum company. Jean Hunt recalled that as an infant he harbored a fascination with light bulbs.[5] His abilities manifested themselves early, including an aptitude for piano and a deep studiousness. While a boy, he commandeered a mail-order radio course that his grandfather was enrolled in, inspiring a life-long interest in electronics tinkering. Awarded a gold medal by the National Guild of Piano Teachers at age eleven, Hunt responded to a question from a news reporter about his process for composing: "I just hear them in my mind, I don't whistle them or hum them or anything. I just find them on the piano."[6]

Aside from music, Hunt was attracted to esoterica, exploring the spiritual philosophies of Vedanta and Rosicrucianism in his early teens by poring over the relevant offerings at the public library and joining the Vedanta Society and Ancient and Mystical Order Rosæ Crucis by mail. He was soon inspired to launch his own correspondence course, taking out advertisements in the local paper and eventually attracting truth-seekers to his family home, much to the chagrin of his parents. Hunt channeled his experiences with mail-order religious organizations into his teenage affinity group the Fine Arts Music Society, run by himself (referred to as "The Instructor-Counselor"), his future life partner Stephen Housewright ("The Administrator"), and a revolving cast of classmates and friends. Emulating the structure of the religious enterprises that Hunt had joined as a preteen, down to the production of membership cards, the society published *Lachesis*, a quarterly publication featuring essays and reviews. A stunning piece of juvenilia, the journal introduced a number of elements that Hunt would carry through his artistic career. For starters, there was its title: named after the Greek Fate said to have "broken the thread of life," *Lachesis* was the first in a long line of references Hunt chose primarily for the sound of the word, enhanced by its mysterious mythological resonance. (Hunt named his dog after Hermes, the Greek messenger of the afterlife and the namesake of the "hermetic" philosophical tradition.)

Friends recall Hunt's virtuosity across musical styles, a muscle he no doubt flexed while performing at Veterans of Foreign Wars halls, cocktail parties, and clubs—gigs he picked up beginning in his mid-teens. He had frequent stints at the Montmartre Club, one of several strip joints found along Commerce Street in downtown Dallas, a stone's throw from Jack Ruby's Carousel Club, where Hunt also occasionally worked.[7] By the late 1950s, Hunt's musical interests were geared more toward contemporary new music—namely the work of Pierre Boulez, John Cage, and Karlheinz Stockhausen— though he never shied away from generating a little extra income by playing jazz and popular music. These worlds intersected, as Hunt would recount to friends later in life, when he treated dancers to performances of Stockhausen before the clubs opened to the public. Hunt also began to accompany the local duo Dick and Patty Hill, a trumpet player and soprano, respectively, who would pick up Hunt for shows while he was still a high-school student and with whom he would perform into the 1970s. As a jazz musician, Hunt admired the idiosyncratic voicing and spontaneity of Art Tatum, and often played in small groups around town with the vocalist Phillip Barbosa, the Ted Stanford trio, which included Ted's wife, Anita Stanford, and occasionally with the trumpeter and vocalist Bart Bartelmehs. In 1959, while rehearsing for a jazz gig that would take place at a local gay bar, Hunt contacted Philip Hughes, a bass player who would become a frequent collaborator throughout the '60s, enlisting him to join the ensemble. Hughes, Hunt, and the drummer Don Hall, would for a few brief years make up the Jerry Hunt Trio, an avant-garde jazz group that would perform Hunt's compositions in addition to the standard repertoire.[8] Hughes would later refer to Hunt as "the kind of musician you meet once in a lifetime."[9]

In 1961, Hunt and Hughes organized a recital at the Oak Cliff Society of Fine Arts in Dallas, presenting their own "improvisational compositions" before an audience of friends and family. The

A FESTIVAL OF CONTEMPORARY MUSIC

Thursday, April 11, 1963 8:00 p.m.
   John Cage; Roman Haubenstock-Ramati;
   Morton Feldman; Henri Pousseur;
   Toshiro Ishiyanagi.

Saturday, April 20, 1963 3:00 p.m.
   Morton Feldman; Earle Brown; Karlheinz
   Stockhausen; Christian Wolff; Roman
   Haubenstock-Ramati.

Thursday, April 25, 1963 8:00 p.m.
   Sylvano Bussotti; Karlheinz Stockhausen;
   Cornelius Cardew; Mauricio Kagel;
   Morton Feldman; John Cage.

Friday, May 3, 1963 8:00 p.m.
   John Cage; Mauricio Kagel

All programs will take place in the
   auditorium of the
   Dallas Public Library

THE DALLAS PUBLIC LIBRARY

Library Music Committee

presents

A FESTIVAL OF CONTEMPORARY MUSIC

Program I

Library Auditorium

April 2, 1963   8:00 p.m.

PROGRAM

Interpolation (1959) – – – – – – – – – – – – – – Roman Haubenstock-Ramati 1919-
        Carol Regland, flute

Folio 1953/54 – – – – – – – – – – – – – – – – – Earle Brown 1928-
  Four Systems for Piano
  December, 1952

     Jerry E. Hunt, piano; Patrick Simpson, violoncello; Gerald Warfield,
     oboe; Eugene Vollen, baritone horn; Joseph Davis, clarinet; Charles
     Pearson, guitar; Tim Wilburn, celeste.

Sonata No. 3 (1960) – – – – – – – – – – – – – – – – – Pierre Boulez 1925-
  Trope
     Jerry E. Hunt, piano

INTERMISSION

Atlantis (1959) – – – – – – – – – – – – – – – – – – Morton Feldman 1926-

     Gerald Warfield, conductor; Sharon Wiegel, flute; Albert Gower,
     bass clarinet; Thomas Wirtel, trumpet; Larry Blassingame, horn;
     Tony Valentine, trombone; Robert McGrew, xylophone; Dennis
     Alexander, vibraphone; Patrick Simpson, violoncello;
     Margaret O'Dell, piano.

Cartridge Music (1960) – – – – – – – – – – – – – – – John Cage 1912-

     Margaret O'Dell, Gerald Warfield, Jerry E. Hunt, percussion.

Program for A Festival of Contemporary Music, Dallas Public Library, April 2, 1963.

concert in many ways presaged Hunt's future work. The program notes announced that "Mr. Hunt and Mr. Hughes" would be offering "spoken commentary on the compositions and on improvisation in the arts." The pedagogical aspect of the program may have been a considered choice given what was likely the adventurous nature of the young artists' work. Or perhaps the commentary was an early example of Hunt's performative exegeses—clarifications of his work that tended to only further confuse his listeners due to his fast-talking, idiosyncratic, and technical turns of phrase. More a mirror than a cipher, Hunt's pataphysical musings on the contingent and temporal nature of his practices, the systems behind them, and the conditions of their presentation maintained a high level of abstraction.

Hunt and Hughes's program for the Oak Cliff recital reveals the duo's intellectual bent in 1961. Hunt was clearly still under the spell of Rosicrucianism. The title of "Enochian Calls XI–XVI" (ca. 1961) alludes to John Dee's Enochian grids,[10] which Hunt would use as an aleatoric device and reference in later compositions such as "*Sur* (Doctor) John Dee" (1966). "Lashtal" (ca. 1961) refers to the "thelemic magick" of Aleister Crowley, another writer (and spiritual charlatan) with whom Hunt became infatuated around 1960.[11] The program concludes with Hunt's interpretations of Hughes's "Fragments I" and "Fragments II" (both ca. 1961) and an improvised "incidental music" piece laid down behind Hughes's reading of Pierre Louÿs's erotic poem "Leda (Or the Glory of Blessed Darkness)" (1898). As Hughes recalls, the concert went off without a hitch, though he remembers feeling a tinge of unease reading Louÿs's poem to the Dallas audience, mostly friends and family, on account of the presence of the Oak Cliff caretaker's young daughter in the front row.

In Hunt's late teens, he studied with local instructors, notably the distinguished pianists Silvio Scionti and Paul van Katwijk, the latter of whom had been a director of the Dallas Symphony Orchestra as well as a dean at Southern Methodist University (SMU). Later in life, Hunt expressed some indifference toward their tutelage, recalling, "The people I studied with were really quite incidental and accidental." When Hunt began to think about college, van Katwijk encouraged him to study under the premiere Béla Bartók interpreter György Sándor, then teaching at SMU. An informal audition was arranged, and an impressed Sándor offered Hunt a full scholarship. Shortly before Hunt was to matriculate, Sandor became embroiled in a scandal involving two female students,

BRANDEIS UNIVERSITY

The Brandeis University Music Club

presents

A Concert of New Music

by

JERRY E. HUNT, Pianist

assisted by

Phillip Krum, *pianist*

Alvin Lucier, *conductor*

and the

Brandeis University Chamber Ensemble

Friday, November 15, 1963   Slosberg Recital Hall

8:30 P. M.

Program for A Concert of New Music, Brandeis University, Waltham, Massachusetts, November 15, 1963.

precipitating his departure from the school and quashing the under-the-table arrangement with Hunt.

In the absence of a formal mentorship, Hunt was voracious in his independent exploration of cutting-edge music, engaging a number of composers by mail. He turned to the work of John Cage and David Tudor, both of whom he approached, apparently unsuccessfully, as potential teachers.[12] Hunt familiarized himself with Cage's work by buying scores from Edition Peters USA, and in 1964 he met him at Texas Tech University in Lubbock at a performance by Tudor.[13] This encounter sparked a lifelong correspondence, and Hunt often hosted Cage on his later trips to Texas. In his late teens, Hunt also communicated with a number of Fluxus composers, most notably George Maciunas, acquiring unique scores that he would perform and premiere. According to his friend and collaborator James "Jim" Fulkerson, Hunt also sought out Stockhausen as the German composer was stopping over at the Houston airport, hoping to clarify some of the pitch constellations on an unpublished score Hunt had received from Universal Edition. "So, unannounced, Jerry drove down to meet him. He explained the problem and handed Stockhausen the score. Stockhausen held it up, looked at the constellation, closed his eyes, touched his hand to forehead and said, 'The pitches there should be . . .' and proceeded to name all of them."[14] Hunt, his friends would recount, went on to premiere and often perform a number of Stockhausen's "Klavierstücke" compositions.

With Sándor and SMU out of the picture, Hunt followed Hughes to the University of North Texas (UNT), where on March 26, 1962, they shared billing for "A Program of American Experimental Music." The concert presented Hughes's "Fragments I–III" (1961) and Hunt's "Energy Discharges" (1962), along with Hunt's rendition of Earle Brown's "Four Systems" (1954) and John Cage's "Concert for Piano and Orchestra" (1957–58), as well as pieces for small ensembles by fellow students Morgan Powell and Gerald Warfield.[15] While many of Hunt's earliest student compositions relied on the straightforward application of compositional techniques such as serialism or atonality, some of the works on this program showcase his interest in arcana, such as his "Enochian Calls" series (ca. 1961) and "Energy Discharges." Much as Cage used the divination techniques of the *I Ching* to inform his work, Hunt began to experiment with Elizabethan magic as a compositional prompt, particularly the angelic tablets of Edward Kelley and John Dee. This device notably surfaces in the composer's first major works, "*Sur* (Doctor) John Dee" (1963) and "Tabulatura Soyga" (1965), graphic scores that pay

Hunt and Houston Higgins, ca. mid-1960s. Photographer unknown.

homage to the scholars' diagrams. Hughes soon took off for graduate studies at Brandeis University in Waltham, Massachusetts, and Hunt, dissatisfied with the curriculum at UNT, dropped out after a few semesters: "They thought [twelve-tone was] a waste of time, he could do that at home with a hand calculator or something, but he certainly shouldn't have to do it here. What we want him to learn is sixteenth- to eighteenth-century counterpoint. Those rules never made a lot of sense to me because it seemed like . . . they were conventions that had outlived the 1890s ideas."[16] Hunt complemented his studies by experimenting with psychedelics and amphetamines, responding in part to his mystical bent: his final semester in Denton ended unceremoniously after a bad trip inspired a fellow classmate to streak, leading to a run-in with the police.

Hunt resettled in Dallas, first living with his parents and then with Housewright and friends Steven Jamieson and Elizabeth Cherry. After Housewright went to college in the fall, Hunt eventually moved back in with his parents. While dedicating himself to rigorous independent study in contemporary music, he continued to earn his living by gigging at various clubs and presenting complex programs of new music around town. In April 1963, he organized an ambitious five-day program at the Dallas Public Library, presenting works by Pierre Boulez, Earle Brown, Sylvano Bussotti, John Cage, Cornelius Cardew, Morton Feldman, Roman Haubenstock-Ramati, Toshi Ichiyanagi, Mauricio Kagel, Bo Nilsson, Karlheinz Stockhausen, and Christian Wolff with musicians from the University of North Texas Symphony Orchestra and the Dallas Symphony Orchestra.[17] In addition to acting as musical director of the encyclopedic event, Hunt performed in almost all of the pieces, and on some evenings was the sole performer for the entire program.

At a pataphysics conference that same year organized by Roger Shattuck, Hunt met Philip Krumm, a San Antonio–based composer two years his senior. Inspired by a *Time* magazine article on John Cage and encounters with Philip Corner (then stationed at Fort Sam Houston), Krumm had been organizing new music concerts in South Central Texas with his high-school classmate Robert Sheff (later known as "Blue" Gene Tyranny). Hunt and Krumm became fast friends, and within months they traveled to Brandeis University at the invitation of Phil Hughes to perform a concert of works by Ashley, Cage, and themselves. (On the way, they stopped off in New York and stayed with Krumm's friends Dick Higgins and Alison Knowles.) Alvin Lucier, who had just started teaching at Brandeis, conducted the ensemble; he has recalled that their concert, the first of its kind at the school, caused "quite a stir." "Do I remember correctly," he recently wondered, "that they [had] strewn the concert hall with toilet paper?"[18] Audio recordings of the concert corroborate the prankishness, ending with an uproarious boogie-woogie performance by Hunt to the distant sounds of ersatz chickens and audience laughter.[19] The pair was set to perform a new music concert in Dallas a week later, on November 23, but their plans were aborted by the assassination of President John F. Kennedy.[20]

Benefiting from a knack for showmanship that became evident early in his career, Hunt was able to garner a bit of press for his relatively obscure engagements throughout Texas. Both the *Dallas Morning News* and the *Dallas Times Herald* covered his Festival of Contemporary Music at the Dallas Public Library in 1963. The following year, a critic for the *Fort Worth Star-Telegram* wrote a somewhat quizzical response to a recent Hunt recital that gives a window into Hunt's local reception:

> The fun and games began when Hunt, a 21-year-old composer-pianist from Dallas with the studious air of a divinity student, strode briskly to the piano and began to adjust an electronic sounding device above the keyboard. The audience fell hushed, anticipating the music to come. Instead of playing, however, the performer continued to putter with the gadget, using curiously stylized gestures and movements. Then, with a feather duster, he began to tidy up the piano's legs and top. "Look—he's going to take it apart," a shocked whisper floated up from the rear of the hall as Hunt began to loosen and retighten the hinges of the lid with a screwdriver. Turning abruptly, the pianist seized a plastic-bottomed chair and, with a startling clang, dumped a handful of metal junk scraps on the seat. Still wearing a stiff poker face he shook hands with spectators in the first row and started a bent nail passing through the audience. Returning to the piano, Hunt bowed formally, the hint of a grave smile dancing in his eyes. He had just "played" the first "new music" selection on the program, George Brecht's "Eight Piano Transcriptions."[21]

Hunt often mused on his attempts to present obscure and demanding pieces of contemporary music to uninitiated audiences in the

MUSIC SINCE 1950   DALLAS COLLEGE   FALL 1966

LECTURES WITH MUSIC - DAVID AHLSTROM

GUEST PERFORMERS: JERRY HUNT, HOUSTON HIGGINS,
THE JUVEY GOMEZ TRIO

PROGRAM ONE: EARLY TWENTIETH CENTURY MUSIC

SEPT. 21, 1966   JERRY HUNT, PIANIST

ERIK SATIE	VIRITABLE PRELUDE FLASQUES (POUR UNE CHEIN) 1. SEVERE REPRIMANDE 2. SEUL A LA MAISON 3. ON JOUE (AUG. 1912)
ARNOLD SCHOENBERG	SIX LITTLE PIANO PIECES OP. 19 (1913)
ERIK SATIE	VIEUX SEQUINS ET VIELLES CUIRASS (1913) CHEZ LE MARCHAND D'OR (VENIS L3 C.) DANSE CHIRASSEE (PERIOD GRECQUE) LA DEFAIT DES CIMBRES (CAUCHEMAR)
IGOR STRAVINSKY	PIANO-RAG-MUSIC (JUNE 1919)
ERIK SATIE	PREMIER MINUET (1920)
DARIUS MILHAUD	SAUDADES DO BRAZIL - (1922) SUITE OF DANCES FOR PIANO 1. SOROCABA; 3. LEME; 5. IPANEMA 7. CORCOVADO; 11. LARANJEIRAS

- - - - - - - - - -

PROGRAM TWO: OTHER EARLY TWENTIETH CENTURY MUSIC

SEPT. 28, 1966   JERRY HUNT, PIANIST; HOUSTON HIGGINS, CLARINETIST

ALBAN BERG	FOUR PIECES FOR CLARINET AND PIANO	(1913)
IGOR STRAVINSKY	THREE PIECES FOR SOLO CLARINET	(1918)
BELA BARTOK	MIKROKOSMOS	(1926-37)V.V.
DARIUS MILHAUD	SONATINE FOR CLARINET AND PIANO	(1927)
ANTON WEBERN	VARIATIONS FOR PIANO, OP. 27	(1936)
PAUL HINDEMITH	SONATA FOR CLARINET AND PIANO	(1939)

Program for David Ahlstrom's Lectures with Music, Dallas College, fall 1966, [1].

Dallas area, an experience that would color his own compositional practice and his understanding of the relationship between performer and audience. In an interview with Gordon Monahan years later, he recalled that he would often play Brecht's music to "prime up" the audience before going into the "big works," where he'd "rip the lid off [the piano] and throw the vibrator into it."[22] Throughout 1965, Hunt continued to perform his own work along with his new music repertoire. On a program at the Dallas Museum of Fine Arts, presented in conjunction with the local chapter of Mu Phi Epsilon, in 1965, Hunt performed Brecht's "Incidental Music" (1961), Ichiyanagi's "Music for Piano No. 2" (1959), Stockhausen's "Klavierstück VI," (1954–55/1961) Cage's "Variations III" (1962–63), and a work of his own, "Unit 2 w/ stabile for continuous topogram" (ca. 1965). That same year, Krumm invited Hunt to participate in a television and radio simulcast on KLRN in Austin called *The Music Hour*, where Hunt performed one of his *Helix* pieces alongside an improvisatory saxophone piece by Ed Vizard. As Hunt's reputation grew, he began to expand his community of musicians in and around Dallas.

*   *   *

Through his piano instructor Paul van Katwijk, Hunt was introduced to David Ahlstrom, a former student of Henry Cowell and the conductor of the Dallas Symphony Orchestra. Ahlstrom also served as a faculty member at SMU, and in turn connected Hunt to a network of like-minded artists and musicians on campus. Toni Beck, a choreographer and head of the university's dance department, attended one of Hunt's recitals in the mid-1960s, and in 1966 hired him as the musical director of her dance company at SMU. He soon became her primary accompanist and later her company's music director; his duties ranged from routine mood music during her classes to intricately composed works for piano and electronics. He also met Houston Higgins, a clarinetist and composition student who would become Hunt's chief collaborator of the period, as well as Higgins's future wife, the vocalist Juliet "Jill" Leatherwood, who was not formally associated with the school but sang in its choir and studied independently with SMU faculty member Lloyd Pfautsch. Though Hunt lacked the typical credentials, he started teaching at the university in 1966 as a guest lecturer on contemporary piano music and served as the director of its Electronic Music program from 1967 to 1973.

Top: Hunt and Ron Snider, late 1960s or early '70s. Photographer unknown.
Bottom: Hunt with his electronics equipment, 1967. Photo: Staff photographer for the
Dallas Morning News.

On February 13, 1966, Ahlstrom invited Hunt to be the guest pianist for the Southwest premiere of Cage's "Atlas Eclipticalis" (1961–62) and "Winter Music" (1957), two of the composer's early aleatoric pieces.[23] The program also presented the world premiere of Gordon Mumma's "Le Corbusier" (1965), a new work commissioned by the SMU ensemble. Judging by Ahlstrom's program notes, it seems that Mumma was already familiar or in touch with Hunt, and had suggested that he be in charge of all the tape and electronic elements.[24] Ahlstrom, along with Hunt and Higgins, formed the Dallas Chamber Ensemble that same year and presented a program with the tenor Thomas Council in June that included a performance of Hunt's "*Sur* John Dee with Infrasolo 3 (Cadenza)" (ca. 1963).[25] (The program also promises a concert of Charles Ives piano music to be performed by Hunt the following Sunday.) The group would remain active for the next few years—its rotating members often included Leatherwood Higgins—presenting a new music repertoire of music by Feldman, Ives, and Cage mixed with Hunt's friends Philip Krumm and Philip Corner.

Hunt had already begun incorporating electronics into his own work as a student at UNT. Hughes recalls that when Hunt presented his piece "Energy Discharges" at the university in 1962, it included a taped electronic section whose execution was bungled by the technical assistants, Peggy O'Dell[26] and John Maus, who were confused about how the sound system worked and kept increasing the volume in the lobby to no effect in the auditorium.[27] While the Dallas Chamber Ensemble continued to present concerts, Hunt began to give multimedia performances in his capacity as musical director of the SMU dance department. These live collaborations were more adventurous than the rehearsals had been and foreshadowed Hunt's interest in interactive systems. An interview with the *Dallas Morning News* illustrated with a photograph of Hunt—"an intense 24 year old that talks almost as fast as he thinks" sitting by a cord-littered stack of oscillators and synthesizers—gives a taste of Hunt's interest in new technologies that would eventually "change the structures of the symphony orchestra completely."[28] The article goes on to describe Hunt and Beck's upcoming contribution to Dance '68, a program that took place at SMU on December 7 and 8, 1967. Their performance of "Through a Glass Darkly" (1967) was listed on the program with Hunt as the sole composer and Beck as choreographer, along with other personnel. "Hunt has taken some music he has written and coupled it with several new ideas. While the dancers on stage are creating the mood choreographed for them by Toni Beck, their movements will trigger various light and sound

Audio Visual Studio/Ensemble (Hunt and Houston Higgins), Highland Park Town Hall, Dallas, 1969.
Photographer unknown.

effects programmed by Hunt into various electronic devices. These effects are predictable and not improvisational although the same total effect that emerges during the first performance may not reappear during the second performance."[29]

In the fall of 1966, Ahlstrom delivered the series "Lectures with Music" at Dallas College and invited Higgins and Hunt to be the main instrumentalists interpreting the European and American music that illustrated Ahlstrom's points; for one lecture, "Jazz, First and Third Streams," Higgins and Hunt were joined by the Juvey Gomez Trio, a jazz outfit led by a former drummer for Gene Vincent.[30] The full program started with two lectures, both titled "Early Twentieth Century Music," that were focused on European composers such as Béla Bartók, Erik Satie, Arnold Schoenberg, and Igor Stravinsky. Next came the lecture "The European Experimentalists," on Boulez and Stockhausen. The fourth presentation (which may or may not have included Hunt) was a staged version of Robert Ashley's "Evening" from his opera *In Memoriam . . . KIT CARSON* (1963), performed by students in the class "Music and Theatre." The following week, Hunt gave recitals for the lecture "The American Experimentalists" that comprised works by Christian Wolff, Henry Cowell, and Cage, and ran an excerpt from a concert tape of the ONCE Group performing Ashley's symphony *In Memoriam . . . CRAZY HORSE* (1964) and Joseph Byrd's *Homage to Jackson Mac Low* (1965). The series concluded on November 16 with "a concert for greater Dallas" presented by Ahlstrom, Higgins, and Hunt, of over twenty-five works by Brecht, Cage, Mumma, Giuseppe Chiari, Walter De Maria (*Surprise Box*, 1960), Houston Higgins ("Golden Spoon," 1966), Hi-Red Center, Alison Knowles, Takehisa Kosugi, Mieko "Chieko" Shiomi, Tristan Tzara, Jacques Vaché, and Hunt himself ("Puncture [Pre Cis]," 1949[31] and "Jerry's Scrap Box and Tape Recorder," ca. 1966). In addition to what was listed on the program, the concert featured a number of "unannounced compositions by La Monte Young, Joseph Byrd, Jackson Mac Low, Nam June Paik, and others." The event, which was likely fairly raucous, boasted simultaneous and consecutive performances, a strategy that Hunt and Ahlstrom would use again the following year for a multimedia event with the SMU dance department, and a concept that resonates with Hunt's interest in sampling and memory as it informed later performances of his own work.[32] Hunt's dog, Hermes, also took part in the concert, realizing George Maciunas's "Music for Every Dog" (1961) and somehow taking part in Cage's "Fontana Mix" (1958).[33]

Hunt was beginning to make inroads with a national network of new music composers. In 1966, he traveled to the San Francisco Tape Music Center to realize some of his electronics-based pieces, and he eventually acquired a Buchla synthesizer. Through Krumm, who was studying at UC Davis, Hunt became privy to the nascent magazine *Source: Music of the Avant-Garde*, submitting three of his compositions to its inaugural issue in 1967. The magazine eventually published "*Sur* (Doctor) John Dee," although Hunt would later complain to Jim Fulkerson that the editors had mistakenly combined all three scores, mangling them to the point of incomprehensibility. Hunt was also beginning to catch the attention of local patrons: at a recital at the Oak Cliff Society of Fine Arts, he met Paul A. Srere, a noted biochemist, and Oz Srere, who both became crucial benefactors. He also became acquainted with Avlona and Douglas Taylor, the latter a pianist for the Dallas Symphony Orchestra and scholar of the Rubaiyat, who lent the group film projectors and non-Western instruments.[34]

Hunt's activities in the Dallas Chamber Ensemble were increasingly varied and boundary-pushing, and his loose affiliation of players was rechristened the Audio Visual Studio/Ensemble. Its membership expanded. In 1967, percussionist Ron Snider, then a student at UNT, reached out to Merrill Ellis, the head of the electronic music department, with questions about Earle Brown's composition "Hodograph I" (1959). Perplexed by the blank sections in the score, Snider asked, "What, what does this mean? What is this?" As Snider recalls, Ellis replied, "Well, I don't know. But I can tell you who would—this fellow in Dallas named Jerry Hunt."[35] Snider then approached Hunt, who did, in fact, understand how Brown utilized the sections. They struck up a friendship, and soon thereafter began formal collaborations. By 1967, the Ensemble included Hughes, Higgins and Leatherwood Higgins, and Ron Snider and his wife, Joan Snider. Gordon Hoffman, a highly skilled technician affiliated with Texas Instruments, served in an advisory capacity. The group's repertoire was becoming more far-flung: in 1970, Hunt and Higgins produced a concert of tape music and organ by the Dutch composer Ton Bruynèl.

Hunt and Higgins (and occasionally Hughes, once he returned to Dallas) pooled their resources for a shared studio space on Lovers Lane and Inwood, dubbed the Green Shack. Higgins contributed reel-to-reel players, while Hunt set up his Buchla and homemade oscillators. With the technical assistance of Hoffman, Hunt also hand-built more complex equipment, keeping up to date in advances in audio synthesis through his subscription to Bernie Hutchins's

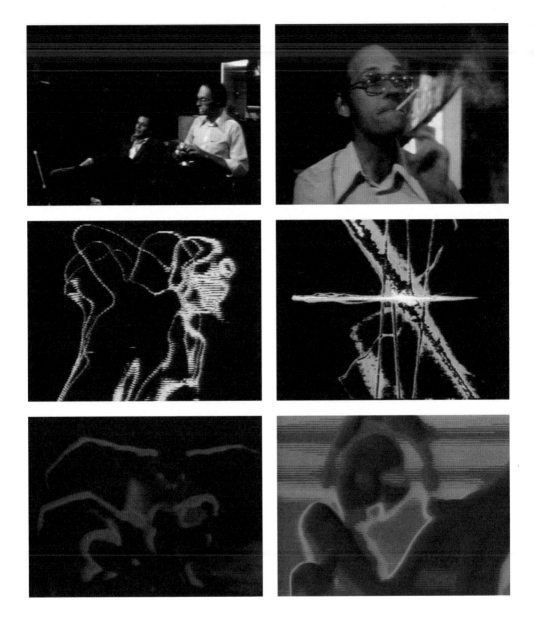

Stills from Jerry Hunt and David Dowe's *Procession*, 1973, video, color, sound, 30 minutes. Courtesy Electronic Arts Intermix (EAI), New York.

music engineer newsletter *Electronotes*. Composers must eat, and Hunt eased the financial strain of his experimental activity with more conventional money-making ventures. His mother had come into a modest windfall, which helped support him, and he continued to perform in bars and social halls. Hunt and Higgins also attempted to hawk their electronic music and composition services to local radio stations, a sideline that Hunt maintained until his final years, contributing synthesized music to industrial videos and public television.

* * *

In 1967, Hunt was brought on to direct a new electronic music program at SMU, and soon after his appointment was introduced by Beck's husband Paul Bosner, a television producer at KERA, to David Dowe, a young video artist on the faculty who was beginning to experiment with nonrepresentational televisual images using feedback and video synthesis. Dowe was fresh from San Francisco, where he worked as an intern for Brice Howard at the National Center for Experiments in Television (NCET), an incubator for the possibilities of TV funded by the Rockefeller Foundation and Corporation for Public Broadcasting. Dowe explained that their assignment at the center was to "make artful images and music in a new way, with electricity."[36] In addition to flirtations with commercial work, as well as Hunt's own explorations in developing systems for his compositions and performance, Dowe and Hunt's main activity was the creation and distribution of nonrepresentational videos for home viewing. NCET was in the process of establishing satellite labs across the United States, and in 1970 the two secured funding to establish the Video Research Center on campus in an unused underground space beneath the football stadium bleachers.

Hunt's own compositional voice was maturing, and in January 1972 the Audio Visual Studio/Ensemble performed his "Quaquaversal Transmission" at the studio of his friend the painter Salle Werner Vaughn. Unlike his prior compositions, which maintained a more traditional distance between composer and performer, this new piece was a "performance system"—a premeditated set of electronic relationships, some automated and some controlled, that triggered audio and visual phenomena devised specifically for the group. (In plainspeak, it was his electronics rig.) Through his association with *Source*, Hunt additionally had his scores published by Austin's Composer-Performers imprint and was able to reach the small but far-ranging international network of emerging experimental composers. That summer, the ensemble was set to perform at the International Carnival of Experimental Sound (ICES), an ambitious multiday festival produced by Harvey Matusow, his then-wife Annea Lockwood, and the editors of *Source* at the Roundhouse in London. The festival was a famously fraught endeavor: Matusow, a notorious huckster who had previously been an informant for the Federal Bureau of Investigations, had promised prepaid chartered airplanes for the global performers, which summarily fell through, and the trip was further complicated by Hunt misplacing his passport. Bandmates Ron and Joan Snider, foreseeing catastrophe, stayed back once the group reached New York, while Hunt and Higgins narrowly made it overseas. Their performances together were increasingly dramatic and performative; David Rosenboom, who attended the performance, has described Hunt "manipulating ropes, causing heavy objects to move over the heads of audience members and making extraordinary sounds along with video synthesis."[37]

Between 1973 and 1975, Hunt's efforts were focused primarily on his collaborations with David Dowe. Hunt helped design both the studio's synthesizer setup and Dowe's video tools, which included a rudimentary color quantizer, an oscilloscope, a primitive 3D transform module, and other synthesis technologies. The duo produced two taped works: *Procession* (1973), an abstract "electronic ballet" made with video synthesizers, featuring dancers Kim Pauley and Clyde Evans; and *Aur Resh* (1973), a video feedback piece for twelve cameras and fourteen monitors named after the Hebrew phrase for "let there be light." That same year, Hunt and Dowe also produced *A Visit to the Center*, a demonstration tape that showed the two artists and the technician Marvin Druckler tinkering with their studio setup and producing an improvised demo of plucky electronic country music.[38] These videos were included in a compendium of works in a nationally syndicated broadcast, and used in demonstrations of the Center's activities shown at the Carpenter Center for the Visual Arts in Cambridge, Massachusetts, and the Museum of Modern Art in New York as part of "Open Circuits: An International Conference on the Future of Television" in 1974.[39]

Hunt's worldview and work at the Video Research Center would take on metaphysical dimensions familiar to cybernetics devotees at the time, in keeping with his own past esoteric pursuits. Alongside the video works created in collaboration with Dowe, meant for wide distribution, Hunt started to use the duo's electronics rigs for his own compositional process: he developed two interrelated setups, one known as the Haramand Plane and the

Hunt and David Dowe, from an article in the *Dallas Times Herald* on the Video Research Center at Southern Methodist University (SMU), University Park, Texas, 1974. Photo: Paul Iverson.

Poster for The Metaphysical Circuit, Bob Hope Theatre, SMU, 1973.

other a derivative system, the numbered compositional series called the Cantegral Segment(s), which would form the basis for his live performances for the better part of the decade.[40] In 1977, *Synapse* magazine published Hunt's reflection on his and Dowe's audiovisual collaborations, which detailed the design of the custom-made interactive systems that enabled the Haramand Plane and Cantegral Segment(s).[41] The article alludes to Hunt's higher aspirations for these projects, notably his enthusiasm for the nascent possibilities of his interactive systems, which allowed for a dynamic interplay between visual and sonic outputs and inputs, creating a relationship that was more responsive than preprogrammed sequencers or randomizers. Hunt stresses that these systems are "responsive mediums (though not fully 'intelligent' in the cybernetic sense) of information *exchange* and *extension*."[42] He goes on to point out that his and Dowe's work with these systems had reoriented their understanding of, and approach to, composition. He describes "composition as performance," akin to improvisation within a set of variable conditions—a concept that resonates with his early scores. Hunt concludes the *Synapse* article by noting the parallels between his explorations with electronic systems and biological systems of perception: "Pattern-structuring formalities emerge which relate to a procedure which approaches one of my long felt enthusiasm for electronic means—an almost colloquial and at once multidimensional/global exchange of aspects of the perception of living."[43] A year prior, in an interview for *D, The Magazine of Dallas*, Hunt similarly connected his work with electronics to perception and consciousness: "Electronics is fascinating precisely because it's so close to us. It simulates how the human mind works: it's a flow of protons."[44]

While it should come as little surprise that Hunt was a card-carrying member of the Cybernetics Society at the time, his most direct exchange with the field came from his 1973 visit to Scotland with Dowe. Hunt had received funding from the Scottish Arts Council and the British Computer Society to develop "Haramand Plane: parallel/regenerative" (1973) that year, and the duo traveled to Edinburgh in August to realize a performance of the piece. While there, Hunt also presented a paper, "An Adaptive Controller System for Interactive Composition," at the Computer Arts Society–sponsored conference "Interact: Man Machine Society" at the University of Edinburgh. Here they most likely first encountered the animal geneticist Conrad Hal Waddington, a researcher at the University of Edinburgh since 1947, who had expressed interest in the duo's work at the Center. It is unclear who contacted whom first or whether Waddington was involved in their invitation to the conference. Though Dowe no longer recollects their exchange, in *A Visit to the Center* he and Hunt discuss their recent correspondence with Waddington. As Dowe recounts in the video, Waddington had explored a relevant phenomenon in his own research regarding the "random flow of electrons in the synaptic passages of animals and human beings," which Dowe interpreted as a study in "how we make sense of chaos." Dowe and Hunt speculated on the archetypal nature of the images they were producing—comparing them to mandalas or the patterns that appear on the inside of your eyelids when you gently press on them.

Before their trip to Scotland, the duo had been using their collaborative techniques in live performance. With funding from the Center, they produced an ambitious light show at the university's Bob Hope Theatre in 1973. "The Metaphysical Circuit" featured dancer Katie McGuire, a student of Toni Beck, responding to live improvised music and video synthesis from both Dowe and Hunt as well as from the San Francisco video artist and composer duo Stephen Beck and Warner Jepson. The video components were projected using an Eidophor, at the time the only large-scale projection system, imported from Switzerland. Hunt and Dowe were able to drum up some local interest in their work, with a handful of articles in local papers painting Hunt as an eccentric genius chain-smoking in the Center's SMU Ownby Stadium basement. As Beck recalls, the show was a considerable success, selling out the theater many shows over, its run extended to meet audience demand. By his estimation, the performance marked the "first time a large-screen video display was used onstage [for a] theatrical performance."[45]

For the most part, however, the duo's more conceptual ambitions flew below the radar of local audiences, and Hunt for one did not shy away from describing to journalists the financial difficulties they encountered in their line of work. Dowe, for his part, lamented the technical difficulties in the Center's first live program, which created a "long sequence that bored even him. 'Putting together a program that would "communicate with people" has been a slow and painful process—like an identity crisis every day.'"[46]

Escaping difficult times in Texas, Dowe and Hunt traveled to New York in April 1973 for the first International Computer Arts Festival. They performed "Heisenberg/Eyes" and "Electric Exo-Sketch," complex improvisations that made use of motion-sensor input that captured muscle movements.[47] The program also lists "Harrinan Playing," an early appearance, however misspelled, of Haramand Plane. As the '70s progressed, the funding from the Rockefeller Foundation that supported nonrepresentational video, and helped to fund NCET and its satellites, began to dry up.[48] In 1975, Dowe and Hunt were invited by composer David Rosenboom to York University, in Toronto, to demonstrate their system in a daylong durational performance. Dowe's clearest memory is of the frugality of the trip; he recalls eating linguini that Hunt cooked in a motel coffee pot. "We did everything on the cheap," says Dowe. "There was no money to go around."[49] SMU's Video Research Center closed shop the next year, and Dowe found production work at KERA through Paul Bosner. The shuttering of the Center, meanwhile, marked a distinct turning point for Hunt, who began to further explore the compositional possibilities of dynamic electronic systems.

While working at the Center, Hunt had become increasingly disenchanted with his first instrument of choice, the piano, and mostly forewent performances on the instrument when in front of the national music audiences to which his work began to cater. According to numerous artist biographies written in the 1970s, Hunt claims to have officially ended his "work as pianist" in 1969.[50] During the next decade, he would contend with the instrument only in private recitals, the one exception being his 1979 composition "Lattice." In 1977, Hunt gave a talk/recital titled "Death of the Piano" at the Highland Park home of the Sreres, the patrons who had taken a shine to him a decade earlier.[51] Later broadcast on KERA, courtesy of Paul Bosner and reporter Billy Porterfield, Hunt's performance was simultaneously a survey of conceptually (and physically) challenging pieces for piano by Arnold Schoenberg and Alexander Scriabin as well as a meditation on Hunt's own disillusionment. "I can see my relationship both personally and politically and particularly financially with the piano going off down into a kind of no-man's-land to which there's no return," he confessed, bemoaning the ubiquity of keyboard controllers in electronic music and praising unique input techniques like David Rosenboom's brainwave biofeedback. While "Death of the Piano," like many of Hunt's performances, embraced slapstick and humor, the underlying concepts were rigorous and reflective of new developments in cybernetics and philosophy that Hunt was engaged with at the time. As he states in the opening of the *Synapse* article, "The early independent work and my work with David [Dowe] for the past five years has substantially reinforced my original intuition that the composing activity can powerfully operate and should operate in ways which are not dependent upon the patterns of feedback and

40

feedaround through one special orientation of thought (action and process)." Hunt's disavowal of the keyboard (and music's concomitant "special orientation of thought") paralleled his interest in new cybernetic systems that allowed the performer to corporally, directly, and seamlessly compose. Like Rosenboom employing electroencephalography to situate the physical body as an instrument, Hunt introduced optical sensors compounded with solid-state memory systems as the basis of his work during the next chapter of his career.

With Hunt's interest in composing for traditional instruments waning, he found renewal in his approach to performance through an engagement with Cage's work.[52] As touched on earlier, the musical content of the older composer's aleatoric compositions was of less interest to Hunt than the philosophical implications of these works in relation to music and life. Thinking back on his own development in the late '70s, Hunt said: "I might have given up music altogether if it hadn't been for John Cage and the new emphasis he gave to communication."[53] Cage's reframing of the concert as situational—highlighting the active exchanges between the composer and the audience—would resonate with Hunt's own cybernetics-tinged understanding of the concert as, in his objective terminology, an "interactive transactional system."

By his own account, Hunt turned a corner in 1978, the year he says he began to compose "interrelated electronic, mechanic, and social sound-sight interactive transactional systems"—a further crystallization of his ideas.[54] As he embarked on a series of solo endeavors, he took the theatrical elements he had introduced in previous collaborative works with Houston Higgins, David Dowe, and Audio Visual Studio/Ensemble to new heights. Hunt began utilizing found percussive instruments and talismanic staffs designed by his friend the sculptor David McManaway, as well as a newly developed audio interface utilizing optical sensors alongside components of the recently released Chess Challenger microcomputer to retranslate audio signals and information into a multifarious system of output patterns.[55] Performative components like guttural vocals and dramatic facial contortions became even more pronounced as video systems were eliminated from his setup and Hunt relied on bodily gestures to captivate his audience. His electronics systems became even less straightforward, with listeners often observing that they were unsure which gestures triggered what. Hunt also played up a fast-talking, pataphysical-circumlocutory persona, both in interviews and program notes, befuddling his audiences, to his own somewhat amused reaction. In a 1980 interview

Hunt performing at Roulette, New York, 1985. Photo: Lona Foote.

with Jane van Sickle, he said, "I know that some people think my music is highly intellectual because I always provide program notes which are complicated in the abstract sense, but the complicated notes provide the full range of alternate music structures."[56] Hunt certainly grasped the obscurity of his work, and dealt with the complexity (and non-transmissibility) of his ideas, with self-deprecating humor.

In 1979, Hunt started a record label, Irida Associates U.S.A. The label was a serious attempt to document his and his peers' activities, though he would often couch its promotion in tongue-in-cheek provocation, referring to it as a "vanity project" aimed at a "tax loophole." Hunt borrowed *irida*—the Sinhala word for *sun*, associated with the name of a pre-Buddhist sun god—from a Sri Lankan art gallery in Berlin owned by his high-school classmate Fred Reisman, who helped support the label. Between 1979 and 1980, Irida put out five records that enlisted Hunt's peers, including former *Source* editors Larry Austin and Dary John Mizelle, the trombonist and composer James Fulkerson, and the Dallas-based free improvisation group BL Lacerta. (A sixth and final release, a compilation of works for Synclavier by students of Austin, came in 1986, at which point Hunt abandoned the endeavor.)

The label's first two records were *Texas Music*, a compilation featuring Hunt's work alongside that of Jerry Willingham and Philip Krumm, and *Cantegral Segment(s)*, a body of solo compositions derived from his Haramand Plane procedure (both albums 1979). Hunt's contribution to *Texas Music* is "Lattice" (1979), whose composition is based on the geometric principles of the titular subject. The resulting score is gamelike and theatrical in a manner that would come to characterize performances like the Cantegral Segment(s). "Lattice" includes an additional layer of sounds created by attaching small metal objects and bells to the performer's wrists and ankles. In a radio interview with Charles Amirkhanian recorded around the time of the release, Hunt made assurances that the piano was not prepared and that there was "no funny stuff inside."[57] According to Hunt's instructions, each performance of "Lattice" should be adaptable to the architecture and resonance of the room in which it is performed, a premise he would explore in the years to come through the employment of optical sensors.

Hunt's solo album on Irida, *Cantegral Segment(s) 16.17.18.19. / Transform (Stream) / Transphalba / Volta (Kernel)*, collects a series of shorter compositional procedures that highlight one of his signature maneuvers: the layering and reworking of his own compositions and methodologies through sampling of prerecorded materials as well as the combination of actions defined by specific prior scores.[58] Hunt describes the composition "Transform (Stream)" (1977), for example, as a "transformation of material of 'Cantegral Segment 16' in combination with material from 'Cantegral Segment 7.'"[59] He goes on to say that "Cantegral Segment 16" "consists of material for human voice, as a primary source" and that "Cantegral Segment 7" "consists of material defining performance of sounds produced by impulse-activated semiresonant mechanical assemblies. 'Transform (Stream)' uses derivatives of continuant fricatives from the allo-phonic sequence of 'Cantegral Segment 16,' articulated using two components of the assemblies of 'Cantegral Segment 7.'" This is a wordy way of giving instructions for the performer to wordlessly breathe a series of phonemes, as described in "Cantegral Segment 16," into a semi-resonant object, as described in "Cantegral Segment 7," which is in principle what the recording sounds like.

Though "Haramand Plane: parallel/regenerative" was developed at the Video Research Center with Dowe, the Haramand Plane system differs from Dowe and Hunt's previous collaborative work, in which the two artists would separately improvise within their respective visual and sonic domains. Haramand Plane, by contrast, was intended to showcase Hunt's increasingly distinctive performance style, with which he would trigger various electronic sensors. Dowe recalls his former collaborator "creating talismanic signs and symbols with his hands, [making] exaggerated facial gestures, shaking, wiggling, being possessed, and all of that stuff," a prototype for Hunt's later seance-like solo spectacles.[60] The program notes from Hunt and Dowe's trip to York University are telling in relation to Hunt's research with Dowe at the time. Most notably, in Hunt's biographical text, he writes in the third person to trace a lineage from his early work to the Haramand Plane. "Since his composition *Sur* Dr. John Dee, which utilizes changes in the performance environment, Mr. Hunt has been concerned with adaptive and interactive processes in musical composition and performance. His current work involves various systems for predicting and selectively altering the histories of performance processes as composition and their specific application in audio and video generating systems."[61]

This compositional procedure would serve as a springboard for Hunt's solo endeavors and lay the groundwork for his methodology over the succeeding decades. On February 18, 1978, Hunt presented the piece again at the Festival of Contemporary Performing Arts at the School of Music at the University of Illinois Urbana-Champaign. This time, the piece was billed as the "Haramand Plane (overlay) 1972, 1976 Transhelix 1972" and performed alongside two of his

Jerry Hunt
Birome (Zone) Cube
Sound Installation,
Museum of Fine Arts, Houston
New Music America

Jerry Hunt's technological sex machine installation begins sensing your presence the moment you walk into the *Birome (Zone) Cube*. Black vinyl walls with patchwork quilts contain sound within the cube, the inner sanctum. A strange walk-in cube made temporary as if to protect itself from the corporate mausoleumness of the museum's slick environment, this audio/video installation makes it all apparent what is right and wrong with avant-New Music-garde today. Because of the immense cost of new music technological innovation, the forefront has shifted from the artists and universities to the corporations; it's with the commercial field that the power rests. But thankfully there's a certain socio-economic fringe element that controls something called ideas.

What makes this work interesting is the approach it takes to the technology it uses. A machine with memory interacting with whoever stimulates it, responding with unknown motives. In the corner of the *Birome (Zone) Cube* a small bedroom lamp is

Jerry Hunt, *Birome (Zone): Cube*, (Exterior and Interior Views), 1986, Museum of Fine Arts, Houston. Photo: Robert Riffle.

tied to a table. Several wall mirrors reflect the images emanating from the two video monitors hidden in the recesses of the black vinyl walls. In the other corner a macrowave machine (normally used for home security) puts out direct contours, detecting pattern changes of any movement in the cube. In the center of the cube, resting on an altar, is a figure almost human, almost carrot, complete with fur-lined orifices. This humanoid form responds to one's slightest touch; numerous heat and pressure sensors lie just beneath its artificial flesh. All of which is fed into an altered chess computer program; a specific pre-programmed audio, where distinct, recorded video patterns controlled by six transports of sixteen tracks, utilize eleven hours of visual material as a memory source. Through tone-coding, the machine links auditory sequences, jumping up and down various skill levels. A transport time window of control exists, with entry points and exit points. The image-find can be reached depending on skill orientation and mind type—some people are more accustomed to technology than others.

The dark abstract images pass across the video, in unison with squawks and electronic noises—or perhaps they're human—all manipulated in some uncontrolled delay system. Is this reaction I'm seeing and hearing coming from my strokings of this humanoid or is it part of some other person's fingering hours ago? It's all complex and unclear, but what is clear is Mr. Hunt's motives—to push a button and then have no idea what randomness will appear. As Jerry Hunt says, "things are not random, just dense."

Clipping from a review in *Artscene* of Hunt's installation *Birome (Zone): Cube*, Museum of Fine Arts, Houston, April 5–13, 1986.

Cantegral Segment(s): "Cantegral Segment(s) 7, 17" (1975, 1976) and "Cantegral Segment(s) 16, 18" (1976, 1977).[62] In the program notes for the Urbana performance, Hunt's description of the Haramand Plane reads as follows: "Haramand Plane is a procedure for generation by recording characteristic histories and allowing these histories to accumulate in context defined relationships. The material consists of a history of components of work produced 1965–1977."

Hunt would describe his 1963 composition "*Sur* Dr. John Dee" as a work "utilizing changes in the performance environment" and would draw a continuum between this and his exploration of "adaptive and interactive" systems that enabled Haramand Plane and Cantegral Segment(s).[63] Hunt's approaches to interpreting his scores and performing with his electronic systems drew on the theatrical mnemonic techniques of Robert Fludd. As Hunt recalled to Guy De Bièvre, "What's fascinating is, even though [Fludd's system is] arbitrary, it is a closed system but it's as workable as a modern idea about memory and about time and about the representation of events and the layering of different patterns of memory, whether it has to do with musical sound or whether it has to do with images."[64] Hunt's employment of mnemonic techniques in his own work was not about recalling past sounds and events as such, but about activating perception and interpretation. Scores (and likewise electronics configurations) were not consulted to reproduce repeatable results but rather to serve as paths for the evolution and combination of ideas and materials that in partnership with one another would solicit new works—new iterations in response to new environments. Hunt would accordingly put his scores into new relationships with one another, creating pieces like "Cantegral Segment 18.17" (1979) or "Transphalba" (1979), a piece derived from "Cantegral Segment(s) 18" and "19." On another level Hunt saw his own work on stage as a mirror of dynamics of the audience's relationship to his performance; both sets of "transactional" relationships would provide another perspectival layer that could be folded into the content of the "work." Hunt had experimented in the '60s with "sampling" other composers' work in live concerts, presenting simultaneous performances of multiple compositions, and once with multiple rock bands playing concurrently in a mall parking lot. These "simultaneous and consecutive" performances can be seen as analogue "live" versions of Hunt's own later work. His later repurposing of previously recorded performances, densely edited and layered on magnetic tape, developed over the decade, eventually introducing solid state memory (SSM) systems in his electronics rigs. SSM would become commercially available in

46

the late '70s, permitting Hunt to call on and combine samples of manipulated and prerecorded materials live during performances, a slightly more sophisticated version of techniques he had already developed using tape cartridges and complex signal chains.

The late 1970s saw another substantial turning point in Hunt's work: the emergence of a national funding structure for which geographical diversity was a boon. After years of striving for national recognition, at the turn of the decade Hunt found an unexpectedly eager audience. "The change came, I think," he later remarked, "with the federal government entering the arts. Suddenly there was an idea of representation, or de-regionalization, or stimulation of regionalism."[65] The inaugural New Music America in 1980, for instance, marked a decided shift. Born out of a weeklong concert series at the Kitchen probing "downtown music" by composers such as Julius Eastman, Charlemagne Palestine, and Steve Reich in 1979, the concept developed into an annual festival hosted by a different city each year. Hunt performed Haramand Plane at the first iteration in Minneapolis, which Tom Johnson reviewed in the *Village Voice*: "I recall that the light was very dim, that Hunt kept walking downstage to whack a large cardboard box with a curious stick, that he rattled some unidentifiable objects in one hand for a while, that a recording of electronic sounds sometimes accompanied him from the loudspeakers, that there seemed to be no explanation for anything that happened and that I was simultaneously fascinated and disturbed."[66]

Hunt was generally entering an era of heightened formal ambition in his compositions, most notably with *Ground* (1980–84), a cycle of works born from an attempted "opera." It is relevant that he was familiar with the composer-performer Robert Ashley, having previously encountered many of Ashley's early works, such as the theater-piece *In Memoriam . . . KIT CARSON* and the tape composition "The Wolfman" (1964). The two had even crossed paths briefly at ICES '72. As composers, they shared a number of interests: a commitment to wily theatrics, a sardonic approach to the conceptual issues of post-Cagean music, a love of colloquial American speech, and even a fascination with the Rosicrucians—Ashley cites Frances A. Yates's *The Art of Memory* (University of Chicago Press, 1966) as a key inspiration for his video *Perfect Lives* (1977–83).[67] Like Ashley's signature work of the era, portions of which were released in 1977 for the album *Private Parts*, *Ground* was first intended to be a "television opera" built around an ensemble cast. Loosely based on George Eliot's 1860 novel *The Mill on the Floss*, the work weaves cryptic repeated phrases from the book against a shambolic

Hunt at the festival New Music America, Houston, April 1986. Photographer unknown.

electronic backdrop. Hunt staged versions of *Ground* with a new ensemble, featuring local performers Vicki Lynn, Peter Mood, and Jane van Sickle, and also performed it as a truncated solo performance at Mills College in Oakland and KPFA in San Francisco..

In part through the momentum generated by his performance in Minneapolis, Hunt received offers to perform at alternative arts spaces in New York, a city with a provincial musical culture that he had found difficult to break into in his earlier years. He played gigs at the Kitchen and Roulette, often staying (and occasionally collaborating) with dancer Sally Bowden, a former student of Toni Beck who was then a member of the Merce Cunningham Dance Company. In 1982, Hunt telephoned into one of Cunningham's "Events" to play a version of his "Quaquaversal Transmission." (At the same time, he advertised in *Computer Music Journal* private telephone performances of the piece—provided the listener bought a custom phone line splitter.) In 1983, Hunt participated in New Music America in Washington, DC, albeit remotely from a sound studio in Austin, Texas. In an early use of satellite for telematic music, Hunt performed "Phalba (stream): extractive" (1983) with the festival's codirector Joseph Celli, a composer and oboist he had met at the 1980 iteration; the system was too expensive to soundcheck, and was thus played truly "live," and mercifully without apparent hiccup.[68] The two would remain in close contact for the remainder of Hunt's life: Celli invited the composer to play at the subsequent New Music America in 1984, on his home turf of Hartford, Connecticut, and later released a CD of Hunt's music, *Ground: Five Mechanic Convention Streams* (1992), and a posthumous VHS tape on his label OODiscs.

As Hunt gained a national profile on the new music scene, he retreated from the local context in Dallas. Wanting to dedicate as much time as possible to composition, he sought to minimize his professional obligations, having already moved on from his affiliation with SMU in 1973. As part of his frugality, Hunt and Housewright relocated to Hunt's parents' farm in Canton, Texas in 1980, where the couple converted an unused barn into a home, using spare parts from an abandoned airport and installing do-it-yourself plumbing and air-conditioning. Hunt continued to contribute occasional incidental music for local radio and television, even enjoying a stint as the music director of *With Ossie and Ruby* (1980–82), a half-hour variety show hosted by Ossie Davis and Ruby Dee that David Dowe was directing for KERA-TV. Other odd jobs followed: through Gordon Hoffman, Hunt provided technical support on the development of an organ chip for the Carrollton-based circuit manufacturer Mostek, and through Paul Bosner, he composed synthesized mood music for a series of instructional videotapes distributed by a local community college. He continued to perform annual recitals at the Sreres' home, with a repertoire ranging from late Romantic preludes to novelty rags by Zez Confrey, and the couple would often send him home with envelopes of cash. In general, however, Hunt directed most of his energies toward tinkering with his audiovisual setup—aided in part by technological novelties like the Amiga computer and microprocessors—and developing his compositional voice.

Hunt's newly freed-up schedule allowed him to maintain a consistent travel itinerary in the mid-'80s. At the 1984 American Society of University Composers at Ohio State University—an odd outing that featured, alongside measured performances of academic music, a mordant keynote address by Frank Zappa titled "Bingo! There Goes Your Tenure"—Hunt demonstrated "Ground: Haramand Plane" on a bill with Pauline Oliveros, a particularly fierce proponent of his work. That same year, she recommended Hunt for a residency at Yellow Springs Institute in Chester Springs, Pennsylvania, where he was paired with the chamber group Relâche to develop a new piece. "He wasn't necessarily keen to work with the whole ensemble," recalls the group's artistic director, Joseph Franklin. "He didn't think that way."[69] Franklin remembers the composer immediately narrowing in on close collaborations with vocalist Barbara Noska and flautist Laurel Wyckoff, using the whole of the residency to craft a suite of pieces with the pair. "His way of working was more of a one-to-one relationship building," notes Wyckoff, who admitted some bewilderment about his processes—a not-uncommon claim from interpreters of Hunt's music. "I didn't understand very much about what he was trying to do, I have to say."[70]

Intensive partnerships of this sort became increasingly frequent in Hunt's work. He attended the Newfoundland Sound Symposium in 1986, an eight-day series of workshops and performances also attended by Oliveros and the Belgian duo Godfried-Willem Raes and Moniek Darge, among others. Hunt conducted a lecture on his compositional practice and gave a characteristically frenetic demonstration of his solo act, but it was an off-the-cuff duet with Toronto-based stand-up comedian Sheila Gostick that festival-goer Gordon Monahan recalls as the week's "show-stopper."[71] In this largely improvisational spectacle, a costumed Gostick sang a rendition of "You've Never Been This Far Before" by Conway Twitty—a favorite singer of Hunt—while the composer slinked around the

BIROME (ZONE):CUBE- JERRY HUNT

HOE DE INSTALLATIE TE GEBRUIKEN.

DE 'STROOM' WORDT GEACTIVEERD OF STOPGEZET DOOR MET DE HANDEN IN BEPAALDE
PATRONEN BOVEN HET CENTRUM VAN DE MANNEQUIN TE BEWEGEN; DE BESTAANDE TOESTAND
IS AFHANKELIJK VAN HETGEEN ERVOOR GEBEURD IS EN KAN DERHALVE NOG ACTIEF ZIJN OF
OP HET PUNT STAAN TE BEGINNEN.

DE INHOUD VAN DE STROOM VAN GELUIDEN EN BEELDEN WORDT VERANDERD DOOR EEN
OPTELSOM VAN ALLE KEREN DAT OVER HET VOORSTE, ZICHTBARE GEDEELTE VAN DE
MANNEQUIN WORDT GETIKT EN GEWREVEN: HET BEWEGINGSPATROON DAT WERD GEVOLGD, DE
RELATIEVE DRUK EN TIJDSDUUR VAN DE BEWEGINGEN WORDEN TESAMEN OMGEZET IN DIRECTE
EN VERTRAAGDE VERANDERINGEN. VERTRAAGDE, LANGDURIGE VERANDERINGEN WORDEN
VOORTGEBRACHT DOOR FLUISTEREN OF HUILEN (STRESS) IN DE BUURT VAN HET OPPERVLAK
VAN DE MANNEQUIN EN/OF DOOR LANGDURIGE OMHELZING. MAAK ZACHTE KLOPPENDE OF
WRIJVENDE BEWGINGEN MET BEIDE HANDEN.

DE WISSELWERKING KOMT HET BEST TOT UITING ALS ER SLECHTS EEN PERSOON

TEGELIJKERTIJD NAAR BINNEN GAAT.

HOW TO USE THE INSTALLATION.

THE STREAM IS ACTIVATED OR STILLED BY PRODUCING PATTERNS OF MOVEMENT WITH THE
HANDS ABOVE THE AREA OF THE MANNEQUIN CORE: THE CURRENT STATE IS DEPENDENT UPON
THE RECENT HISTORY AND STATE OF THE STREAM AND MAY BE ACTIVE OR STILL UPON
ENTRY.

THE CONTENT OF THE SOUND-VISION STREAM REFLECTION IS VARIED BY AN ACCUMULATIVE
HISTORY OF STROKING AND RUBBING THE FRONTAL EXPOSED PORTION OF THE MANNEQUIN
SURFACE: STROKE PATTERN, RELATIVE INTENSITY AND DURATION ARE TRANSLATED
TOGETHER TO PRODUCE IMMEDIATE AND REMOTE CHANGE. REMOTE, LONG-TERM CHANGES ARE
PRODUCED BY WHISPERS OR CRIES (STRESS) NEAR THE MANNEQUIN SURFACE AND/OR
SUSTAINED EMBRACE. USE GENTLE STROKING OR RUBBING WITH BOTH HANDS.

INTERACTION IS OPTIMIZED IF PARTICIPANTS ENTER SINGLY, ALONE

Program notes for Hunt's installation *Birome (ZONE): Cube*, Het Apollohuis, Eindhoven, Netherlands,
April 22–May 22, 1988.

room, turned the lights on and off, and whacked objects against the floor. Housewright suggests the act was a foreshadowing of Hunt's later collaboration with Karen Finley, a performative turn driven by freewheeling, improvisatory theater.[72]

Generally, Hunt was refining his interest in the extra-musical elements of performance. In interviews throughout the '80s, for instance, he was fond of admitting his appreciation for pop music. Though such a sensibility was nothing new for Hunt—he chalked up the reverberating, dense quality of his work to his fondness of Phil Spector and the Supremes, and previously claimed that he adapted Cantegral Segment(s) from a single Elvis Presley song—he was increasingly citing the mainstream pop-star system as a model worthy of deep consideration. "The avant-garde has been redefined in a completely different avenue, and that's in commercial, techni-cally sophisticated dealings with masses of people in Top 40 global rock," Hunt told Monahan, explaining that he was particularly impressed with pop's ability to import contingent cultural imagery into international contexts.[73] While Hunt pointed to a number of musicians he felt epitomized this phenomenon—including Cyndi Lauper, Madonna, Stevie Wonder, and Vanilla Ice—he was most taken with Prince. "He's created a kind of a religion, which is this bizarre mixture of almost Hollywood glitz, sex, and Middle American puritanical religion mixed together in this incredible combination with this very basic rhythm and blues foundation," he elaborated in an interview.[74] In a way, these artists were mirrors of Hunt's attempts to build immediate languages, and motivated him to further cultivate his own onstage charisma.

There were occasional outlier projects that strayed from his usual performance paradigm. *Cyra* (1984), a collaboration with the Brooklyn Philharmonic and accordionist Guy Klucevsek that premiered at the Brooklyn Academy of Music, was a rare work for a traditional orchestra, although in customary Hunt fashion, it featured an extended coda that had Hunt banging on an amplified suitcase. He briefly flirted with a series of pieces based on the tango rhythm, performing variations in disparate evenings with Bowden, Klucevsek, and BL Lacerta. Between 1985 and 1987, Hunt was inter-mittently occupied with composing a piece for two Synclaviers, a commission for the University of North Texas's Center for Electronic Music and Intermedia (CEMI) parlayed by Larry Austin. *Fluud* (1985), the composer's sole work for the Synclavier, was based on polymath Robert Fludd's occult text *Monochordum mundi syhiphoniacum* and his theory of rarefaction and condensation—the belief that the universe was guided by dual "austral" and "boreal" forces. A dense, stuttering, process-oriented work, the piece was an ordeal for Hunt, who found the synthesizer's interface frustrating, privately referring to it as a "big expensive piece of crap."[75] He performed *Fluud* at a Composers' Forum evening at Dia Art Foundation in New York. (Much to his chagrin, he was responsible for transporting a Synclavier by airplane, which he found to be a logistical nightmare.) He realized the piece with theatrical flourish, making faces as he played, controlling a light with a pedal, and placing small objects like a plastic heart and mirror on the back of his hands.

In spring 1986, New Music America came to Houston—a four-hour drive from Canton, practically in Hunt's backyard compared to the Northeast engagements he was used to flying to. Jerry McCathern, the director of the city's annual Houston Festival, had attended the 1984 Hartford New Music America iteration, where he proposed that his organization offer a future venue. Oliveros, a Houston native, was selected as the artistic director, and Michael Galbreth, a local performance artist and one half of the duo The Art Guys, was engaged to oversee the logistics. Hunt was invited to participate in the selection committee, as was his colleague Larry Austin, who edited the festival's catalogue. As the centerpiece of a citywide arts festival celebrating Houston's sesquicentennial, the seven-day event was the New Music Alliance's most ambitious incarnation yet in terms of scope and attendance. Featuring over one hundred participating artists, it was spread out across over a dozen partnering venues (including the Houston Astrodome) and began with a parade along the city's downtown, led by cellist Tom Cora that fed into a performance of John Cage's "Ryoanji" (1983–85).[76]

While the festival featured many of the usual suspects in new music—in addition to Cage and Oliveros, stalwarts like Annea Lockwood and downtown New York figures like Leroy Jenkins, Joan La Barbara, and Phill Niblock speckled the lineup—the selection of artists was intended to demonstrate the breadth of Texas's homegrown music and performance scenes. The opening night spotlighted Shirley Clarke's newly completed documentary *Ornette: Made in America*, centered on the Fort Worth jazz saxophonist and the opening of the Caravan of Dreams performing arts center he led, while one of the festival's marquee events featured "Blue" Gene Tyranny and Ned Sublette (San Antonio and Lubbock natives, respectively) performing idiosyncratic country-western tunes. An afternoon panel was dedicated to defining the "avant-garde music of the Third Coast," and the closing ceremony programmed Sonic Youth alongside local punk unit Culturcide and polka ensemble

Brave Combo. Many of Hunt's close compatriots participated: Jim Fulkerson performed trombone in the inaugural Cage piece, Austin presented the video piece *Ludus Fractalis* (1984)—which juxtaposed spoken-word elements by Hunt and a processed video of a mime performance—and BL Lacerta played an outdoor improvisation at the city's Tranquility Park.

Hunt did not perform at the festival, a curious omission given the general excitement around his frenetic live spectacles. His early "Preparallel" (1964–65) was included in an exhibition on graphic scores at the art center DiverseWorks, and he participated in a midweek symposium on the topic of "sight and sound" alongside artists Pat Oleszko, Bonnie Sherk, and Jim Pomeroy, a sly Texas-born conceptual artist who shared Hunt's background in home-brewed electronics.[77] Most substantially, Hunt contributed to the festival's sound installation component, in which over a dozen artists, including Stuart Dempster, Ellen Fullman, and Alvin Lucier, were invited to create site-specific works across the city. At the Museum of Fine Arts, Houston, Hunt premiered his first installation, *Birome (ZONE): Cube* (1986), developed in close collaboration with David McManaway; it was a beguiling room-sized "memory cabinet" featuring scattered objects, television monitors, electronic sound, and a large doll-like mannequin, and was felt by some to be a highlight of the festival.

As McManaway's found and sculptural assemblages had been an aspect of Hunt's performances since the late '70s, it was not a significant jump to arrange these in an exhibition space. *Birome (ZONE): Cube* was like a slow-moving adaptation of Hunt's live shows: visitors throughout the day triggered sensors of various sorts that recorded data points that were input into a system of Hunt's design, said to be based on the rules of Rosicrucian chess and John Dee's scrying grids. Thus, viewing the installation would influence its behavior in nonobvious ways. Seemingly random electronic samples and computer-generated sigils cycling on a television monitor would be dictated by audience movements from hours earlier, thereby frustrating the effort to understand the internal logic of the piece. The work's processes were not observable, enabling it to function as a near-parody of the "interactivity" touted by other sound art works presented at the festival.

Consistent with his ambivalent approach to contemporary currents in the experimental music scene, Hunt expressed a wry skepticism of the sonic installations that were becoming increasingly fashionable throughout the '80s. In an interview with Guy De Bièvre, Hunt described such works as "Victorian scientific experiments that are displaced, that have been brought forward and updated slightly with modern electronics and put into a gallery setting instead of a well-to-do gentleman's backyard in his country estate."[78] *Birome (ZONE): Cube* reveled in Hunt's fascination with obsolete sciences, beginning with its reliance on Enochian processes. The work served as a virtual catalogue of mnemotechnics: the construction of the room harkened back to both the early eighteenth-century cabinet of curiosities and the speculative, Renaissance-period Memory Theater; the sigils served as a form of graphical mnemonics; and the audiovisual component was guided by the Z80 microprocessor, which in Hunt's eyes was practically an electrical reification of Giordano Bruno's sixteenth-century *Ars Memoriae*. At the center of the *Birome (ZONE): Cube* installation stood a McManaway-designed mannequin, which Hunt referred to as a "homunculus"—the final frontier of alchemy.

Hunt's participation in New Music America and downtown venues like the Kitchen and Roulette bolstered his quasi-mystical reputation overseas; like many left-field figures of his generation, he found a receptive audience in Western Europe. Following Hunt's 1984 performance in Hartford, Connecticut, sound artist John Driscoll and music curator Matthias Osterwold invited the composer to participate in a 1986 multiday festival in Berlin called Music with Memory, which showcased musicians utilizing then-novel microprocessing units, but scheduling conflicts prevented Hunt from attending. He would not make it to Europe until 1988, when the Dutch composer Paul Panhuysen, who had performed at the Houston iteration with his group the Maciunas Ensemble, asked Hunt to restage *Birome (ZONE): Cube* at Het Apollohuis, an experimental arts space in Eindhoven. Around this occasion, Hunt organized a two-month tour that took him to Middelburg, Berlin, Cologne, Ghent, and Brussels. The German composer Werner Durand attended the Berlin performance, which prominently featured the mannequin from the *Birome (ZONE): Cube* installation and consisted of Hunt repeatedly taking on and off his wool jacket and hanging it on a chair. It was "beyond theater and performance," Durand recalls.[79]

Due to Hunt's reliance on the extra-musical components of his work, the question of whether or not he was in fact a composer was not infrequently broached. By the early '90s, only a minority of Hunt's output resembled "composition," with re-performability ranking low on Hunt's list of priorities. Most of his solo performances were highly variable, contingent on how much equipment he could carry in a suitcase, and he made many crucial artistic decisions on the fly in response to the technical capacity and shape of the particular venue. If pieces were scored, the scores primarily took the form of written or verbal instructions, sigilic graphic notations, or audiocassette demonstrations sent to performers by mail. Hunt himself seemed conflicted about the nature of his creative identity. He would tell William Duckworth that by the late '80s he no longer played music as such. "I don't think music really has much to do with sound," he clarified. "The material of music is sound, but the significance of music to people is not the sound."[80] Later in the interview, however, he reported that he still thought of himself as a composer. When asked on another occasion by the Dutch psychoacoustician Leon van Noorden if he considered what he did to be above all music, he replied, "Yes I do. The visual and gestural components of what I do I regard as subordinate to and dependent upon the sound stream. The visual and gestural parts are signals, overlays of the course of development that the musical stream takes."[81]

For Hunt, his late-period performances were about managing the multivalent relationships that exist within the frame of a concert space, a role he compared to that of a priest mediating between an audience and an abstraction—in Hunt's case, instead of God, the abstract force was musical convention. He saw each of these relationships, which the cyberneticist in him referred to interchangeably as signals, as fundamentally interrelated, and his job as being to tune them, akin to the live processing he had done in tandem with David Dowe a decade earlier.

Particularly in the final four years of his compositional career, Hunt was a prolific collaborator, often inviting musicians he would meet on tour to join in future projects, possible performances, and long-term correspondence. In Ghent, Hunt enchanted the staff of the arts space Logos Foundation, befriending its founders Godfried-Willem Raes and Moniek Darge as well as its staff members Guy De Bièvre and Maria Blondeel. Hunt and Blondeel, an intermedia installation artist, would exchange letters for years, their rapport culminating in *Bitom (fixture:plane)*, 1992, an installation that features stereoscopic light work by Blondeel, and plans for further collaborations that were cut short by Hunt's death. Despite having veered away from traditional instrumentation in his own performances, he would sustain prolonged communication with musicians such as the San Antonio–based violinist Jane Henry, the flautist Jerry Willingham, and the trombonist Jim Fulkerson, in many cases sending work-in-progress scores by cassette tape in order to nurture future, speculative performances.

Stills from Jerry Hunt, *How to Kill Yourself Using the Inhalation of Carbon Monoxide Gas*, 1993, video, color, sound, 20 minutes.

The Netherlands made a special impression on Hunt, who not only sent frequent lengthy updates to Paul and Hélène Panhuysen for the remainder of his life but also studied Dutch in preparation for a permanent, though ultimately unrealized, move to the country. On his first visit, in 1988, he became fixated on the cartoons of Marten Toonder, particularly the anthropomorphic bear-and-cat duo Olivier B. Bommel and Tom Poes. Back in Texas, he'd often read Toonder comics—as well the wildly popular Dutch-language *Donald Duck* magazine, which Housewright gave him a subscription to—in order to brush up on the language. (Hunt also took great interest in the psychosexual works of the Dutch writer Gerard Reve.) Certainly the country's amply funded arts organizations attracted him, as did the Dutch role in the seventeenth-century mystical science that served as a backdrop to much of his work. He could hardly wait to return, and arranged a four-week Christmas trip in the country that same year, during which he performed at both a new music festival in Rotterdam and Het Apollohuis in Eindhoven and vacationed with Housewright in Middelburg and Amsterdam. In Amsterdam, the two were able to reconnect with Jim Fulkerson and his wife, Mary, who were in the process of immigrating to the Netherlands.

In Rotterdam, Hunt met the downtown New York performance artist Karen Finley, with whom he felt an immediate connection; by the fall of that year, the two were on stage together at New Music America in New York, somewhat incongruously booked as part of a "computer music extravaganza" night at Merkin Concert Hall. Their performance, "Babalon (String)," featured Hunt's usual cere-monial object manipulation—rattles, bells, light bulbs, and mirrors, as well as a long shofar—while Finley threw chocolate candy into the audience and scream-recited her performance-poetry. "It was unexplainable and irreducible, like most of life's significant events," wrote Kyle Gann, covering the event for the *Village Voice*.[82]

In 1990, McManaway and Hunt collaborated at a local art space in Dallas on a second installation, *Birome: Fixture*, a compar-atively sparse setup that featured objects scattered around a TV monitor. At the opening, Hunt performed "[Trapani: stream] a+b," a pair of pieces meant to eulogize two sets of recently deceased friends. Part *a* was in memory of Houston and Jill Higgins, his early collaborators, who had died within two weeks of each other; Jill had succumbed to melanoma, while Houston, a hemophiliac who was sickly for much of his adulthood, perished from liver disease. Part *b* was dedicated to Jack Briece, a young composer then based in Santa Fe who shared Hunt's penchant for esoterica; before Briece's untimely death from AIDS-related complications in 1989, the two had intended to collaborate on an ambitious TV installation and live performance.[83]

Hunt continued to tour, though intermittently. In the spring of 1990, he embarked on an ambitious "Maritime Tour" of Canada, stopping in Sackville, Halifax, Charlottetown, Fredericton, and Moncton, and later in the year returned to the Netherlands. In addition to the Panhuysens and the Fulkersons, Hunt had befriended a number of other artists based in the country, including the composer Joel Ryan, a director at the Studio for Electro-Instrumental Music (STEIM) in Amsterdam. Hunt had hoped to develop, with Ryan and STEIM, a MIDI controller based on his performance system, although it did not come to fruition. Hunt was a resident artist and guest lecturer at the Hogeschool voor de Kunsten in Arnhem during the spring of 1991, and used his extended period in Europe to fulfill engagements in Vienna and elsewhere. His final performance abroad was in Frankfurt in the fall of 1992; he was scheduled for another semester in Arnhem, but it did not materialize due to the rapid progression of his illness. He left behind a wake of unfinished or uninitiated collaborations, including plans to perform with Ryan and to present new installations with Maria Blondeel. He had collaborated, by mail, with Paul Panhuysen on a bizarre installation titled *Marten Toonder's Studio*, 1993, which featured live goats and an accompaniment of their amplified vocalization; in his final trip to Europe, Hunt traveled to Eindhoven to help install the work, but a miscommunication prevented him from seeing it through. The work was realized in the entrance of a former dairy factory in 's-Hertogenbosch a couple weeks after Hunt's return to Texas, just months before his death.

Starting in the late '80s, Hunt experienced persistent fatigue and shortness of breath. He was in the early stages of emphysema, a condition caused and exacerbated by his heavy smoking, which he largely refused to curtail even as it began to affect his work. His symptoms would often become more pronounced during his spirited live performances; at his 1988 show at Het Apollohuis, a panting Hunt jested to the audience, "I'm getting too old for this. Next year, I'll be on videodisc."[84] In the final years of his life, Hunt gradually replaced his highly intensive solo setups with less physically demanding mediums like installations and duo collaborations, and increasingly relied on video—a return to the beginnings of his career, when he soldered video synthesis units, though he had yet to produce a stand-alone moving-image work of his own.

Initially, Hunt treated video as a supplement to performance, to solve what he saw as a fundamental limitation of live music: the audience's attention had nowhere to fix while the music played. (Hunt himself admitted feeling bored while watching solo instrumentalists.) He was particularly intrigued by the possibilities of laser disc, with its low cost and potential for nonlinear storage and recall. Enlisting the services of a Dallas-area electronics store, ECI Video, chiefly with the assistance of a young technician named Shawn Sterling, Hunt shot close-ups of himself wearing a frilly Elizabethan collar and playing and gesturing with his performance objects. His hope was to project the images behind him during his shows, sputtering through them in real time, likely using the same dynamic timecode system as his *Birome* installations. He also shot a striking piece called *Birome (Zone): Hemisphere* (1992), intended to accompany music, in which he zoomed in on the details of his skin with a magnifying glass and slowly scanned the entirety of his body. Resembling in equal parts '70s body art à la Bruce Nauman and the steady precision of a NASA space probe, the video transformed each crevice, freckle, and hair into an abstract field of pale color and texture, occasionally interrupted by discernible features such as the composer's anus. Hunt told Housewright that it contained the most "narrative interest" of any of his video works.[85]

Since their collaboration at the 1989 New Music America, Hunt and Karen Finley had been working to get a far more ambitious project off the ground. *The Finley-Hunt Report* (1992–93) was a taped performance that fused live psychodrama, video, and Hunt's electronic music. Its production is storied: In 1990, Finley submitted an application to the National Endowment for the Arts seeking funding that, along with three other applications, was awarded and then rescinded by NEA chairman John Frohnmayer. The agency, then under siege by the Republican party and culturally conservative religious groups for its acceptance of sexually explicit art, buckled under the pressure, denying Finley the grant by citing her frequent use of nudity. Frohnmayer's decision prompted a media circus and later a prolonged legal dispute culminating in a Supreme Court hearing. The fact that Hunt sat on the NEA panel that had approved the grant only heightened the controversy; Hunt penned a letter to the agency, expressing his disgust with its decision and refuting the alleged conflict of interest. The letter was cutting: "The actions of the NEA and the National Council make me a liar and/ or a tool of political manipulation," it concluded. "I am not the first and won't participate as the latter."[86]

Despite the obstacles, in the summer of 1992 *The Finley-Hunt Report*, a droll satire of television talk shows, had a weekend run at the Kitchen, where it drew on the frenzy of the cultural controversy;

one segment mashed up real-life footage of a TV reporter's interview questions to Finley, omitting the artist's responses. Hunt provided his contributions—a sweeping sampled-based score and videos of his domestic surroundings—from his home in Canton.[87] On a visit to Hunt's Texas ranch in the spring of 1992, Finley had taped monologues he conducted around the property. On the same occasion, they traveled together to Dealey Plaza and the nearby Texas School Book Depository, from which John F. Kennedy was shot, an event that was again swirling in the cultural consciousness after the success of Oliver Stone's *JFK* (1991). The two soon plotted a collaboration they would title *LBJ*, a "documentary opera" on the life of Lyndon B. Johnson, featuring the assassination as a crucial inflection point. It was intended to incorporate real-life sound recordings of Johnson with dramatic interpretations of his mother and the First Lady by Shelley Hirsch, and to be filmed across locations in Texas. It never came to fruition.

Hunt had, meanwhile, reconnected with David Dowe, who had taken a gig as an instructor at a strip-mall for-profit college in Dallas called Video Technical Institute (VTI), which shared its facilities with a veterinary certification program. Using Dowe's equipment and modest studio, Hunt shot four realizations of his work specifically for video. *Birome [zone]: plane (fixture)* demonstrates his stage antics—gesticulating on a stool and trying to balance a slew of objects as occasional walls of sound whirr; *Transform (stream): core* features his disembodied head sporting a ruff as he performs a deceptively complex work for solo whistling and electronics; *Talk (Slice) Duplex* is a scored conversation between Hunt and his young associate Rod Stasick, trading off their dialogue according to a preprogrammed woodblock sound, placing it somewhere between Hunt's algorithmic composition and his work with Finley; *Bitom [fixture]: topogram (core)* features Hunt in medical scrubs with a stethoscope, "inspecting" performance artist Michael Galbreth—noteworthy subject matter given Hunt's lifelong avoidance of doctor's offices and his deteriorating health. These four works, all from 1992, represent the clearest video documentation of the composer's performance style, notoriously difficult to capture on tape and here reformatted to fit inside the television screen. (Given the works' medium-specificity, Stasick has described them as "translations.") Never publicly screened during Hunt's lifetime, they were posthumously distributed as a commercially available VHS tape by OODiscs.

It appears that Hunt, in his final days, was hoping to ramp up his creation of single-channel videos with the ambition of producing experimentally minded work for television. His unrealized *LBJ* had been construed as an opera for "home viewing."[88] Echoing

Robert Ashley's 1976 series *Music with Roots in the Aether*, an experimental documentary that interviewed a different composer in each episode, Hunt put in an unsuccessful application to the Independent Television Service (ITVS) for *Art in Flight*, a documentary to be codirected with David Dowe that sought to profile five American expatriates. Each segment would feature a "confrontational interview" and site-specific performances that would help explain why Europe was more supportive of artists than the United States. The proposed participants—Arnold Dreyblatt, James and Mary Fulkerson, Shelley Hirsch, and Joel Ryan—were all close collaborators with Hunt, and the proposal seemed in part engineered to provide Hunt with the funding he needed to travel overseas and follow through on long-standing joint projects.

At this time, Hunt's health took a dramatic turn for the worse. In early 1993, his breathing difficulties had become so severe that he sought medical advice and was diagnosed with advanced lung cancer. He refused treatment and began research on best end-of-life practices, which he conducted with the same meticulousness he brought to his self-built electronics rigs. Before the Thanksgiving holiday, he rented a camera from ECI, and on November 27—three days shy of his fiftieth birthday—recorded his final video, *How to Kill Yourself Using the Inhalation of Carbon Monoxide Gas* (1993), an instructional tape running down all the relevant safety precautions and considerations, such as the deliberate placement of signs to alert those who might discover the body. Shortly thereafter, Hunt took his life, leaving behind instructions on how to edit the video.

The unrealized works Jerry Hunt left behind ranged from near-complete fragments—such as *Melody*, performed posthumously by the S.E.M. Ensemble at Paula Cooper Gallery in 1994—to open-ended propositions, such as loose plans to work with interactive software. In the year following his death, he was eulogized in several memorials that featured tribute performances by his many friends and peers. These performances included 77 Hz's *Telephone Calls to the Dead* and Shelley Hirsch's "virtual duet" with Hunt, both of which incorporated videos of the late composer—fitting for someone who derived much of his inspiration from "scrying," or divining messages from the beyond. Though by the end of his life Hunt was an agnostic, treating many of his early mystical revelations as mere compositional tools, his work seemed to tap into something at the very edges of the mortal coil. Instead of crystal balls, mandalas, or automatic writing, he used makeshift electronics, light bulbs, and David McManaway's wands. Musical sounds came to Hunt throughout his life as transmissions from the pleroma: "I just hear them in my mind, I don't whistle them or hum them or anything. I just find them."

Hunt at his home near Canton, Texas, with his and David McManaway's wands, 1982.
Photo: Stephen Housewright.

Notes

1 Gordon Monahan, "A Half Hour Behind Means They're Slightly Ahead," *Musicworks* no. 36 (Fall 1986): 11.

2 Stephen Housewright, *Partners* (New York: Blank Forms Editions, 2021), 148, 177.

3 Jerry Hunt, in "Jerry Hunt in discussion with staff and students of CNDO (1991)," *Jerry Hunt* (Exeter, UK: Arts Archives, 1993), 5.

4 Jerry Hunt, in "Jerry Hunt in discussion with staff and students of CNDO."

5 Housewright, *Partners*, 45.

6 Jerry Hunt, in "Wacoan Wins National Contest," *Waco Times-Herald*, May 4, 1955.

7 Hughes recalls that in the early fall of 1963, a few months prior to the Kennedy assassination and Ruby's own notoriety, Hunt recounted working for Ruby during lunchtimes at one of his clubs; the dancers and Hunt were obliged to perform to an empty room so that customers wouldn't find the stage empty when they arrived. Philip Hughes, email to the authors, October 6, 2021.

8 Philip Hughes and Stephen Housewright, emails to the authors, September 30 and October 1, 2021.

9 Philip Hughes, interview by the authors, April 30, 2021.

10 John Dee, *Liber Logaeth* (1583).

11 Hughes recalls that Hunt had handwritten scores that sketched the general direction of the two pieces performed with the trio, "Spiritus Niger" and "Lashtal," but that the pieces could generally be considered improvisational. The trio went on to perform Hunt's work to an unreceptive audience at a multi-act benefit concert at the American Federation of Musicians Local 147 later the same year. As Hughes recounts, he and Hunt had been praised beforehand by a critic in the *Dallas Morning News* who had yet to hear them perform, causing eager anticipation in the audience. Upon hitting the stage, they were quickly ushered off.

12 In an undated letter, most likely from the early '60s, Hunt writes to David Tudor: "Let me thank you for the pleasure of those performances of yours which I have enjoyed. My knowledge of your work, due to my present geographical situation, is quite limited, but of that I know of I have found excellent. Not knowing your attitudes regarding teaching (which I find particularly a morbid pastime), I am writing somewhat redoubtably. As I wrote Mr. Cage under separate mail, I can conveniently be in New York at any time within the next seven months. If I might meet you and talk with you regarding this matter, I would be most indebted. Whatever financial arrangements you find necessary I will attempt to negotiate." Jerry Hunt, letter to David Tudor, n.d., courtesy Getty Research Institute, Los Angeles (980039).

13 Organized by Lowell Cross at Texas Tech, the event took place at the Coronado Room of the Student Union Building on Monday, May 4, 1964, starting at 8:15 p.m. Remembering the event, Cross has written: "The Lubbock 'reception' of the performances of the Ichiyanagi and Cage pieces was even more uproarious than that in Austin. For *Variations II and III*, John Cage had contact microphones attached to practically everything that he planned to use, including an old mechanical typewriter upon which he typed, and with which he made great use of the right-margin bell and the return lever. He taped a contact microphone to his throat and drank water, staring at the audience in the most deadpan manner imaginable as the highly amplified sounds of his water-swallowing cascaded over the loudspeakers. Knowing what was coming from having witnessed the Austin performance, I could scarcely contain myself (I was supposed to have been 'assisting' by operating the sound system) as he progressed to the next 'Variations.' He clipped a contact microphone to his cigarette holder and smoked. I understood the underlying reason for the cigarette holder, because John Cage had already told the Sassers and me that his doctor had told him 'to get as far away from cigarettes as he could.' In any event, the amplified sounds of his smoking via the cigarette holder were but mere wisps of audio-frequency information in comparison to the water-swallowing. Next, he attached a contact microphone to his eyeglasses, put them on, and read." Lowell Cross, "Remembering David Tudor: A 75th Anniversary Memoir," accessed August 19, 2021, https://bop.unibe.ch/EJM/article/download/6118/8360/.

14 James Fulkerson, "Hunt, Irida Records, The Barton Workshop, and Me," *Irida Records: Hybrid Musics from Texas and Beyond, 1979–86* (New York: Blank Forms Editions, forthcoming), 52.

15 At a recital on April 12, 1962, Hunt presented Hughes's "Preludes," Susan Calvin's "Romanza," and his own "Structures" (all works ca. 1962) with an ensemble that featured Hughes. Interestingly enough, Hunt's instrumentation on "Structures" is given as piano and electronic continuum.

16 Jerry Hunt, in Guy De Bièvre, "It Would Be Great to Be Regarded as the World's Greatest Meringueist: Jerry Hunt Interviewed by Guy De Bièvre (Spring 1988)," audiotape edited for publication in the current volume, 274. The interview was conducted in preparation for publication in Dutch in *Logos-blad* (September 1988).

17 "Library Sets Avant Garde Music Series," ca. April 1963. Clipping, possibly from the *Dallas Times-Herald*.

18 Alvin Lucier, email to the authors, February 25, 2021.

19 Through his association with the ONCE Festival, Robert Ashley, and Gordon Mumma, Krumm would presumably have introduced Hunt to Ashley's "Maneuvers for Small Hands" (1961), which Hunt performed at Brandeis along with his own composition, "Helix 1963 w/ Theatre Function" (1963), Krumm's "May 62" (ca. 1962), and pieces by George Brecht, Toshi Ichiyanagi, and Karlheinz Stockhausen.

20 Philip Krumm, interview by the authors, March 10, 2021.

21 Grover Lewis, "Sounds of the Times: Critics Vary on Recital," *Fort Worth Star-Telegram*, 1964. Clipping, precise date unknown.

22 Jerry Hunt, interview by Gordon Monahan, 1986, tape 1, side B, courtesy Gordon Monahan.

23 Handwritten notes on the program for "Southern Methodist University School of the Arts Present SMU Orchestra February 13, 1966" suggest that Hunt was present for "Winter Music."

24 Typewritten notes inserted into the program read: "It might make good use of the talents of Jerry Hunt (who I knew would be on hand for the 'Winter Music' anyhow) in the sound control area. Sound control today is by Jerry Hunt, who is the co-conductor, being in charge of all tape and electronic elements as well as the concertante group."

25 Hunt's piece is listed on the program as "*Sur* John Dee with Infrasolo 3 (Cadenza)," which appears to be a variation on or iteration of a score he submitted to *Source: Music of the Avant-Garde*, which published it the following year under the title "*Sur* (Doctor) John Dee," in what Hunt alleged was an incomplete and incorrect reproduction. The piece is dated 1963 on Hunt's works list, but the dating there is often inaccurate due to repetitions in the titles and lack of original dated scores. The complete score for "*Sur* (Doctor) John Dee" has yet to be uncovered.

26 Peggy O'Dell, whom Hunt had met at UNT, became a close friend of Hunt's (and, later, of Housewright's as well).

27 Phil Hughes, email to the authors, May 4, 2021.

28 Unidentified author, "Electronic Composer Sees Music Revolution," *Dallas Morning News*, November 19, 1967.

29 Unidentified author, "Electronic Composer Sees Music Revolution," *Dallas Morning News*.

30 Ahlstrom's jazz lecture, disconcertingly, starts with Bill Evans's arrangement of Victor Young's "When I Fall in Love" and Debussy's "Reflections sur l'eau," followed by a romp through a "demonstration of the styles of Duke Ellington, Oscar Peterson, Red Garland, and Lenny Tristano." It concludes with Michael Zwerin's notorious interview with Cage, in which the composer discusses his distaste for jazz and rock, first published in the *Village Voice* on January 6, 1966. ("The form of jazz suggests too frequently that people are talking—that is, in succession—like in a panel discussion or a group of individuals simply imposing their remarks without responding to one another.") The interview was reprinted as "A Lethal Measurement" in *John Cage: An Anthology*, ed. Richard Kostelanetz (New York: Praeger Publishers, 1970), 163–64. One can only imagine that Ahlstrom's tone was somewhat pejorative. It is certainly worth noting that,

in both attitude and format, the program followed in the footsteps of Cage's "History of Experimental Music in the United States," an article that set the historical narrative that affirmed the prominence of Cage and certain white colleagues. As George Lewis notes, the article "articulated a model that eschewed any contact with African American forms." George Lewis, *A Power Stronger than Itself: The A.A.C.M. and American Experimental Music* (Chicago: University of Chicago Press, 2008), 378.

31 The 1949 date is either a joke or a typo, as Hunt would have been six at the time.

32 In a 1991 interview conducted by the Center for New Dance Development in Arnhem, Netherlands, Hunt recalls his first "experimental performance," which included eight bands playing simultaneously for the opening of a shopping center in Texas: "The first [experimental performance] that was really shocking, but which would not be shocking by modern standards, was that we provoked a police riot. We had been asked to do a concert for the opening of a shopping center. A large number of rock bands were involved, about eight. Unfortunately, the rock bands didn't know that they were not going to play separately but were going to sort of play at once. We did things in the middle which created the direction and controlled their amplifiers." Jerry Hunt, in "Jerry Hunt in discussion with staff and students of CNDO."

33 "Tape Recorder" appears in lieu of a performer's name on the program, followed by the phrase "(Realization by Jerry Hunt's dog's Jerry)," suggesting Hunt's involvement.

34 Douglas Taylor, who shared a fascination with esoterica, showed Hunt his original research on the subject; this included photocopies of John Dee and Edward Kelley's *Liber Mysteriorum Sextus et Sanctus*, the angelic tablets that would guide the electronic processes of much of Hunt's later work.

35 Ron Snider, conversation with the authors, June 24, 2020.

36 Jerry Hunt and David Dowe, *Procession*, 1973, video, Video Research Center, Dallas.

37 David Thompson, *The International Carnival of Experimental Sound* (self-published, 2017), 118.

38 Jerry Hunt and David Dowe, *A Visit to the Center*, 1973, video, produced by KQED/NCET, San Francisco.

39 "Open Circuits: An International Conference on the Future of Television" took place at the Museum of Modern Art, January 23–25, 1974, and brought together curators, artists, and critics working in the emerging field of video. The event included screenings, panel discussions, and the presentation of papers around the themes of the production, distribution, and exhibition of video. A collection documenting the conference was subsequently published as *The New Television: A Public/Private Art* (Cambridge, MA: MIT Press, 1977).

40 Both Haramand Plane and Cantegral Segment(s) started out as audio/video collaborations with Dowe, but Hunt soon began presenting these projects as solo performances.

41 Hunt's Haramand Plane and Cantegral Segment(s) refer to both the systems he designed and his compositional procedures. Jerry Hunt, "Audio Video Synthesis," reproduced in this volume, 185–94. Originally published in *Synapse* no. 6 (March/April 1977): 26–29. Page references are to the current volume.

42 Hunt, "Audio Video Synthesis," 192.

43 Hunt, "Audio Video Synthesis," 192.

44 "Of course, how do we know what 'human' is? I ask that whenever people tell me that electronic music they've heard sounds like it was made by a machine." Jerry Hunt, in Willem Brans, "Jerry Hunt's Electronic-Musical Genius," *D, The Magazine of Dallas*, May 1976, 34.

45 Stephen Beck, conversation with the authors, October 28, 2021.

46 David Dowe quoted in Susan Barton, "Art: Television Is its Canvas," *Dallas Times-Herald*, January 10, 1974.

47 Dimitri Devyatkin, *The 1973 International Computer Art Festival*, program (New York: The Kitchen, 1973), 6. The festival ran from April 1 to April 14.

48 To give a sense of the overall economics of the situation, Dowe recalled in an interview that SMU provided space and administrative support for academically relevant matters

related to the VRC. He was paid as a lecturer in the university's Television department, while Hunt was on salary in the Dance department and eventually as the head of the Electronic Music department. The National Center for Experiments in Television made Dowe a Fellow and provided an additional stipend for the work he was doing at the VRC at SMU. NCET also provided a small budget for operations, which Dowe directed toward a stipend for Hunt. The Rockefeller Foundation provided a one-time $5,000 stipend for travel and expenses related to lectures and performances at other universities in the region. NCET provided additional support when Hunt and Dowe helped with productions for training and broadcasting, such as honorariums, travel, and other expenses. David Dowe, interview by the authors, September 30, 2020.

49 David Dowe, interview by the authors, March 9, 2020.

50 Hunt uses the phrase "work as pianist" in a number of biographies printed in the '70s. This may reference both his professional work in dance halls and strip joints and his modernist recitals.

51 Beginning in 1975, recitals of this sort became a nearly annual affair and were rare showcases of Hunt's piano stylings.

52 Even so, Hunt would continue to collaborate with a handful of instrumentalists over the next decade. He met James Fulkerson in 1976 at the Intermuse Festival, an academic conference comprising a series of performances and talks at the Chinsegut Hill Manor House (then affiliated with the university), organized by Larry Austin. Hunt, Dary John Mizelle, and Fulkerson all presented new works; Mizelle premiered "Polyphonies I," a semi-improvisational work for shakuhachi and electronic tape, later included in his Irida release. Fulkerson writes that he was impressed by the combination of theoretical depth and humor in Hunt's performance. Their encounter proved to be formative for both artists, and Fulkerson would go on to be one of the primary interpreters of Hunt's compositions in the years to come. For more information on Intermuse and Hunt's collaboration with Fulkerson, see Fulkerson, *Irida Records* (New York: Blank Forms Editions, forthcoming).

53 Jerry Hunt, in Bernard Brunon, "Jerry Hunt," *Artspace* 10, no. 4 (Fall 1986).

54 Jerry Hunt, liner notes for *Ground: Five Mechanic Convention Streams* (OODiscs, 1992).

55 Chess Challenger was a dedicated chess microcomputer with an Intel 8080 CPU commercially released in 1976. See Gordon Monahan, "Stompin' and Beatin' and Screamin': An Interview with Jerry Hunt by Gordon Monahan," reprinted in this volume, 219–40. Originally published in *Musicworks* no. 39 (Fall 1987): 6–11. Page references are to the current volume.

56 Jerry Hunt, in Jane van Sickle and Seaon Coburn, "Interview: Jerry Hunt," *Dallas Studio*, February 1981.

57 For more on "Lattice," see Kumpf and Maxin, "Transformations for Electromechanical Reproduction." It's also worth noting that above and beyond playing the piano, Hunt's use of architectural spaces and the physical attachment of sounding objects to the instrumentalist have parallels in the optical sensor systems he would be employing in his instrument-less solo work, the gestural movements of the body becoming sounds interacting with, rather than preparing, the piano. See Charles Amirkhanian, "An Interview with Jerry Hunt," *Morning Concert*, KFPA, November 6, 1980, https://archive.org/details/MC_1980_11_06/MC_1980_11_06_A_ed.wav.

58 It is also worth noting that Krumm claims that his piece "Sound Machine" on the *Texas Music* compilation is essentially a Hunt piece, utilizing a similar layering and remixing strategy that employed past performance recordings of "Sound Machine" as its source material. Philip Krumm, interview by the authors, March 10, 2021. Hunt corroborated this in his description of the piece in Amirkhanian, "An Interview with Jerry Hunt."

59 Jerry Hunt, liner notes for *Cantegral Segment(s) 16.17.18.19. / Transform (Stream) / Transphalba / Volta (Kernel)*, Irida, 1979.

60 David Dowe, conversation with the authors, March 11, 2021.

61 Jerry Hunt, program notes for "Jerry Hunt and David Dowe in a concert of live video and sound synthesis with intermedia theater," York University, Toronto, 1975. Jerry Hunt archives, courtesy Stephen Housewright.

62 The two pieces listed as "Cantegral Segment(s)" have different numbers associated with them. Perhaps as with "Transform (Steam)," which was also presented as part of this program along with "Kelley: (Drape)," Hunt was combining and layering aspects of both "Segment(s)" for the performance.

63 Hunt, program notes for "Jerry Hunt and David Dowe in a concert."

64 Jerry Hunt, in De Bièvre, "It Would Be Great to Be Regarded as the World's Greatest Meringueist," 251.

65 Jerry Hunt, in Monahan, "Stompin' and Beatin' and Screamin'," 47.

66 Tom Johnson, "New Music America Takes Over a Town," Village Voice, June 25–July 1, 1980.

67 Kyle Gann, Robert Ashley (Champaign: University of Illinois Press, 2012), 64.

68 Program notes for Joseph Celli, Phalba (Revisited), Experimental Intermedia Foundation, New York, March 19, 1994.

69 Joseph Franklin, conversation with the authors, August 20, 2021.

70 Laurel Wyckoff, conversation with the authors, August 20, 2021.

71 Gordon Monahan, interview by the authors, April 22, 2020.

72 Housewright, Partners, 195.

73 Jerry Hunt, in Monahan, "Stompin' and Beatin' and Screamin'," 223.

74 Jerry Hunt, in De Bièvre, "It Would Be Great to Be Regarded as the World's Greatest Meringueist," 269.

75 Jerry Hunt, letter to Gordon Hoffman, August 16, 1987. Jerry Hunt archives, courtesy Stephen Housewright.

76 Houston Festival Foundation, New Music America 1986 (Houston: Houston Festival Foundation, 1986), https://0836f2f1-c746-430e-b8e7-c266264baefb.filesusr.com/ugd/b4072f_60ab765228cc4ebeb6232a89e54bb9b0.pdf.

77 Following the festival, Jim Pomeroy and Hunt kept in touch, and Pomeroy soon arranged to visit Hunt's studio with video artist Ed Tannenbaum. In 1990, Pomeroy relocated from San Francisco to Arlington, Texas, putting the pair in closer contact until his untimely death in 1992 after suffering a concussion from a fall.

78 Jerry Hunt, in De Bièvre, "It Would Be Great to Be Regarded as the World's Greatest Meringueist," 259.

79 Werner Durand, conversation with the authors, July 15, 2021.

80 Jerry Hunt, interview by William Duckworth, 1990, hand-edited manuscript, Jerry Hunt archives, courtesy Stephen Housewright.

81 Jerry Hunt, in "Interview between Leon van Noorden and Jerry Hunt," Jerry Hunt: Birome (ZONE): Cube and Birome (ZONE): Cube [frame], brochure (Eindhoven, Netherlands: Middelburg Bureau of Culture and Het Apollohuis, 1988).

82 Kyle Gann, "Drips and Chocolate," Village Voice, December 12, 1989.

83 On November 30, 1989, the evening before World AIDS Day, a one-day sound installation constructed by Hunt was performed at the Dallas Museum of Art as part of its Day Without Art. The works were similarly dedicated to Briece.

84 Jerry Hunt, performance at Het Apollohuis, Eindhoven, Netherlands, December 23, 1988, Videocassettes (VHS), 98 minutes and 59 min. Het Apollohuis archive, courtesy ZKM | Center for Art and Media, Karlsruhe, Germany.

85 Housewright, Partners, 267.

86 Hunt's letter to the NEA is reprinted on page 346 of the current volume.

87 Hunt's electronic score was released posthumously on Tzadik Records as Song Drapes (1999). The album also featured assorted unrealized work interpreted by Finley, Shelley Hirsch, and Mike Patton, as well as an arrangement by Michael Schell that paired a precomposed piece by Hunt with an audio-taped phone call by Lyndon B. Johnson.

88 Jerry Hunt and Karen Finley, "LBJ Proposal," reprinted on page 352 of the current volume.

Hunt, late 1950s or early '60s. Photographer unknown.

NORTH TEXAS STATE UNIVERSITY

SCHOOL OF MUSIC

presents

Student Recital Series

February 14, 1962   10:00 a.m.   Recital Hall

Nocturne, E Major .... *Chopin*

Ellan Smith, piano

Grand Duo Concertant .... *C. M. von Weber*

Andante con moto
Allegro con fuoco

Kenneth Flory, clarinet
James Rivers, piano

Romance in F♯ .... *Schumann*

Clyde Hudgins, piano

Heavenly Father .... *J. S. Bach*

Ann Allen, soprano
James Rivers, piano

Structures .... *Jerry E. Hunt*

Fred Sautter, trumpet
Bob Grace, saxophone
Phil Hughes, string bass
Jerry Hunt, piano
and
electronic continuum

Program from Student Recital Series, North Texas State University School of Music, Denton, February 14, 1962.

Jack Hospers welcomes new Chamber members to the luncheon March 5. They include the Ted Stanford Trio, left to right surrounding the bass fiddle, Anita Stanford, Jerry Hunt, Ted Stanford. *First row,* left to right: Hal Mayer, Bennie McKee, Doug Kelly, Jim Allen, Mr. and Mrs. Van Hoesen, Robert Weathers. *Second row,* left to right: John Croxall, Merl Scheffey, L. L. High, Winfield Morten, J. L. Fountain, Jearl Brown.

Hunt with Jack Hospers and new Chamber members, March 1963. Photographer unknown.

The Dallas Museum of Fine Arts

and

Mu Phi Epsilon

Present

JERRY HUNT, *Pianist*

● ● ● ●

DALLAS MUSEUM OF FINE ARTS

Sunday, May 30, 1965   4:00 P. M.

● ● ● ●

PROGRAM

Incidental Music..*George Brecht*

Music for Piano No. 2 ....*Toshi Ichiyanagi*

Klavierstuck VI..*Karlheinz Stockhausen*

● ● ● ●

INTERMISSION

● ● ● ●

Unit 2 w/stabile for continuous topogram......................*Jerry Hunt*

Variations III ....*John Cage*

● ● ● ●

Programs Courtesy of

WHITTLE MUSIC COMPANY

2733 Oak Lawn – Dallas, Texas – Phone LA 1-0208

Flier for Hunt concert, Dallas Museum of Fine Arts, May 20, 1965.

THE DALLAS PUBLIC LIBRARY

Library Music Committee

presents

A FESTIVAL OF CONTEMPORARY MUSIC

Program II

Library Auditorium

April 11, 1963   8:00 p.m.

A FESTIVAL OF CONTEMPORARY MUSIC

Remaining programs in the series:

Saturday, April 20, 1963   3:00 p.m.

Thursday, April 25, 1963   8:00 p.m.

Friday, May 3, 1963   8:00 p.m.

All programs will take place in the
auditorium of the
Dallas Public Library

PROGRAM

Intersection # 3 (1953)   Morton Feldman
                                     1926-
                  Jerry E. Hunt, piano

Concert for piano and voice   John Cage
   with Fontana mix (1957-58)   1912-

                  Jerry E. Hunt, piano
                  Donald Cowan, bass-baritone
                  John L. Maus, technician

INTERMISSION

Duet I (1960)   Christian Wolff
                                     1934-
           Jerry E. Hunt, Tim Wilburn, piano

Sapporo for 16 performers   Toshi Ichiyanagi
                                     1934-
                  Jerry E. Hunt, conductor

Handbill for Program II of A Festival of Contemporary Music, Dallas Public Library, April 11, 1963.

THE DALLAS PUBLIC LIBRARY

Library Music Committee

Presents

A FESTIVAL OF CONTEMPORARY MUSIC

Program III

Library Auditorium

April 20, 1963   3:00 p.m.

PROGRAM

34'46.776" (Prepared Piano)   John Cage
   (1954)   1912-

Jerry E. Hunt, piano

February Pieces (1961)   Cornelius Cardew
                                    1936-

Jerry E. Hunt, piano

INTERMISSION

Last Pieces (1959)   Morton Feldman
                                    1926-

Jerry E. Hunt, piano

Quantitaten (1958)   Bo Nilsson
                                        1937-

Jerry E. Hunt, piano

A FESTIVAL OF CONTEMPORARY MUSIC

Remaining programs in the series:
Thursday, April 25, 1963 8:00 p.m.
   Friday, May 3, 1963 8:00 p.m.

All programs will take place in the
auditorium of the Dallas Public Library.

Handbill for Program III of A Festival of Contemporary Music, Dallas Public Library, April 20, 1963.

THE DALLAS PUBLIC LIBRARY

Library Music Committee

presents

A FESTIVAL OF CONTEMPORARY MUSIC

Program IV

Library Auditorium

April 25, 1963   8:00 p.m.

PROGRAM

Klavierstück No.XI (1957)   Karlheinz Stockhausen
                             1928-

Jerry E. Hunt, piano

Durations 2 (1960-61)   Morton Feldman
                             1926-
        Patrick Simpson, cello
        Jerry E. Hunt, piano

Durations 4 (1960-61)   Morton Feldman
                             1926-
        Lutz Mayer, violin
        Patrick Simpson, cello
        Jerry E. Hunt, vibraphone

INTERMISSION

Five Piano Pieces for   Sylvano Bussotti
    David Tudor   1931-

Jerry E. Hunt, piano

Music Walk (1958)   John Cage

Jerry E. Hunt, Margaret O'Dell, James Rivers

The last program in the

FESTIVAL OF CONTEMPORARY MUSIC

will take place on
Friday, May 3, 1963 8:00 p.m.
in the auditorium of the
Dallas Public Library

Handbill for Program IV of A Festival of Contemporary Music, Dallas Public Library, April 25, 1963.

THE DALLAS PUBLIC LIBRARY

Library Music Committee

Presents

A FESTIVAL OF CONTEMPORARY MUSIC

Program V

Library Auditorium

May 3, 1963   8:00 p.m.

PROGRAM

Atlas Eclipticalis (1961-63)   John Cage
                                      1912-
          Chamber ensemble
        Jerry E. Hunt, conductor

0' 00"   John Cage
                                      1912-
        Jerry E. Hunt, performer

Octet 1961 for Jasper Johns.   Cornelius Cardew
                                      1936-
          Chamber ensemble
        Jerry E. Hunt, conductor

INTERMISSION

Transicion II (1958-59)   Mauricio Kagel
  For pianist, percussionist   1931-
  and 2 magnetic tapes.

          Jerry E. Hunt, piano
          Roger Staley, percussion
          John L. Maus, technician

Handbill for Program V of A Festival of Contemporary Music, Dallas Public Library, May 3, 1963.

Above and following pages: Hunt, Houston Higgins, and David Ahlstrom performing at two locations around Dallas, mid-1960s. Photographer unknown.

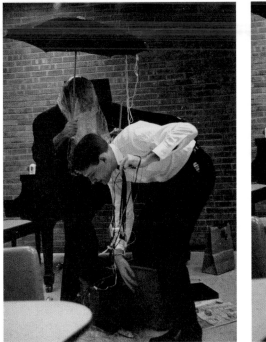

THE ENTERTAINMENT DIVISION
of SPECIAL SERVICES

presents

JERRY E. HUNT

IN CONCERT

MARCH 20, 1966 • 7:00 P. M.

YELLOW BARN THEATRE
FORT POLK, LOUISIANA

Program for Hunt concert at Yellow Barn Theatre, Fort Polk, Louisiana, March 20, 1966.

Mu Phi Epsilon Alumnae

and

Dallas Art Association

present

JERRY HUNT, Pianist — HOUSTON HIGGINS, Clarinetist

•   •   •   •

DALLAS MUSEUM OF FINE ARTS

Sunday, November 6, 1966   4:00 P. M.

•   •   •   •

PROGRAM

The Anti-Abolitionist Riots of the 1830's and 1840's	*Charles Ives*
Madrigal I	*Henri Pousseur*
Klavierstucke 7-8	*Karlheinz Stockhausen*
Mimetics (Metapiece) w/	*Mauricio Kagel*
Samaym	Houston Higgins
Plate w/ Theatrefunction 3a	Jerry Hunt
Sound Machine	*Philip Krumm*

•   •   •   •   •

Variation IV	*John Cage*
Rhapsody I	*Claude Debussy*

•   •   •   •

Programs Courtesy of

WHITTLE MUSIC COMPANY

2733 Oak Lawn Avenue — Dallas, Texas — Phone LA 1-0280

Flier for Hunt and Houston Higgins concert, Dallas Museum of Fine Arts, November 6, 1966.

The Dallas Chamber Ensemble

Presents in Concert

JERRY HUNT, PIANIST
JILL LEATHERWOOD, SOPRANO
HOUSTON HIGGINS, CLARINETIST

Oak Cliff Society of Fine Arts
28 February 1967   8:15 .P.M.

Piano Pieces 1952, 1955, 1956a, 1956b
Extensions III   Morton Feldman
        Mr. Hunt

Theatre-Function IV (1963) Coelum philosophorum   Jerry Hunt
        Miss Leatherwood, Mr. Higgins

As pure to begin   Philip Corner
                Mr. Hunt, assisted by
        Miss Leatherwood, Mr. Higgins

Sound Machine   Philip Krumm
        Mr. Higgins, Mr. Hunt, Miss Leatherwood
        (Instruments courtesy of Douglas and Avlona Taylor)

Three-Page Sonata   Charles Ives
        Mr. Hunt, assisted by Mr. Higgins

for Vivaldi (1965)
    w/ Planispheric Surface   Jerry Hunt
        Electronic version for instrumental
        consort, bridge and ring modulator,
        noise generator.
            Miss Leatherwood, Mr. Hunt, and
            Mr. Higgins

DALLAS CHAMBER ENSEMBLE
P. O. BOX 47163
DALLAS, TEXAS 75247

Program for Dallas Chamber Ensemble performance, Oak Cliff Society of Fine Arts auditorium,
Dallas, February 28, 1967.

CONCERTS ONE AND TWO

JERRY HUNT, Pianist   HOUSTON HIGGINS, Clarinetist

Metapiece (Mimetics)
Mimetics (Metapiece)

Mauricio Kagel, 1961
For Piano. This piece may be performed as a solo, or simultaneously, intermittantly, sequentially
with any other 20th C. work.
Mr. Hunt and Mr. Higgins have composed materials to be performed
with the piece.

Klavierstück VI
Plus Minus

Karlheinz Stockhausen
Klavierstück VI (1954-55) was re-
vised in 1961. Mr. Huht plays the
1961 version. Plus Minus (1963)
is for 2 - 7 players and is realized from the score by the players.

Electronic Music for Piano
with 0'0"
Fontana Mix

John Cage
Electronic Music for Piano (1964)
is realized by using composing
means of Atlas Eccliptocalis. 0'0"
(1962) is part of a larger work;It
is to be performed alone or simultaneously with other activities.
Fontana Mix (1958) provides material
for audio-visual presentations. This
version is instrumental-theatrical.

Sur (Doctor) John Dee

Jerry Hunt, 1966
Dr. Dee: Astrologer-Magician-
Physician-Writer, Court of Elizabeth I.
The piece is and enchantment for
0-11 people (or multiples of the
prime from 0-11). Musical material:
Tabulatura Soyga.

Madrigale I

Henri Pousseur, 1966
For clarinet alone.

Ebullism

Joseph Byrd, 1966
For clarinet and piano. Commissioned
by the Dallas Chamber Ensemble.

Star Chamber

Philip Krumm, 1966
For 2 or more musicians. This piece
was also commissioned by the DCE. It
exists in various versions for various
number of performers.

Program for Hunt and Houston Higgins concert at an unidentified venue, mid-1960s.

PROGRAM THREE: THE EUROPEAN EXPERIMENTALISTS

Oct. 5, 1966   JERRY HUNT, PIANIST

KARLHEINZ STOCKHAUSEN	KLAVIERSTUCK VII	(1954)
KARLHEINZ STOCKHAUSEN	KLAVIERSTUCK XI	(1956)
PIERRE BOULEZ	TROPE	(1958-)
SYLVANO BUSSOTTI	FIVE PIANO PIECES FOR DAVID TUDOR (1958)	
	(No.'s 1, 2 AND 3 ONLY)	

- - - - - - - - - -

PROGRAM FOUR: MUSIC AND THEATRE

Oct. 12, 1966

"EVENING" FROM IN MEMORIAM KIT CARSON (OPERA)
(STAGE VERSION, DECEMBER, 1965)

ROBERT ASHLEY

PERFORMED BY MEMBERS OF THE CLASS, WITH SIMULTANEOUS
PLAYING OF A TAPE RECORDED PERFORMANCE BY THE DALLAS
CHAMBER ENSEMBLE. (JULY 10, 1966)

- - - - - - - - - -

PROGRAM FIVE: THE AMERICAN EXPERIMENTALISTS

Oct. 19, 1966   JERRY HUNT, PIANIST

CHRISTIAN WOLFF	FOUR PIECES FOR PREPARED PIANO	1952
HENRY COWELL	BANSHEE	
	AOLIAN HARP	
CHARLES IVES	ANTI-ABOLITIONIST RIOTS	1908-9
JOHN CAGE	CARTRIDGE MUSIC	1960
	MR. HUNT	
ROBERT ASHLEY	IN MEMORIAM CRAZY HORSE	1964
JOSEPH BYRD	HOMMAGE TO JACKSON MACLOW	1965

(THE LAST TWO WORKS ARE TAPE RECORDINGS
OF ONCE GROUP PERFORMANCES.)

Above and following pages: Program for David Ahlstrom's Lectures with Music, Dallas College, Fall 1966, [2–5].

PROGRAM SIX: JAZZ, FIRST AND THIRD STREAMS

Nov. 2, 1966   PART I (LIVE) JAC MURPHY AND THE JUVEY GOMEZ TRIO
               JUVEY GOMEZ, DRUMS; GIL PITT, BASS; JAC MURPHY, PIANO

RAVEL   LE GASPAR DE NUIT (LE GIBET)

               WHEN I FALL IN LOVE (ARR. BILL EVANS)

DEBUSSY   REFLECTIONS SUR L'EAU

DEMONSTRATION DUKE ELLINGTON
OF THE STYLES OSCAR PETERSON
     OF   RED GARLAND
               LENNY TRISTANO

JAC MURPHY   FELICIA'S THEME

               THE ARISTOCRATS' THEME (FROM THE INCIDENTAL
               MUSIC FOR "SPARKS FLY UPWARD")(COMPOSED LAST
               FALL FOR SMU THEATER DEPT.)

               PART II (RECORDED)

ANDRE HODEIR   AROUND THE BLUES

                    MODERN JAZZ QUARTET AND ORCHESTRA

GUNTHER SCHULER VARIANTS ON A THEME OF THELONIUS MONK
                    (CRISS-CROSS)

ROBERT ASHLEY   WOLFMAN WITH JAZZ
                    (TAPE AND SMU GROUP)

JOHN COLTRANE'S NATURE BOY

               PART III

AN INTERVIEW (ABOUT JAZZ) WITH JOHN CAGE
                  (VILLAGE VOICE JANUARY 6/66)

PROGRAM SEVEN: JAZZ AND ROCK (A READING AND A LECTURE) (BOTH
                                          WITHOUT MUSIC)
Nov. 9, 1966

I   AN INTERVIEW WITH JOHN CAGE (CONTINUED)

II   THE LIVELINESS TO BE OBSERVED IN MUSEUMS
      THE SPECTATOR SPORTS
      FROM POPULAR TO SPECIALIST GAMES
      TEACHING SOCCER
      OTHER MUSEUMS

                - - - - - - - - - -

PROGRAM EIGHT:

Nov. 16, 1966

                    A CONCERT FOR GREATER DALLAS

          SIMULTANEOUS AND CONSECUTIVE PERFORMANCES OF WORKS

               FROM THE NON-SPECIALIST LITERATURE.

            HOUSTON HIGGINS, JERRY HUNT, DAVID AHLSTROM
           (THE ORDER BELOW WILL DEFINITELY NOT BE FOLLOWED)

GEORGE MACHIUNAS   MUSIC FOR EVERY DOG (1961)   MR. HUNT
               (REALIZATION BY JERRY HUNT'S DOG HERMES)

ALISON KNOWLES   MESH (1961)   MR. HUNT

WALTER DE MARIA   SURPRISE BOX (1961)
               (PERFORMER TO BE ANNOUNCED)

GEORGE BRECHT   LAMP EVENT (1961)   MR. HUNT

GEORGE BRECHT   EIGHT PIANO TRANSCRIPTIONS
                                   (1961)   MR. HUNT

GORDON MUMMA   SMALL SIZE MOGRAPH (1962)   MR. HUNT

HOUSTON HIGGINS   GOLDEN SPOON (1966)   MR. HIGGINS

JERRY HUNT   PUNCTURE (PRE CIS) (1949)   MR. HUNT

T. KOSUGI   MICRO 1 (1963)   MR. HUNT

                    (CONTINUED)

96

PROGRAM EIGHT: (CONTINUED)

JOHN CAGE	FONTANA MIX (1958)	TAPE RECORDER
	(REALIZATION BY JERRY HUNT'S DOG'S JERRY)	
ICHIYANAGI	I B M ('61)	MR. AHLSTROM
TRISTAN TZARA	SIMULTANEOUS POEM FOR THREE READERS	
	MR. HUNT, MR. HIGGINS, MR. AHLSTROM	
THOMAS SCHMIDT	ZYKLUS (1963)	MR. AHLSTROM
GEORGE BRECHT	SUNDOWN EVENT (10:00 P.M. VARIATION)	
	(TO BE PERFORMED BY ALL PERSONS PRESENT ON INSTRUCTION.)	
C. SHIOMI	AIR EVENT (1964)	MR. AHLSTROM
LAMONTE YOUNG	FOR HENRY FLYNT (1960)	MR. HIGGINS
HI RED CENTER	FOR FRED RAULSTON (1910)	MR. RAULSTON
DICK HIGGINS	LECTURE NO. 6 (1963)	MR. AHLSTROM
ERIK SATIE	SELECTED READINGS	VARIOUS PERFORMERS
JACQUE VACHE	SELECTED READINGS	VARIOUS PERFORMERS
ERIK SATIE	LE PIEGE DE MEDUSE	

BARON MEDUSE.......MR. HUNT
POLYCARPE..........MR. AHLSTROM
(DANCE OF THE MONKEY...BY HOUSTON HIGGINS)

G. BRECHT	INCIDENTAL MUSIC (1961)	MR. HUNT
GUISEPPI CHIARI	LA STRADA (1964)	MR. HUNT
JOHN CAGE	0' 00"	MR. HIGGINS
LA MONTE YOUNG	(TITLE TO BE ANNOUNCED)	MR. HIGGINS
JERRY HUNT	JERRY HUNT'S SCRAP BOX	MR. HUNT
		AND TAPE RECORDER

OTHER COMPOSITIONS BY LA MONTE YOUNG, JOSEPH BYRD,
JACKSON MACLOW, NAM JUN PAIK (AND OTHERS) TO BE
ANNOUNCED.

Hunt with Houston Higgins and Jill Leatherwood, ca. 1960s. Photographer unknown.

audio visual studio/ ensemble

2311 glencoe / p. o. box 28428 / 214/827-8435 / dallas, texas

Jerry Hunt
Houston Higgins   Directors

Highland Park Town Hall
4700 Drexel Ave.

Sunday, 27 April 1969
3:00 P.M.

Admission: $1.50

ELECTRONIC INSTRUMENTAL/THEATER

Above and overleaf: Program for Audio Visual Studio/Ensemble, Highland Park Town Hall, Dallas, April 27, 1969.

La Strada (1964)   Giuseppe Chiari
  to George Maciunas

Sette Fogli (1959)   Sylvano Bussotti
  Nr.5 Lettura di Braibanti per voce sola

Aus den Sieben Tagen (1968)   Karlheinz Stockhausen
  Richtige Dauern 7.Mai
  Unbegrenzt   8.Mai
  Treffpunkt   8.Mai

Solo for Voice 2 (1960)   John Cage
  w/ Cartridge Music (1960)

                    intermission

Samaym (1966)   Houston Higgins
  w/ Preamble (1965) realization by Douglas Taylor

Etude No. 3 (1963)   Phillip Hughes

Last Pieces (1959)   Morton Feldman

Tabulatura Soyga (1966)   Jerry Hunt
  w/ Continuous Sphere (1963)

              Audiovisual Studio/Ensemble wishes
              to extend special thanks to Gordon
              Hoffman, electronics design/engineer,
              for his technical assistance and
              for the electronic instrumentation
              he has designed for the studio.

              Oriental instruments, film, film
              projectors courtesy of Douglas Taylor

              Intermission refreshments will be
              served courtesy of AVSE

              Intermission music courtesy of
              Phillip Hughes (Furniture Music)

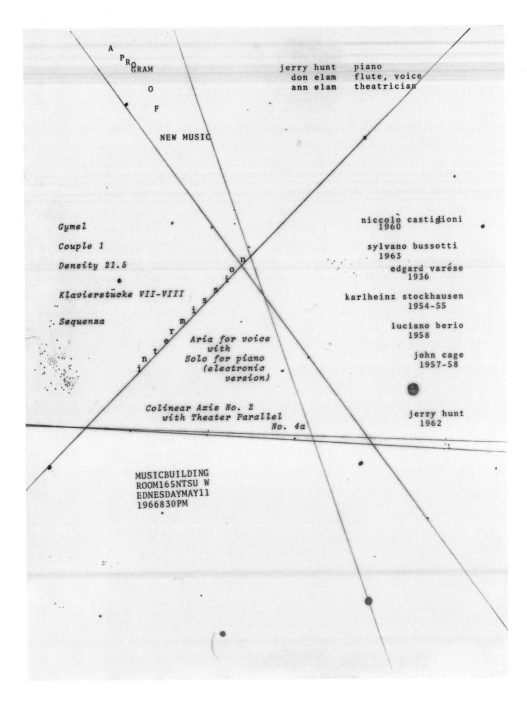

Poster for A Program of New Music, University of North Texas, Denton, May 11, 1966.

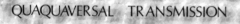

QUAQUAVERSAL TRANSMISSION

electronic aural + visual

audio visual
studio/ensemble

29 and 30 January 1972
8:00p.m. Saturday
3:00p.m. Sunday

Admission

JERRY HUNT, HOUSTON HIGGINS, PHILLIP HUGHES
GORDON HOFFMAN - DESIGN ENGINEER
Ron Snider, percussionist
Jill Higgins, vocalist   GUEST ARTISTS

at the Studio of Salle Werner
4501 Cole Ave.
Dallas , Texas
$2.50

Poster for Quaquaversal Transmission, studio of Salle Werner Vaughn, Dallas, January 29–30, 1972.

Hunt and Salle Werner Vaughn at Werner Vaughn's studio, Dallas, ca. 1970s.

Hunt at Salle Werner Vaughn's studio, Dallas, ca. 1970s.

Hunt preparing dinner for Gordon Hoffman (bottom, foreground) and others at his Swiss Avenue home, Dallas, mid-1970s. Photographer unknown.

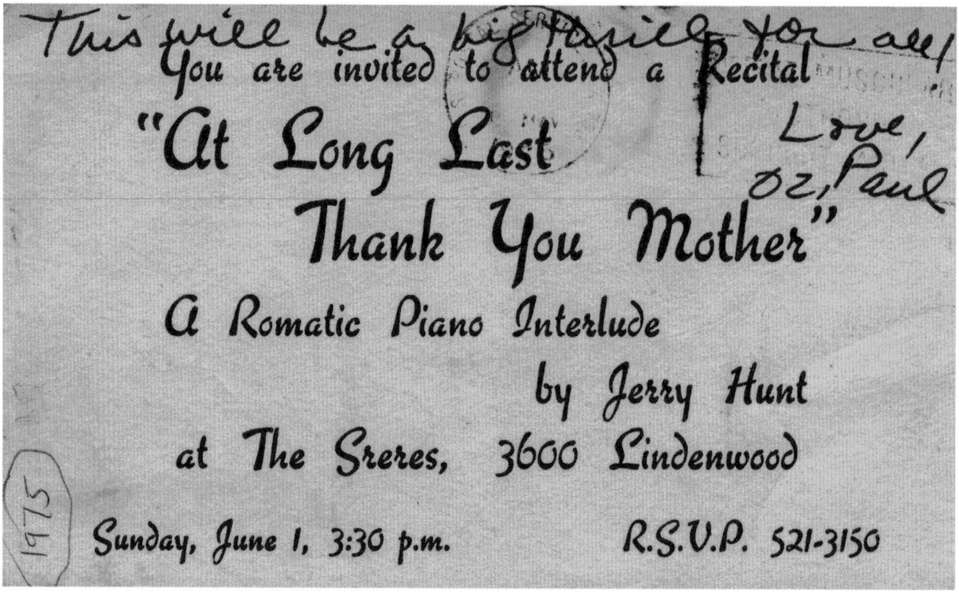

This will be a big thrill for all!

You are invited to attend a Recital

"At Long Last

Love,
Oz, Paul

Thank You Mother"

A Romatic Piano Interlude

by Jerry Hunt

at The Sreres, 3600 Lindenwood

1975

Sunday, June 1, 3:30 p.m.

R.S.V.P. 521-3150

Invitation to At Long Last Thank You Mother, home of Oz and Paul Srere,
Dallas, June 1, 1975.

UNIVERSITY OF ILLINOIS AT URBANA-CHAMPAIGN
The School of Music

FESTIVAL OF CONTEMPORARY PERFORMING ARTS

Jerry Hunt

Haramand Plane (overlay) 1972, 1976
Transhelix 1972   .

Cantegral Segment(s) 7, 17 (1975, 1976)

Cantegral Segment(s) 16, 18 (1976, 1977)

(pounding)   (1977)

Transform- (stream) (1977)
   in memoriam, Clarence Edward Hunt (1912-1977)

Kelley: (Drape)   (1976)

Music Building Auditorium, Saturday, February 18, 1978, 8:00 P.M.

Program for Festival of Contemporary Performing Arts, University of Illinois at Urbana-Champaign, February 18, 1978.

THE MUSIC OF
JERRY HUNT

CANTREGAL SEGMENT(S)   17.   16.   18.   19.   21.

Pounding   (CS 17)

(volta-kernel)   (CS 16)

(transphalba)   (CS 19)

Transform(Stream)   (CS 16.17)

Kelly: (Drape)

Album cover artwork for *Texas Music* (Irida, 1979).

Album cover artwork for Hunt's *Cantegral Segment(s)* (Irida, 1979) by Salle Werner Vaughn.

Above and overleaf: Special edition album cover artwork for *Cantegral Segment(s)* (Irida, 1979) by Salle Werner Vaughn.

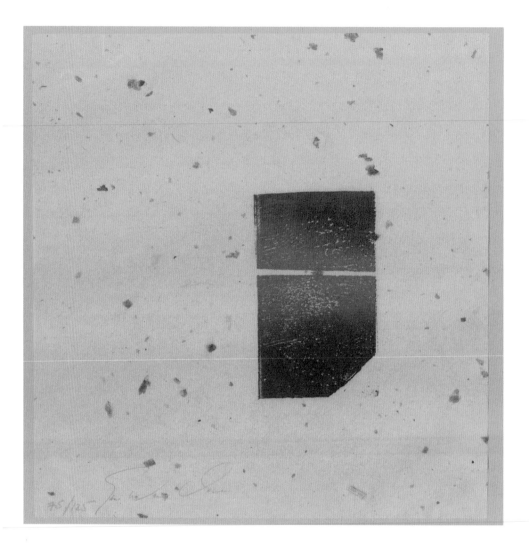

75/125

112

PREMIÈRE
OF
JERRY HUNT'S
FIRST RECORDING
PIANO PIECE
SUNDAY, OCT. 7, 1979
2:00 P.M.
AT HOME OF
OZ & PAUL SRERE
3600 LINDENWOOD
DALLAS, TEXAS 75205
R.S.V.P.
IF NOT COMING 521-3150

Invitation to Première of Jerry Hunt's First Recording Piano Piece, home of Oz and Paul Srere, Dallas, October 7, 1979.

Hunt at the piano, 1980. Photographer unknown.

Within the image:

JERRY HUNT
Quaquaversal Transmissi...
(PHALBA) overlay

Texas Performance Grou...

appearance

Jill Higgins
Peter Mood
Jane Van Sickle
Vicki Lynn

special insert   Sally Bo...

appearance (announ...

photo: Lora Dobkins...

...xas
...te
...27, 1979

...Arts Festival

Flier for the concert Quaquaversal Transmission (PHALBA) by Texas Performance Group, Fair Park, Dallas, September 27, 1979.

Southern Methodist University

Meadows School of the Arts

DANCE DIVISION

Margo Jones Theater
September 7, 1980 at 4:00 p.m. and 7:30 p.m.

SELF-PORTRAIT
- - - for dancer
- - - for composer

"- - to know the person hidden beneath the mask"

dancer: Jean Marc Baier   composer: Jerry Hunt

Sections:

1. "We're Watching You, America"
2. Illusions on "illusion"
3. Shedding A Layer
4. "You are one of the elected few who had the right stuff"
5. Me - You & Me - Me
6. Aftermath
7. Inviting You To The Present

Choreographer: Toni Beck

Assistant to the
  Choreographer: Daphne Rathouse

Lighting & Scene
  Designer: Tom Korder

Assistant to the
  Designer   Gary Archer
                              Jerry Bevington
                              T. Jean Ray

Statement by the choreographer:

"I am involved with surface, not idea; with texture,
 not structure; mood, not thought- - - "

                Toni Beck

Program for a performance of *Self-Portrait* by Toni Beck with Hunt, Southern Methodist University Meadows School of the Arts, Dallas, September 7, 1980.

Above and following pages: Hunt and Stephen Housewright at their home outside of Canton, Texas, ca. 1980. Photographer unknown.

MR JERRY HUNT
in person

PLAYING

★RAGS
★PLAIDS
★RHYTHMS

at

OZ & PAUL'S
3600 LINDENWOOD

SUNDAY
NOV. 8

2:00 PM
BE THERE!

★

Flier for Hunt's concert Rags, Plaids, Rhythms, home of Oz and Paul Srere, Dallas, November 8, 1981.

Above and following pages: Hunt performing at Roulette, New York, 1982. Photo: Lona Foote.

Poster for Hunt's concert Stompin' Beatin' and Screamin', Sheldon Ballroom, Saint Louis, February 10, 1988.

Jerry Hunt, mid-1980s. Photo: Bob Riffle.

Above and overleaf: Hunt performing at Roulette, New York, 1985. Photo: Lona Foote.

Festival program featuring Hunt and Alvin Lucier concerts, Künstlerhaus Bethanien, Berlin, presented with Freunde Guter Musik Berlin e.V., May 27–28, 1988.

Program for Hunt's Maritime Tour, April 3–13, 1990.

Hunt in the Netherlands, 1993. Photographer unknown.

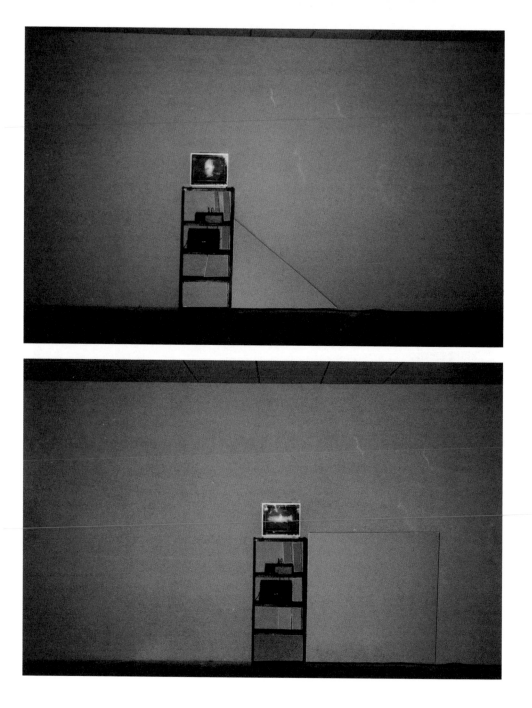

Collaged photos documenting Jerry Hunt and David McManaway, *Bitom: Fixture*, 1989, mixed media with video and sound. Installation views, 820 Exposition, Dallas, March 18–March 24, 1990.

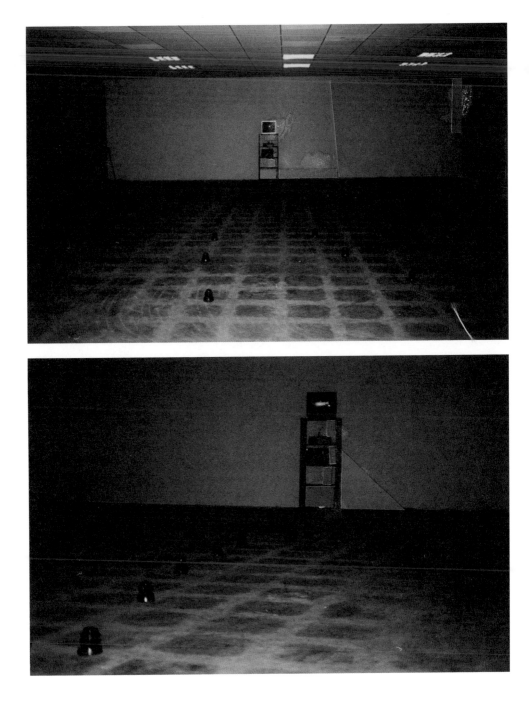

133

Jerry Hunt

somewhat nearby, a
David McManaway piano

Paul & Oz Srere
3600 Lindenwood
Dallas Texas

Sunday October 27, 1991 2:00PM

Flier for Hunt and David McManaway's performance "somewhat nearby, a," home of Oz and Paul Srere, Dallas, October 28, 1991.

Above and overleaf: Contact sheet from a photo shoot in the backyard of Hunt and Stephen Housewright's home on Swiss Avenue, Dallas, Texas, ca. 1970s. Photo: Houston Higgins.

Above and following pages: Views of Hunt and Stephen Housewright's home near Canton, Texas, 1988. Housewright's study. Photo: Stephen Housewright.

Hunt's music studio.

Hunt and Housewright's bedroom.

Hunt and Housewright's bedroom.

Hunt's music studio.

Hunt and Housewright's kitchen.

Stills of Hunt and Rod Stasick in Hunt's *Talk (slice): duplex*, ca. 1990–94, video, color, 22 minutes.

Stills from Hunt's *Birome [zone]: plane (fixture)*, ca. 1990–94, video, color, 13 minutes.

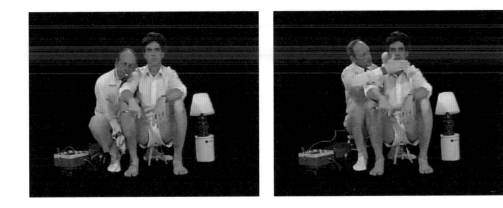

Stills of Hunt and Michael Galbreth in Hunt's *Bitom [fixture]: topogram*, ca. 1990–94, video, color, 11 minutes.

Stills from Hunt's *Transform (stream): core*, ca. 1990–94, video, color, 10 minutes.

Hunt performing in *The Finley/Hunt Report* at the Kitchen, New York, June 11–14, 1992. Photo: Dona Ann McAdams.

LACHESIS:
THE SOCIETY OF FINE ARTS AND SCIENCES

In the late summer of 1958, the teenaged Jerry Hunt and Stephen Housewright began self-publishing *Lachesis*, a mimeographed newsletter associated with the Fine Arts Music Society, an esoteric-aligned arts appreciation club they had formed with high school classmates Elsie Moores and Patricia Tipton. Named for the Greek Moira tasked with measuring the thread of life allotted to each being on earth, the magazine contained writing on art, music, philosophy, religion, Hollywood gossip, and astrology. *Lachesis* was printed by Hunt on a hectograph at his parents' home and distributed mainly to friends and family. Publication began in August 1958 and concluded with a Christmas issue at the end of the year. The following selections include three essays, published across three of the five issues, written by Hunt (the Instructor-Counselor) and Housewright (the Administrator). They have been lightly edited for typographical errors and clarity.

Lachesis-?

Many of you readers do not as
yet know how to pronounce the
name of this organ. It is said
as if it were written-
   (lah-kay-sis)
Lachesis was one of the three
Fates in Greek Mythology who
broke the thread of life.

MANIFESTO

Issued by the Charter Members of the Fine Arts Music Society

The Fine Arts Music Society is hereby constituted as a working society, this day, the 5th of August, 1958 as was conceived by the Charter Members.

The Fine Arts Music Society shall function as a group of interested people who are endeavoring to expand their comprehension and enjoyment of the Finer Arts and Sciences, and are willing to work to bring the fruits of these endeavors to the outside world.

Its powers shall be autocratic and invested in the Administrator who shall direct the work, which shall consist of promoting our understanding and consciousness of the Arts and Sciences dealing with the aesthetic qualities of Life.

These things we proclaim through this Manifesto, and ascertain such by our signatures afixed to this document.

-The Charter Members-

The Administrator
Stephen R. L. Housewright
Stephen Raymond L. Housewright

The Instructor-Counselor
J. E. Hunt
J. E. Hunt

The Secretary
Patricia Carol Tipton
Patricia Carol Tipton

The Superintendent of
Propaganda
Elsie Ann Moores
Elsie Ann Moores

ATTEST:
Mrs. R. L. Housewright

Fine Arts Music Society Manifesto, August 5, 1958.

The Charter of the Fine Arts Music Society

The following orders, rules, and regulations are to be accepted by every member of the Fine Arts Music Society and thusly carried out. Any opposition of the set Charter means an automatic dismissal from the assemblage. Recognizing the preceeding we feel each member must be acquainted with the Charter and exercise their knowledge of it.

The Fine Arts Music Society functions as a group of interested people who are endeavoring to expand their mutual comprehension and enjoyment of the Finer Arts and Sciences.

-The Book of Membership Acceptance-

I. Requirements for Membership

To be qualified for observation a prospective member must have a working knowledge of a self-chosen musical instrument and be willing to exercise this knowledge at Society meetings.
The prospective member, or candidate, must join with a person of the opposite sex, of his own choice. This person is declared a relative. Of course, the inductee must be certain of the relative's qualifications.
The inductee is given one week to declare a relative. During this week he is under observation by the Council of the Society. At the end of this week, if the members of the Council approve the inductee and his relative, they are placed on record for an appointment with the Council. If either member is denied membership, the pair is disqualified, and they must seek admission with another relative. All prospective members must be vouched for by some worthy person. This can be either through personal contact with the Council or through letter of recommendation, which is addressed to the Council Secretary.

If a prospective member can not find a relative, he may appeal to the Administrator . If the Administrator recognizes the appeal, he will be placed on one week observation, and then accepted or rejected by the Council. If he is again rejected, after another attempt with a relative, as one can attempt to affiliate alone only once, he is disapproved, and is disqualified for any other attempt to join. Relatives may try for acceptance over again, but only every six weeks.

II. Procedure for Membership Acceptance

A member of the Society selects a person he thinks worthy of induction. He then notifies the Society. His voucher, the member of the society who notifies the Council, assures the Council of his qualifications. This is based upon the supposition that the person wants membership in the society. After finding a relative, the observation period begins. The relative chosen must have been examined by the Administrator. At the end of this one week period, the Council holds a convocation. The inductee is interviewed by the Council at this convocation, and the decision is announced. The new members must then

Above and opposite: Fine Arts Music Society Charter, ca. August 1958.

participate in a recital designated by the Council.

-The Book of Officiate Organization-

The Administrator-

The Administrator is the autocratic head of the Society, and has the power of dismissal over any of the members. He is the ultimate head of the assigned duties, co-editor of the Society's magazine, and entertainment critic for thee entire Society.

The Administrator is to see that all Society work is done rapidly and efficiently, and that the work is evenly distributed. He lectures at every meeting, at the beginning, and sometime may wish to give a demonstration in the evening's agenda. He notifies the inductees of their acception or rejection and supervises the mailing list. He prepares the membership papers with the aid of the Secretary.

The Instructor-Counselor-

The Instructor-Counselor is to conduct the work of the Society; that is, to teach to all members the principles of the Fine Arts and Sciences advocated by the Society. The Instructor Counselor lectures at all meetings and provides all material which is a part of the work of the Society. He acts as counselor to both Administrator and the Society and prepares and publishes manuscripts and documents for the Society.

The Secretary-

The Secretary does all the stenographic work for the Society and assists the Administrator and the other members of the Coucil in all secretarial work. She is co-editor of the mailing list.

The Superintendent of Propaganda-

The Superintendent of Propaganda is the head of the Society's publications and takes and manages all subscriptions to the Society's magazine. She distributes all the advertisements and material of the Society and prepares the mailing list.

All the above officiates of the Society in the Council must sign pledge cards of their proposed work. They meet at regular, 3 week, intervals. They vote on membership acceptance and rejection. They are the only Charter members of the Society.
The Council must have a working knowledge of the Charter and the rules of the Society.

-Society Expansion-

I. A free copy of the Society's magazine is distributed to each person on the mailing list.
II. Subscriptions may be taken to the magazine at $1.15 per year.
III. The Superintendent of Propaganda is to place ads in various periodicals for the encouragement of membership.
   Expansion should be encouraged at all times and never denied.

Administrator-
Secretary- *Patricia Carol Tipton*

Instructor-Counselor- *[signature]*
Superintendent of Propaganda- *[signature]*

-LACHESIS-

A Monthly Publication of The Fine Arts Music Society, Dallas, Te

---

Volume One, No. 1   August 1958-
Single Copy, $.10   Per Year 1.15

MANIFESTO

Issued by the Charter Members of the Fine Arts Music Society.

The Fine Arts Music Society is hereby constituted as a working society, this day, the fifth of August, 1958 as was conceived by the Charter Members.

The Fine Arts Music Society shall function as a group of interested people who are endeavoring to expand their comprehension and enjoyment of the Finer Arts and Sciences, and are willing to bring the fruits of these endeavors to the outside world.

Its powers shall be autocratic and invested in the Administrator who shall direct the work, which shall consist of promoting our understanding and consciousness of the Arts and Sciences dealing with the aesthetic qualities of life.

These things we proclaim through the Manifesto, and ascertain such by our signatures affixed to this document.

The Administrator   The Instructor-
                                              Counselor

The Secretary   The Superintendent of
                                              Propaganda

The above is a copy of the Manifesto of the Fine Arts Music Society stating its purposes and declaring the existence of the Society as official. It was signed and attested on the fifth day of August, 1958, by the directing Council. Also the Charter was signed and it was distributed on this day. For more detailed information, note page four of this organ.

The average person vaguely knows whether a thing is ugly or beautiful. He determines the degrees of ART by his inborn concepts of harmony and design, concepts which are basic, pure, but yet not capable of functioning on higher planes of artistic expression. Is this basic conception enough? Is it enough to frequently say "yes" or "no," "pretty" or "ugly," "good" or "bad," letting our opinions depend only upon concepts which are undeveloped? Taste is an essential part of man's culture, and it is developed through the agency of the Fine Arts.

The Fine Arts consist of music, dance, sculptury, drawing, painting, drama, poetry, and architecture. These art forms are pleasing to the senses and cause man's emotions to prompt him to a mode of thinking called aestheticism, which is the "philosophy that views and values such appreciation of art as a base for good living." When one of the expressions under one of the headings mentioned above is enjoyed by many people over a period of time, it is considered a true work of art, for any form which can exist under changing concepts may be considered GREAT.

One of the purposes of the Fine Arts Music Society is to develop the taste and color of life. As an attachment to life's routine, the Finer things of life can extend man's horizon, broaden his views, and enlarge his appreciation of the beautiful.

When the mind is developed and channeled, the beauty of life excites the aesthetic emotions, a vibrant, sensory perception into the spiritual realms of the God-given gift of developing appreciation for the truer arts and sciences.

Good channeling of mental faculties leads to the appreciation of the Fine Arts. This mental influx provides the incentive for greater study, which in turn widens one's consciousness of the Finer things of life, and instigates a great love for these finer things. The creative mind is the key to working toward the final condition of man, the consciousness of EVERYTHING.

We must learn this truth and work toward our betterment. This can be attained by GOOD culture and CLEAR thinking. Decisive hammers drive the nail, the nail is driven into the wood of good, taken from the TREE OF LIFE.

We of the Society must stimulate work toward achieving the creative powers of mind, so that the essence of the Finer Arts and Sciences may be accumulated for spiritual growth. This is a reason for a society such as ours, a driving reason that stops not til a GOAL is Attained, each score only increasing the determination.

from *Lachesis*, September 1958

THE RELATIONSHIP BETWEEN MUSIC AND MAN
—Instructor-Counselor

Dear Friends: My articles each month have a very definite aim: to consider the area of the Fine arts AND sciences from three important standpoints: Scientific, Philosophical, and Religious. It is only in this way that we can attain a perfect knowledge of anything we study or attempt to learn. This is my policy, and it shall continue to be my policy so long as I write this column. I strive to educate, to teach the doctrine, the show truth; this is divine.

Part First
The Musical Scale and the Scheme of Evolution:
"As it was in the beginning."

The method by which man developed his potential powers was according to the vehicles which man possesses. The vehicles of man, the three-fold creature, were, and are, the physical body, the mind, and the soul. The method of man's evolution, that is, the descent of the spirit into matter, and its sublimation, or individualization, is according to the musical scale, which consists of seven tones, all of which except two are a full tone apart, the other two being a semitone apart. We shall see later, perhaps, how these semitones cause the universe to function as we know it.

Architecture, which has to do with form, was the first lesson learned by mankind. Form is the basic stimulus to our eyes as well as our other senses. We learn that man's consciousness, or his awareness of existence, was likened unto that of the deepest trance state during this period. All architectural construction from the tiniest structure to the Cosmos itself, is based upon and functions according to Cosmic Law; that is, the great laws which cause life to exist.

Sculpture, which determines the structure and proportion of forms, was the second lesson in the arts given to man. Here was a lesson of greatest importance; it showed him how to change natural forms, from a recognition of pleasing shapes and displeasing shapes. Here his consciousness corresponded to a deep sleep state, or dreamless sleep. Sculptury teaches us how to direct forces so as to give correct shapes to basic forms, which were assimilated from the lesson of architecture.

Painting was the third art given to man, BY HIS OWN ENDEAVORS. His consciousness here corresponded to that of a dreamful sleep. Thus conception of color was possible. (See the previous two months' articles, "Music: The Illusive Art"). Painting is related to primal desire; that is, creative urge, for color shows the first sign of emotions into art, or, emotion as we experience it today, at our present stage in life.

Pythagoras, the great mathematician and occult teacher, taught that creation was called out of chaos and constructed according to the principles of sound harmony and proportion. The seven tones of the musical scale correspond to the heavenly spheres, although vibration has no part in it. The zodiacal signs correspond to the twelve tones of the scale, and have a remarkable significance.

Thus is music significant in the Universe: it is the creator of the Universe, and is expressed in all the Cosmic Works: the stars, the planets, and all other manifestations.

Therefore was music the last lesson, and is yet the lesson being learned, for men are growing unto the Absolute, or God, and are expressing the Creative Power within themselves, and this is a direct manifestation of the Laws of Sound and Harmony.

(to be continued)

—from *Lachesis*, November 1958

THE SOCIETY OF FINE ARTS AND SCIENCES
Dallas 28, Texas

Date: 12/27/58

The following information form must be filled out accurately and completely and filed with the Society Council. Use pen and ink or typewriter to obtain the best legibility. Your cooperation in this matter is deeply appreciated. (If using typewriter: use black or blue ribbon only.)

Name Jerry   Edward   Hunt
     First Name   Second Name   Middle and/or Surname
                  (No initials please)

Address 4661 Sen Medina   Telephone Number DA-7-8639

City & Zone: Dallas, 28   Occupation: Student

State Texas   If student, where parents are employed and
                               official title of their work there:
Emergency Telephone BR-9-3242   Pit Milk Silesman
(To be used if parents cannot be
reached.)   Alfords Warehouse

—Position held in the Society of Fine Arts and Sciences:

Check one; Council Member   Member   Inductee: Present status with Society
                                                 (Do Not Use)
           ☑   ☐   ☐

No. of meetings missed   (Esoteric....)   Amount of your monthly
to above date. 0   (Exoteric....)   dues; 50¢
(To be filled out by you and used in calculation.)

           Signed: Jerry Hunt
                   (Script)

The following questions cannot be completed for some do not apply to you. If this be the case, leave those unappliable ones blank. Thank you.

Have you passed an oral examination as a member (not Council)?
What was your score on this examination (circle one)?   1   2   3   4
(Above: Refer to Society files.)
To date, how many months have you been with the Society as a
Member _____   Council Member 6   Inductee _____

Are you a participant of the Music Instrumental Club? Yes
What instrument do you play in this MIC organization? Piano
If you are not in this music club, what instrument do you play? Piano

Additional or corrective information: (DUE TO THE PROCESSING PLEASE MAKE NO
ERASER MARKS but rather make corrections below:)

Instructor Counselor: To instruct or teach and head the Institute. (Counselor
to Society.)

Hunt's Society for Fine Arts and Sciences information form, December 27, 1958.

Date: *12/27/58*

Administrator
(Do Not Use)

The following information form must be filled out accurately and completely and filed with the Society Council. Use pen and ink or typewriter to obtain the best legibility. Your cooperation in this matter is deeply appreciated. (If using typewriter: use black or blue ribbon only.)

Name *Stephen ___ Raymond ___ Lorenzo Housewright*
First Name ____ Second Name ___ Middle and/or Surname
(No initials please)

Address *10464 Ferguson Rd.* ____ Telephone Number *DA-7-1945*

City & Zone *Dallas, 28* ____ Occupation: *Student*

State *Texas*

If student, where parents are employed and official title of their work there:

Emergency Telephone *TA-3-7196*
(To be used if parents cannot be reached.)

B. L. Housewright; Ven. E.
Kieth, Shipping Clk., RI-1-6371

—Position held in the Society of Fine Arts and Sciences:

Check one; Council Member ☑   Member ☐   Inductee: ☐   Present status with Society; (Do Not Use)

No. of meetings missed   (Esoteric. X.)   Amount of your monthly
to above date. *0*   (Exoteric. X.)   dues; *50¢*
(To be filled out by you and used in calculation.)

Signed: *Stephen B. L. Housewright*
(Script)

The following questions cannot be completed for some do not apply to you. If this be the case, leave those unappliable ones blank. Thank you.

Have you passed an oral examination as a member (not Council)? ____
What was your score on this examination (circle one)?   1   2   3   4
(Above: Refer to Society files.)
To date, how many months have you been with the Society as a
Member ____   Council Member *5*   Inductee ____

Are you a participant of the Music Instrumental Club? *Yes*
What instrument do you play in this MIC organization? *Violin*
If you are not in this music club, what instrument do you play? *violin*

Additional or corrective information: (DUE TO THE PROCESSING PLEASE MAKE NO ERASER MARKS but rather make corrections below:)

Administrator: To guide the proceedings of the Society and manage all other offices.

Stephen Housewright's Society for Fine Arts and Sciences information form, December 27, 1958.

MUSIC: THE ILLUSIVE ART

—Instructor-Counselor

Music is well said to be the speech of Angels.

—Carlyle

Man, when evolving, was given the capability for developing the ear. We learn that sound is the creator of all things. This is imparted in the words of St. John: "In the beginning was the word, and the word was with God, and the word was God." Since sound was such a mighty factor from the beginning of creation, it is feasible that the evolvement of the ear at an early stage of man's evolution was important. The ear, as we possess it today, after thousands of years of evolution, is the most perfect instrument we have.

The ear conveys the impression of conditions outside of ourselves, with exactness to our consciousness and is less subject to illusion than the other sense organs. It is the receiving instrument for all sound vibrations. Everything created emits a definite tone as well as a color. There is an intimate connection between tone and color. In fact, tone is the very agent which produces color.

Listening to the elemental sounds of nature brings us in touch with the keynote of our planet earth. Our consciousness is enriched by the sounds the wind makes in the forest and by the sounds of many waters. From the natural sounds emanating from trees and brooks up all the way to the tunes of celestial harmonies, God's creation is taught and influenced by sound waves.

Sound waves are invisible, yet they have the power to build as well as destroy. We find this corroborated in the Old Testament story of the Battle of Jericho which tells about the sounding of a ram's horn while marching around the walls of the city. Destruction of the walls resulted.

Today we are indeed in debt to the arts, which give us great joy, a Spiritual Joy, which transcends all earthly manifestations with its far-reaching results. Of the arts, music may well be said to be by far the most influential. Pythagoras tells about the music of the Spheres and the true musician knows what he meant by that term. The arts serve to turn man's mind toward the heaven world and to inspire us to become creators ourselves. Music inspires us with a sense of transcendent loveliness of God, the source and goal of all the world. It is the intangible and comes from the home of the Spirit. It conveys feelings from being to being without speech and mind with mind can meet without the exchange of words.

Poets of every land get their inspiration from spiritual realms and they have given us many revealing truths in verse about music. The words of J.G. Brainard when writing about tone:

> God is its author, not man;
> He laid the keynote of all harmonies;
> He planned all perfect combinations,
> And he made us so that we could hear and understand.

(to be continued)

II. MUSIC: THE ILLUSIVE ART
—Instructor-Counselor
(cont.)

Music has more influence on the growth and unfoldment of our being than any of the other arts for it has the power to calm us in times of turmoil and stress as well as the power to stir us into action when it is desirable. It touches our hearts as nothing else can for it is connected with our higher selves and keeps us in touch with the higher world. It is the most potent influence in swaying humanity that is known to us.

Echoes from the passions and emotions of the higher worlds reach us through the agency of the Mind, and most of us here on earth have a longing for the higher and spiritual qualities of the universe. Often when we are privileged to hear great, inspirational music it brings to us memories of the world of tone, our true home, and the depths of the Soul of Man rejoices whenever such melodies reach our ears. WE WOULD ALL BENEFIT BY HEARING GREAT MUSIC AS OFTEN AS WE CAN DO SO. While we are in the terrestrial life we are exiled from spiritual qualities, and we are prone often to lose sight of the beauty and love of God .... "Then comes music, a fragrant odor laden" .... with expressions of the higher world. Like an echo from heaven it reminds us of the Profound Peace of God, the Soul of the Universe, the mystery which searches the heart of Man, and knows all secrets, and elevates us to the world from whence we came, where love, light, and life exist in purity and profundity.

The realm of Thought is the "womb in which is conceived all earthly manifestation." We learn that the Mind is the home of tone and color. Here in this world is conceived the energy counterpart of all physical existence.

The atom is composed of minute vortices of energy electrons. These electrons have their birth in the realms of Mind, since electrons are the first material manifestation of spirit force, the creative energy of God. Thus as these force vortices organize on the earth according to mundane laws, there is set up in the Mental World, or "Psychic Plane" what is known as an Archetype, or spiritual counterpart. This archetypal form in Human Beings is called the Human Aura, which is a Magnetic radiation emanating from the form of Man.

Music is the universal language; it appeals to all regardless of race, creed, or color. It is truly universal. We are well aware that all great music is not for any one people but it speaks to all alike. Music especially has the great mission to unite different peoples since there is no language barrier to hinder in its meaning or understanding. All anyone needs to benefit by these wondrous sounds is the inner feeling for it. Most people respond to melody, rhythm, and harmony. Therefore we can look for music to play a leading part when the different nations finally will have absorbed the lessons which we are to learn on the path of separateness.

If we would properly appreciate great masterpieces of music which genius has bestowed on mankind we will have to take into consideration that it has its origin in Divinity. Unless we are attuned to these great masterpieces, we will not receive the great influx of Cosmic Love and Truth that shows the way to Soul Growth.

But even when conditions in our material lives do not seem conducive to soul growth, ways and means will be found. We can find a little time each day and "build within our own inner self a sanctuary filled with that silent music which sounds ever in the serving soul as a source of upliftment above all the vicissitudes of earthly existence. Having this 'living church' within, being in fact under the condition of LIVING TEMPLES we may turn at any moment when our attention is not legitimately required by temporal affairs to the spiritual temple, not made with hands, and love in its harmony."

"The sun intones his ancient song,
'Mid rival chant of brother-spheres.
His prescribed course he speeds along,
In thunderous ways throughout the years."

Justice and judgement are the habitation of thy throne;
Mercy and truth go before thy face. Blessed is the people

165

That know the joyful sounds;
They shall walk, O Lord, in the light of thy countenance.
—Psalms 89.14 and 15

I welcome questions, comments, and letters regarding my monthly column. Address them to the Society.

—Instructor-Counselor

from *Lachesis*, September 1958

CHIT CHAT-
        cont.

Timely and Contemporary

The following offeratory lists a few
choice entertainment availabilities for
this month: Munch Conducts Wagner on
RCA,...Stravinsky: Rite of Spring, RCA.
...The Short Stories of Saki a book for
"people with a passion for suprise" —
Modern Library...Concerto for Orchestra
by Béla Bartók on RCA.   (November.)

All Classical Music Radio Station

An FM Dallas Radio Station, KSFM, is
currently presenting 19 hours each day,
from 6 AM to 1 PM, of classical music.
This station has been in operation—
off and on—for about three months. On
it have been a review of Symphony performances, an interview with Donald Jo-
hanos and Paul Kletzki, plus numerous
operas. These have been only specialty,
as we are constantly hearing new records
and we have 3 hours a day for request
selections.

CRITICAL NOTATIONS: A CONCEPTION OF THE UNIVERSE, Page 5.

This exploratory article touches but
lightly on the subject of life and also
the universe. It gives us a rudimentary
background of the science of astronomy,
which has only been hinted at in two or
three of the preceeding articles.
Rather than presenting and attempting
to answer many questions, only a few—
the most important ones—are presented
for much thought and consideration.

The Lachesis editors hope to be able
to print the accompanying drawing, also
titled the Universe, and also by the
Secretary. In this drawing you shall see
many allegories, some closely related to
this article on page 5, others not even
remotely associated with it.

We wish to note the article Egyptian
and Islam Music has been postponed, and
will appear in the January issue.

Christmas Music

As mentioned earlier in Lachesis, a
series of Christmas Music Concerts will
be given on two days in the Holiday Sea-
son. These dates are not yet permanent
but if you would be interested in attending one or both of these concerts you
can call or write us and we shall send
them to you.
This kind of music is not the most
popular series of carols and ballads, but
rather a group of long-classical works.
We would be glad to have you attend.
The charge is 10¢.

The Society of
Fine Arts & Sciences
announces
A Series of
Christmas
Music Concerts
At: 10464 Ferguson
          Dallas 28 Tex.
Admission Fee - 10¢
For the program-
Call or write
The Society
at Davis-7-1945

A VISIT TO THE CENTER
Kris Paulsen

This text has been excerpted and adapted from an essay originally published in the Winter 2013 issue of *X-TRA* under the title "In the Beginning, There Was the Electron . . ."

The material of the medium is an electron. Its mass is 1/1835th the mass of a hydrogen atom. Though it moves so swiftly it cannot be perceived by the eyes of man, it is finite. Its effects can be studied upon the surface graphs of oscilloscopes. And these effects are seen as sine curves and waveforms. Synchronization, amplitude, amplification, and modulation are what electronic circuitry is mainly about. It's also about storage and delay.

But mostly, it's all about time.[1]

Television, one version of the story goes, was invented in San Francisco.[2] Philo T. Farnsworth, the fourteen-year-old boy genius who diagramed the device in the early 1920s on the blackboard of his schoolhouse, brought his invention to life several years later in his Green Street workshop. On September 7, 1927, Farnsworth instantaneously beamed a "minimalist straight line" from one side of the studio to the other.[3] The straight line was not a surprising first image for electronic television. It was, in fact, indigenous to the screen, whose images are produced by an electron beam racing back and forth across an invisible raster grid. A year later, Farnsworth's investors were no longer satisfied simply with his conquering of space and time; they demanded profits from the "gadget."[4] Farnsworth then produced another image on the screen for his backers: a dollar sign.[5]

Farnsworth's two early images—the structural line and the dollar sign—neatly sum up the course television would take as a medium. Scientific and artistic experimentation would work at the service of profit. Soon after Farnsworth's successes, American radio broadcasting corporations would become interested in television technology and its potential to capture new markets with "illustrated" radio programs. By the end of World War II, television would take off as a mass medium and become a regular part of the ambient sights and sounds of the American home. Forty years after Farnsworth's transmission, the Baby Boomer generation, the first "raised" on television, had come of age. In the United States, this coincided with the Vietnam War and the protests against it; the civil rights and feminist movements; the 1967–68 marketing of the first portable video camera, Sony's PortaPak; and the Rockefeller Foundation's somewhat sudden decision to sponsor artists' programming on public television. Between 1967 and 1977, the Rockefeller Foundation donated more than $3.4 million to public broadcasting stations (primarily WGBH in Boston, KQED in San Francisco, and WNET in New York and New Jersey) to begin experimental artists' workshops in their television studios.[6] With new funding, new equipment, and a new generation of experimenters, San Francisco, once again, became the site of a televisual revolution.

In 1967, amid these conducive circumstances, Brice Howard moved from New York to San Francisco to become the director of KQED–San Francisco's Rockefeller Foundation–funded artists' workshop, the National Center for Experiments in Television.[7] Under Howard's leadership, NCET produced some of the most outlandish, innovative, and psychedelic work ever to screen on TV. Howard invited a team of young painters, poets, musicians, and engineers to become video artists in residence at the station's lab. Among them were filmmaker and physicist Loren Sears, painter William Gwin, painter William Allan, designer Willard Rosenquist, Beat poet Joanne Kyger, and engineer Stephen Beck. Despite the radical appearance of the videos produced by the NCET artists, Howard predominantly framed the group's work as a formalist investigation into the medium-specific qualities of video and television, which pointed back to Farnsworth's electron lines as well as to a contemporaneous legacy of modernist methodologies in art history and criticism. While it is commonplace to frame the history of video art in the contexts of film, television, and photographic history, Howard and the NCET artists sought to separate the video image from these narratives and explore it as a new, unique artistic medium.

By the early 1970s, this agenda drew critical fire from eminent art-world tastemakers, such as *Artforum* editor Robert Pincus-Witten, who, for one, criticized the abstractionist approach as too conservative. Consequently, NCET work has largely been relegated to the footnotes of video history.[8] At Open Circuits: An International Conference on the Future of Television, the Museum of Modern Art's 1974 conference on the state of the new medium that included abstract, structuralist, experimental video artists and filmmakers, such as Beck, Hollis Frampton, and Stan VanDerBeek, Pincus-Witten described their work and its "deficiencies" as such:

> The generation of artists who created the first tools of "tech-art" . . . [refuse] to acknowledge the bad art they produced. Their art was deficient precisely because it was linked to and perpetuated the outmoded clichés of Modernist Pictorialism, a vocabulary of Lissajous patterns—swirling oscillations endemic to electronic art—synthesized to the most familiar expressionist color plays and surrealist juxtapositions of deep vista or anatomical disembodiment and discontinuity.[9]

For Pincus-Witten, video was an inherently "reproductive" and narrative medium.[10] While he does connect this work to modernist traditions (albeit in their degraded "pictorialist" forms), he neglects to see these investments in formalism as a necessary step in establishing the material properties of video as a medium. The investigations that took place at NCET in the 1960s and '70s were clearly an attempt to practice a mass medium in the register of a fine art by subjecting it to a formalist reduction in the Greenbergian tradition—that is, to take very seriously the specific formal properties of video that distinguish it from the other arts.[11] But the properties that Howard and the NCET artists located as the essential qualities of the medium were at odds with those typically associated with television and video at the time (and since). The Whitney Museum of American Art's first two major presentations of video (David Bienstock's 1971 show, "A Special Videotape Show," and "Video Films" from 1972) were entirely dedicated to abstract work. By 1973, this work had disappeared from TV programming and museum exhibitions, and representation, narrative, and performance-based video art dominated the field, as they have continued to do.

Pointing at the Center

In 1973, KQED produced a curious program entitled "A Visit to the Center."[12] The segment opens with a blurred image that slowly resolves into a set of shapes. Three men—NCET staffers David Dowe and Jerry Hunt and a young visiting artist—are seated in a horseshoe ring of television sets with cameras pointed at the screens. The camera tracks around the outside of the ring and joins the men in the center, at the Center—one of the NCET production facilities. Their voices begin to be audible amid the electric hum of the room and its many devices. The three men are looking at the monitors. A voice rises above the din and says, "Wow. That's nice." Another answers: "Well, what it is, is a thing called feedback." Looking at a TV image unavailable to the presumed at-home viewer, the young man describes what he sees: "It looks like there are two mirrors right next to each other, and you are looking into one of them and it just keeps going." After he speaks these words, and without warning, the viewer's vision is altered: the scene multiplies and stretches into a visual echo corridor of feedback. The broadcast image briefly illustrates their conversation. The men tinker with their cameras, and the scene then slips further into psychedelic swirls—doubled ghost images of the men and brightly colored pinwheels of feedback hover

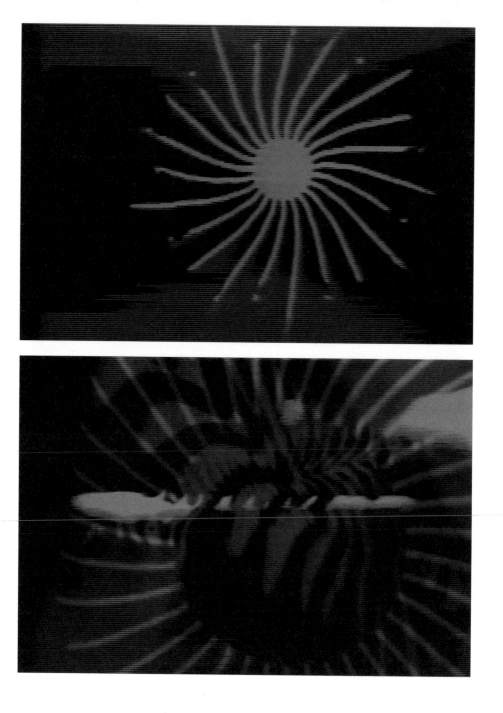

in the empty space of the room. The viewer listens in as the three men talk among themselves. The young man is the uninformed viewer's foil—he does not know what feedback is. Hunt patiently explains the mechanical and mathematical forces that produce video feedback patterns; Dowe translates the technical language for the lay viewer and enacts them with a camera. Like the 1973 home viewer, the visitor sees for the first time an inherent trait of live video.

The camera and its mimetic properties were so inextricably tied up in what it meant to be "television" or "video" that Rosalind Krauss's famous diagnosis of video art in 1976, "Video: The Aesthetics of Narcissism," hinges on the ability of the video camera/monitor system to act like a mirror and thus short-circuit a traditional modernist examination of the medium, exchanging critical reflexivity for narcissistic reflection. For Krauss, this substitution of reflection for reflexivity complicated the possibility for a formalist project in video. Even so, most video artists, she argues, "intended to disrupt and dispense with" the formalist critical tradition and to "render nonsensical a critical engagement with the formal properties of a work, or indeed, a genre of works—such as 'video.'"[13] In her discussion of Vito Acconci's 1971 video *Centers*, Krauss claims the artist attacked both the logic of "pointing to the center" that "[invoked] the internal structure of the picture-objects" and the critical paradigm that "takes seriously the formal qualities of a work, or tries to assay the particular logic of a given medium."[14] However, Krauss will argue that, despite his attacks, Acconci accidentally models and exposes the formal logic of video (as she perceives it) by showing that it is fundamentally a medium of mirroring and narcissism. It is worth noting that while it appears on the video that Acconci is pointing at the center of the viewer's monitor, he must have been, in fact, pointing at the center of the camera's lens when he recorded the tape. Her condemnation of video has to do, I think, with not seeing beyond the representational functions of video. She can conceptualize video based in distortion (e.g. the work of Joan Jonas) and disorientation, but not abstraction or nonobjectivity. This subtle oversight points to a need to reexamine her claims about video, especially with regard to the videos created at NCET during the earliest days of video art.

Electronic video feedback comes in two forms. One is what Krauss describes Acconci doing: using the camera and monitor as an electronic mirror that responds and reacts to a live image. As noted above, however, there are crucial differences between video and

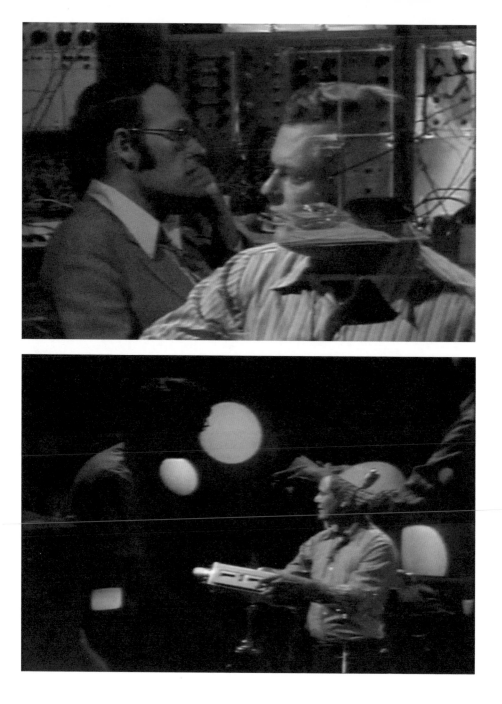

a mirror. One needs to be in front of the camera, rather than the monitor, in order to transfer one's image to the screen. Furthermore, the image that appears on the screen is a true image, not a reversed mirror image, which is why it is so difficult to use a video monitor as a mirror. It is the very opposite of a mirror.[15] That is, one needs to be displaced from the "reflective" surface to see one's own live image. The second form of feedback is more traditional; a system's receiver is placed too close to the input, causing distortion. This form of electronic feedback acts as a mirror, too, but of a different kind. By pointing the live camera at its monitor, one can create a visual mise en abyme in which the image of the monitor recedes infinitely into the space of the monitor, just as with two mirrors facing each other. But each repeating image is a slice of *time* as well as space. Any event captured by the camera will also tumble down the reflective corridor. Slight changes to the camera—tilting it on its side, adjusting the aperture or focal distance, placing an object before it—will echo through the image, pulsing and distorting it. The representational image will begin to tumble and form abstract, psychedelic "mandalas." These "archetypal" forms of the video medium (per Dowe) are a simple means of divorcing the video camera and screen from the iconic and representational codes that usually govern them. In creating these circular, symmetrical patterns, the men self-reflexively and critically "point to the center"—to NCET—as a concrete location for video production and to feedback circular structures as the conceptual framework for understanding video's basic qualities. They point to the very surface of the screen in order to differentiate its specific, unique properties, to indicate where one needs to look to have a different kind of televisual experience, and to make a case for taking the potential of video's electronic formalism seriously. Feedback, and the abstract images that video inherently tends toward, can be a means for the modernist self-assessment that Krauss did not think was likely or possible in the medium.

Rather than focusing on the mimetic properties of the camera and its ability to produce and transmit representational images, which dominated discussions of video's formal character, the NCET artists turned their attention to the abstract, electronic structure of the cathode ray screen. They located the essential properties of video not in the live transmission of a camera image but in the blinking pulse of the electron beam. By attempting to remove the primacy of the camera and its representational powers, Howard and the NCET artists engaged in an unexpected and provocative

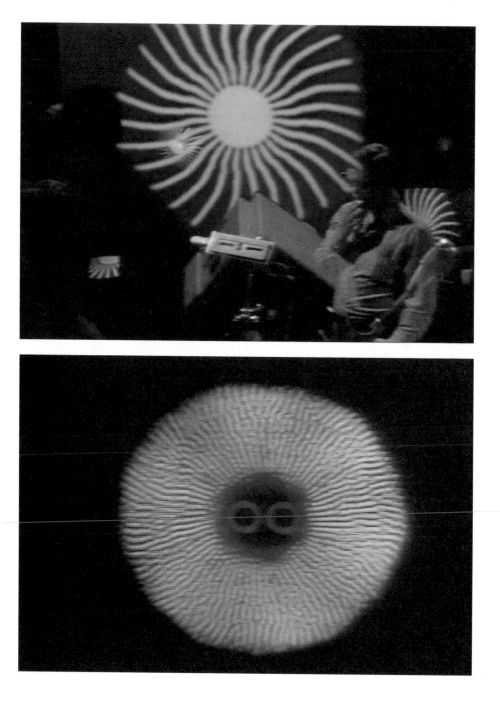

(174, 176, 178) Stills from Jerry Hunt, David Dowe, J.D. Jarvis, and Jno F. Moormann's *A Visit to the Center*, 1973, video, color, sound, 29 minutes. Courtesy University of California, Berkeley Art Museum and Pacific Film Archive.

rethinking of what video was and could be. They created a genre of video based on the screen rather than the camera.

Beyond opening a new avenue for what video art might become, Howard also turned television on its ear. Video and television are closely related material forms—all television images are video images—but as cultural forms they were quite distinct in the late 1960s and early 1970s. Video cameras electronically transmit and reconfigure images on a raster screen for a dispersed audience; video is both the base medium and the recording medium for television. "Video" was regarded as a private, personal medium in contrast to the corporate broadcast and cable systems of "television." While video, like television, could instantaneously transmit its live images from camera to monitor, it could only span the distance of the length of the cord between the camera and the monitor. Additionally, the portable home video cameras that popularized the personal medium were not compatible with broadcast standards, so homemade tapes could not be aired without expensive transfers to broadcast-quality tape or use of a broadcast camera to shoot off of a playback monitor. The artistic medium was, then, largely distinct from the broadcast form of television in terms of distribution and quality. The NCET, as well as the artist-in-residence programs at WGBH and WNET, gave artists unprecedented access to airtime and broadcast-quality equipment. The Rockefeller-funded research programs extended the nascent field of video art into "artists' television."

Most discussions of the essential properties of video as a medium hinge on its ability to transmit real-time *representational* images from one place to another by means of an electronic camera, and television's ability to do so over long distances to a mass audience.[16] NCET artists attempted to drive a wedge between the medium and its representational, cinematic qualities. In their experiments, they also troubled what it meant for an image to be "live." Liveness no longer designated the transmission of a recognizable real-time image of people, places, or things from the TV studio or scene of an event to the monitor, but referred instead to the live action of electrons on the surface of the viewer's screen. By focusing attention on the electronic properties of the cathode ray tube, the NCET artists accomplished the kind of reflexive formalism that linked itself to classical epistemological investigations into the relationship between vision and reality.

Notes

1 Brice Howard, *Videospace* (San Francisco: National Center for Experiments in Television, 1972), 25.

2 As with the inventions of photography and cinema, television had many competing and concurrent inventors. Farnsworth is just one of several men credited with the invention of television. Farnsworth's electronic television, the precursor to today's televisions, followed John Logie Baird's invention of mechanical television by about two years. Vladimir Zworykin, too, patented an electronic television system around the same time as Farnsworth. Farnsworth eventually used his early blackboard drawings of his proposed system to win a patent lawsuit against RCA and Zworykin (Evan I. Schwartz, *The Last Lone Inventor: A Tale of Genius, Deceit, and the Birth of Television* [New York: Perennial/Harper Collins, 2003]). For a history of Farnsworth's invention, see Daniel Stashower, *The Boy Genius and the Mogul: The Untold Story of Television* (New York: Broadway Books, 2002).

3 Steve Seid, "After the Raster: Early Television in San Francisco," in *Radical Light: Alternative Film and Video in the San Francisco Bay Area, 1945–2000*, eds. Steve Anker, Kathy Geritz, and Steve Seid (Berkeley: University of California Press and Berkeley Art Museum and Pacific Film Archive, 2010), 26. Seid astutely connects Nam June Paik's early "prepared television" work, *Zen for TV* 1963, to Farnsworth's first image. In a note, Seid writes, "About thirty-five years later, Nam June Paik would return to this prototypical straight line in his manipulated television sets of the 1960, acknowledging, perhaps unconsciously, the origins of the televised image." Seid, "After the Raster," 26n2.

4 J.J. Fagan, executive vice president of Crocker First National Bank, quoted in Schwartz, *The Last Lone Inventor*, 135.

5 Schwartz, *The Last Lone Inventor*, 135.

6 Marita Sturken, "Private Money and Personal Influence: Howard Klein and the Rockefeller Foundation's Funding of the Media Arts," *Afterimage* 14, no. 6 (January 1987): 9.

7 In 1967, the workshop was called the Experimental Television Center. In 1969, it was renamed the National Center for Experiments in Television.

8 Lucinda Furlong, "Tracking Video Art: 'Image Processing' as a Genre," *Art Journal*, Fall 1985, 234. Furlong writes, "With the exception of Nam June Paik's well-known collaboration with engineer Shuya Abe, the history of video art as it is presently constituted has virtually ignored the work of first-generation tool designers and builders," such as NCET's Stephen Beck and other synthesizer artists, including Dan Sandin, Bill Etra, and Steve Rutt.

9 Robert Pincus-Witten, "Panel Remarks," in Douglas Davis and Allison Simmons, eds., *The New Television: A Public/Private Art* (Cambridge, MA: MIT Press, 1977), 70. Furlong notes that Pincus-Witten's remarks reflect that "no one in art circles wanted to hear about—let alone look at—video that seemed based on the conventions of modern painting" (Furlong, "Tracking Video Art," 334). The turn toward representation and toward the artist's body, while a rejection of this early work, was also a turn toward political engagement with the new technology and the media. But as Furlong points out, Pincus-Witten does give credit to these artists for their inventions, if not formally then technologically. They built and developed the very tools that later video artists would use in their work, long before corporations developed consumer models.

10 Pincus-Witten, "Panel Remarks," 70.

11 Clement Greenberg, writing in 1961, marked out what he saw as the trajectory of modern art. Each medium had specific, essential properties. The task of modernism was to engage in a reflexive self-criticism that exposed these properties. "Each art had to determine, through its own operations and works, the effects exclusive to itself. By doing so it would, to be sure, narrow its area of competence, but at the same time it would make its possession of that area all the more certain." Clement Greenberg, "Modernist Painting," in *Art and Modern Culture*, ed. Francis Frascina and Jonathan Harris (New York: Phaidon, 1994), 309.

12 It is not clear if *A Visit to the Center* ever aired. "The Electronic Notebook" series aired Thursday nights at 10 p.m. in November of

1973. The KQED program guide lists other Electronic Notebooks, but also mentions that some of the segments had aired on previous occasions. When KQED dissolved NCET, they let go of all their paper records and tapes (the latter landed at the Berkeley Art Museum and Pacific Film Archive [BAMPFA]). The BAMPFA archives are incomplete in regard to broadcast schedules.

13 Rosalind Krauss, "Video: The Aesthetics of Narcissism," *October* 1 (Spring 1976): 50.

14 Rosalind Krauss, "Video: The Aesthetics of Narcissism," 50.

15 For a more detailed discussion on video's relationship to mirrors and mirroring, see Kris Paulsen, "Uncanny Confusion: Early Video and the Fantasy of Presence," in *Here/There: Telepresence, Touch, and Art at the Interface* (Cambridge, MA: MIT Press, 2017).

16 See, for example, James Friedman, "Attraction to Distraction: Live Television and the Public Sphere" in *Reality Squared: Televisual Discourse on the Real*, ed. James Friedman (New Brunswick, NJ: Rutgers University Press, 2002); Stephen Heath and Gillian Skirrow, "Television: A World in Action," *Screen* 18, no. 2 (Summer 1977); and Jane Feuer, "The Concept of Live Television: Ontology as Ideology," in *Regarding Television: Critical Approaches—An Anthology*, ed. E. Ann Kaplan (Fredrick, MD: University Publications of America, 1983).

AUDIO VIDEO SYNTHESIS
Jerry Hunt

The following piece by Hunt appeared in the March/April 1977 issue of *Synapse: The Electronic Music Magazine*, a biannual publication centered around synthesized music that included technical news, record reviews, and articles by musicians and technologists. This issue also featured extensive interviews with progressive rock groups the Steve Hillage Band and Todd Rundgren's Utopia, as well as a profile on Greenpeace's efforts to communicate with whales through electronic sound. Hunt's article built on his experiences as codirector, with David Dowe, of Southern Methodist University's Video Research Center, which had closed the previous year. It is a technical summary of his strategies for manipulating audiovisual elements in live synthesis, and serves as an early articulation of his compositional system Haramand Plane.

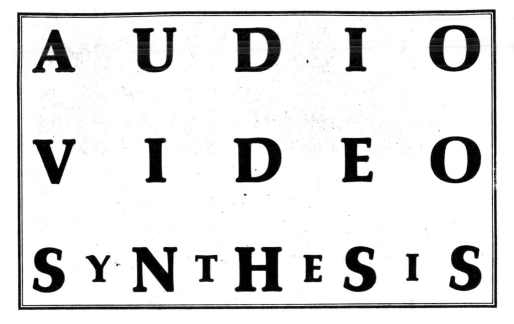

A U D I O V I D E O SYNTHESIS

For me video is a direct, immediate, and natural global extension of the compositional activities associated with sound. I have not and do not now distinguish between electronic and nonelectronic means as a procedural definition. Video is an electronic environment extending from the theatrical reality of producing sound; similarly, audio is an extension from the environmental necessities of sound producing. My background and training have been exclusively concerned with sound production, as a pianist and composer (1950–60) engaging in compositional and performance activities which increasingly utilized electronic resources. David Dowe's specialization of training is visual, and the history of visual thinking in his own development is as extensive as mine has been in an aural orientation. This I think suggests something of the successfulness of our approach for us: the compositional

activity can be highly specialized to take full advantage of the workers involved, and at the same time the system procedure (audio/video together) provides a situation of equivalency in variational decision-making. The method, compositionally and procedurally, of working with interactively adaptive audio-video systems has also led to a reorganization of our thinking habits associated with the disciplines of music, film, painting, sculpture, dance, and theater. From my own independent work before association with David Dowe and the Video Research Center, I have developed a group of procedures and systems for the audio and video components of my compositions. Gradually areas of contact between audition and vision became more clearly self-evident. The early independent work and my work with David for the past five years have substantially reinforced my original intuition that the composing activity can powerfully operate and should operate in ways which are not dependent upon the patterns of feedback and feedaround through one special orientation of thought (action and process). The perceptual, structural, and dynamic modalities of image and sound are profoundly unique and different in sometimes difficult ways. Certainly in regard to the requirements of parameter pattern extraction from signals produced by video cameras and microphones, these differences become exaggerated. The fortunate circumstance of systems for the electronic generation of image and sound is exactly that the parameters required for effective and powerful interactive operation exist in separable, definable, pattern-coherent structures, and the signal formats can easily be made compatible. (Unfortunately, however, this in no way provides solutions to the still-difficult synthesis problems for such systems.) Some aural/visual correlates seem to possess perceptual and/or historically reinforced constants of association—for example, the variation of average luminance in a visual display space and the dynamic variation of the intensity/spectrum relations of sounds through loudspeakers, and image orientation with reference to the viewing frame and sound distribution (regarded in both spatial and spectrum modulation aspects). Even more interesting was the situation in which image (*still*—in a spatially defined viewing space) and sound (rhythmic/melodic *drone*) could be associated over a limited but highly variable range of characteristics. Furthermore, in this special situation provided by electronic systems, the variational histories of developments of characteristic features of dynamic pattern-sequences of sounds and image can become the central compositional procedure. Special attention to two areas of work became necessary to meet the demands of composition in this assumed interactively adaptive situation. First, the systems for signal generation had to be implemented in such a way as to allow selective parallelism of dynamic variation in image and sound and yet provide sufficient control flexibility/predictability to preserve the specific characteristics and integrity of a possibly large repertoire of image and sound development. The audio and video generators were implemented and have been continually modified and updated with the constant objective of increasing the integrity of *ensemble dynamic* parameter variation. (In electronic music systems the greatest problem in emulation has been in this area.) The objective required very early in the development of the signal generating systems a movement away from modular conception to a more integrated global structure. Second, because parameter-structure variations of image and sound develop in dissimilar ways, a system for extraction and analysis of ensemble-pattern over short-time histories was essential. Although unexpected, the results of *direct* interconnection of signals and controls are predictably limited and trivial. The accompanying block diagrams illustrate the organization of the audio and video generating systems, the interactive-adaptive processor used with these systems, and a smaller derivative system of recent design for use with performances involving voice and voice emulation and specialized generators for image-sound.

The *audio generating unit* is a four-voice system organized as a parallel processor. All the function-subunits

A video image created with Jerry Hunt's and David Dowe's audio/video synthesis system.

employ primarily analog electronic technology; all the static programming, matrixing, and routing subunits utilize digital implementations. A ROM[1] plug-in relates an array of 128 switches to major static program changes, allowing continuous performance manipulation. All parameters of all subunit functions are completely electronically presettable and full-range variable. Spectrum specification, formant, frequency, waveform, and amplitude modulation processes are all dynamically interrelated by user-defined specifications. Electronically programmed multiphase function generators operate on all levels of the system subunits and may be dynamically controlled. The input transducer ports accommodate a complement of a pressure/pressure-derivative sensing keyboard or, interchangeably, a similarly responsive band-controller, two three-dimensional foot pedals, and two three-dimensional trackers (one rotary and one similar to a joystick-array). The output structure allows reentry and parallel organization of separate processes and signal channels. A component of the output subunit consists of a generalized delay processor which allows specialized spatial, spectrum, and frequency modulation.

The *video generating unit* is a multiport input system also organized as a parallel processor. The system is completely synchronous: all waveforms and modulation involved in video generation of primary processing loops are related to the composite synchronizing signals[2] employed in NTSC[3] color video. The system generates up to six separate electronic images in the display space (television color monitor), and video camera signals and electronically generated video signals can be simultaneously accessed and accommodated. Subunits of the system perform basic video processing tasks: arbitrary colorization and color modulation, spatial and textural reorganization of the images in the display space, edge/line derivatives and modulation (PNW, PPM, PAM[4]), chroma[5] and gray-scale[6] modulation, etc. The subunits are also isolatable (including external patch interfacing and switching). This feature was necessary to satisfy the requirements of widely divergent applications of the system. Subunits for generating groups of electronically variable waveform sequences produce basic image structures; modulation of these subunits produces images in an arbitrary-scan format. Independent electronic control is available for spatial transformation and translation of images, movement, size and distance, apparent distance, surface and "environment" texture and shading, and viewing angle and color. A scan-conversion subunit performs the format translation for NTSC and is input-output uncommitted to allow electronically generated and camera-scanned signals to be interchangeably processed, mixed, and routed. The scan-converter subunit is an optically coupled system; a selective digital framestore subunit allows the static storage, delay, and processing of limited image feature-extraction components. The final mixture of signals is encoded into the NTSC composite color video[7] signal and displayed over color television monitors, video recorded, and/or broadcast through standard television transmission systems.

The *interactive processor*, like the generating systems, has been continually altered in implementation and structure and has undergone two complete

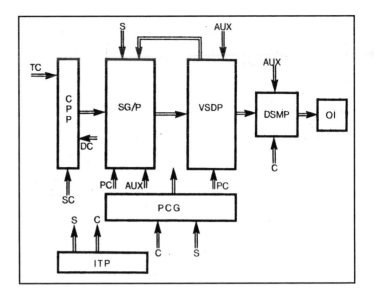

Audio System Block Diagram.
Refer to page 194 for
abbreviation key.

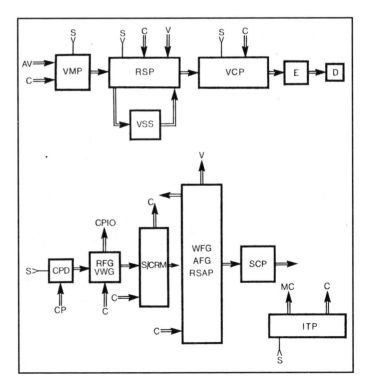

Video System Block Diagram.
Refer to page 194 for
abbreviation key.

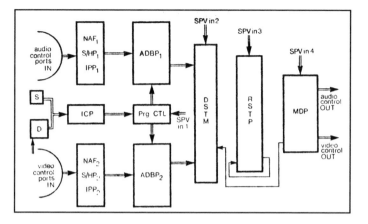

Interactive Processor Block Diagram. Refer to page 194 for abbreviation key.

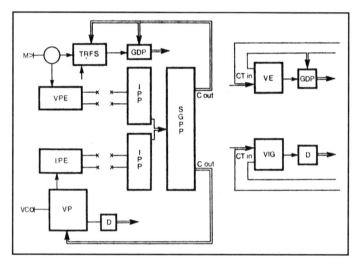

Cantegral Segment(s) Processor with transducer pickup and direct versions.

rebuildings of hardware since 1972. Control signals describing an array of parameter designations to be monitored from the two systems are scaled and modified for electrical compatibility and each routed to one of three varieties of preprocessors. Slope derivatives of dynamically varying controls and synchronizing signals control access to these inputs. The preprocessors perform in each parameter channel a nonlinear adaptive filter[8] function; several channels allow sampling functions and/or delay processing. Programmable weighting and matrixing is then performed to produce groups of unique signal branches. Processors similar to adaptive linear variable-threshold amplifiers[9] are then utilized to generate sequences of parallel pattern codes which are stored in a recirculative memory system. Programmable dynamic "template" models are applied according to program instructions which provide for dynamically variable goals under some arbitrary set of limits. This process is cyclic and continuous and produces, in relation to input signals, output codes which are dematrixed and arithmetically manipulated to generate for the audio and video systems two separate groups of interrelating parameter controls. Preprogram settings establish degrees of parallelism and "goal-pointers" between image and sound parameter designations. The control signals to and from the generating systems are routed using firmware connections and may therefore be arbitrarily assigned to a given channel location. The large system has been employed to produce components of audio/video recorded work, but primarily it has found use as a system for investigation and dynamic real-time performance operation

(*Haramand Plane*). The smaller, derivative special purpose system (used for performance of my *Cantegral Segment(s)* 19, 20 and David Dowe's *Repons*) and its associated synthesis modification systems have been developed since 1975 as a direct outgrowth of the larger system. The signal sources involve microphone and camera transducers (and interchangeably since January 1977 a performable voice-emulator and special image-synthesizer). Image and voice parameter extractors operate on a limited selective range of features to provide strings of signals which control the variation of the processors (and/or generators) with respect to dynamic performance definitions. We do these works frequently on tour since they are more easily transported, adaptable to various circumstances, and require minimum rehearsal and set-up. No specific philosophy of design or technical suppositions have been imposed upon any subunit or system aspect of the devices other than electrical compatibility and all-electronic means. Since the beginnings of our work independently and later together, most of the technical and developmental work has been financed by us directly (with the very important exceptions of the National Center for Experiments in Television in San Francisco at the time of establishing the Video Research Center and, currently, the Rockefeller Foundation). This fact and the important influence of constantly reevaluated cost/performance assessments have been, I now think, frequently fortuitous forces in defining proposed implementations. A further auxiliary observation of increasing importance for me was the byproduct of work on coding and pattern recognition theory during preliminary study for my work *Haramand Plane* (the first of our works interactively executed): an insight into the possibilities of virtual high-level operations using carefully limited computation and storage elements. This observation involves economics in no way related to technical or financial considerations but informs directly the eventual result for electronic art activity generally. Finally, for our work together involving interactive processes, several delightful situations occur. First, because of the system structure of the audio and video generating units, dynamic sequences of deviation from *still* (video) and ornamental *drone* (audio) can be arbitrarily interrelated by a wide range of different variational principles. At the same time complete performance autonomy is maintained. Second, because of the dynamic provisions, both systems are essentially performance instruments (this is important even in recorded, highly editorial modes of working); this fact encourages the finding of ways of working which sometimes closely correspond to the experiences of encounter in visual and auditory space—for the video particularly, a "tactile" element seems to develop as a side benefit. Third, the interactive systems are in no way "sequencers" or randomizers but rather responsive mediums of information *exchange* and *extension*. Although not intelligent in a cybernetically austere sense, the systems have begun to produce for our work some results which suggest several modes of reorientation for us: composition is dynamically related to the responsive cycles of activity required (composition as performance); goal setting and patterning in this dynamic activity of composition dissolves some aspects of the image/sound separation; finally, and most importantly, pattern-structuring formalities emerge which relate to a procedure which approaches one of my long-felt enthusiasms for electronic means—an almost colloquial and at once multidimensional/global exchange of aspects of the perception of living.

[1] ROM—Read only memory.

[2] sync—Synchronizing pulses employed to establish time relationships.

[3] NTSC—National Television Standards Committee—used generally to refer to the electrical and related standards to which American television systems conform.

[4] PWM, PPM, PAM—Pulse width modulation, pulse position modulation, pulse amplitude modulation.

[5] Chroma—the color-information of brightness between black and white in a television display or signal (luminance).

[6] Gray-scale—the graduations of brightness between black and white in a television display or signal (luminance).

[7] Composite color video—a signal containing timing (sync) chroma and luminance information electronically combined.

[8] Nonlinear adaptive filter—a filter whose characteristics vary according to some function of the input/output relationships.

[9] Adaptive linear variable—threshold amplifier—an amplifier whose region of linear amplification varies according to a required characteristic of input/output.

Video System

S sync
Avin auxiliary video inputs
Cin control inputs
Vin primary video inputs
RSP raster-scan processor
VSS video selective frame storage
VCP video colorizer-processor
E encoder (NTSC)
D distribution driver
VMP video mixer/processor
CPD clock processor/distributor
CPIO camera processor-inputs/outputs
RFG raster function generators
VWG video waveform generators
S/CRM signal/control routing matrix
Cout control signals-outputs
WFG waveform function generators
AFG arithmetic function generators
RSAP random-scan arithmetic processors
SCP scan-conversion processor
Vout video outputs
ITP input transducers-processors
MCout matrix/routing controls out
CP clock program (input)

Audio System

TCin transducer controls-inputs
SCin static controls/presets-inputs
DCin dynamic controls-inputs
ITP input transducers/processor
S sync
Cout controls (all) out
PCG programmable control generators
Cin control inputs
PCin program controls-inputs
Aux in auxiliary program or signal inputs
VSDP voicing, spectrum, distribution processors
DSMP distribution and spatial modulation
    processors
OI output interface (mixing, drivers etc.)
CPP control program/processors
SG/P signal generators/modulation processors

Interactive Processor

S sync
D slope derivative generators
ICP input control processor
Prg CTL program control
SPV statis program variables
NAF nonlinear adaptive filters (preprocessor
    subunit)
S/HP sample-hold processors (preprocessor
    subunit)
IPP input signal preliminary processing
    (preprocessor subunit for scaling etc.)
ADBP arithmetic, distributive and "blend"
    processors
DSTM dynamic sequential "template mapping"
RSTP recirculative sequential template processor
MDP matrix decoding processor

Special purpose processor system

M microphone
VC video camera (B&W)
VPE voice parameter extractor
IPE image parameter extractor
VP video processor
D display (distribution drive etc.)
TRFS transversal/recursive filter structure
GDP generalized delay processor
IPP input control parameter processors
SGPP sequential "goal-pointer" processors
Cout control out to TRFS control inputs and VP
    control inputs resp.
CTin control transducers-inputs
VE voice emulator
VIG video image generator

THE DEATH OF THE PIANO
Jerry Hunt

Beginning in the mid-1970s and continuing until shortly before his death, Hunt would perform an annual recital at the Dallas home of biochemist Paul Srere and his wife, Oz, two prominent patrons of the local arts. *The Death of the Piano* was one such performance, hosted by the Sreres in 1977, which took the form of a survey introducing a general audience to modernist piano techniques. The evening was videotaped and broadcast on the Dallas public television station KERA, where Hunt found occasional work as a composer of incidental music, and was produced by Hunt's colleague Paul Bosner and narrated by journalist Billy Porterfield. The lecture showcases Hunt's loquacious explanatory style and exasperation with his initial instrument of choice, offering insight into such key works as *Cantegral Segment(s)* (1973–93) and the composer's compositional influences. The following text has been transcribed from a recording of the broadcast. Auditory and stage cues have been added for clarity.

This is the Srere House in Highland Park, Texas, a venerable and august suburb of Dallas, and these are the Sreres, Paul and Oz. Paul is a scientist and Oz is a mother of four, but beyond that, they are patrons and appreciators of the artists in their community. Every fall, when people turn inward and tempers take a contemplative turn, the Sreres rearrange their furniture and open their house to a group of friends. Everyone comes to sit and listen to one very special man. What he does may vary from concert to concert, but the element of eccentric surprise is always constant. In this recital, Jerry Hunt destroys the piano, if not literally then compositionally. But stick around and see and hear for yourself, as we await Jerry and his guest.

Dallas is not a particularly avant-garde place, but somehow Hunt has managed to mature into one of the most gifted of new composers working in the electronic medium. His friends and admirers include John Cage and David Tudor. *Baker's* biography, the bible of modern living composers, credits Jerry with forty works, a collection esteemed enough to have won for him a Rockefeller Foundation grant.

Hunt has toured Europe and America. You don't have to be a music lover to take to him. One can enjoy Jerry on several levels. Although he insists he is primarily an electronic composer, it will quickly become evident that he is a spellbinding talker with an astonishing knowledge of the whole classical tradition.

So join us now as we attend Jerry Hunt in performance.

PAUL SRERE

Okay, I think we can get started now. Would you please take your seats now?

JERRY HUNT

You've been given some inside information that I don't know yet. I wasn't sure whether I was really supposed to start or not, so we were having a little chitchat here about it. The Sreres have been nice enough, as always, to force me to do these things. So I hope you don't feel like you're being forced yourself. I had a hard time coming up with a program for this and it's gone through about five stillbirths up to the point of doing it now, because little by little I can see my relationship—both personally and politically, and particularly financially—with the piano going off down into a kind of no-man's-land from which there's no return. I can only give you

just the one tiny example, that in preparation for this, regardless of what I do, there's some nineteen strings missing from my piano at the moment and I haven't bothered to have them replaced, if that gives you just a little bit of the idea. Anyway, after a lot of resistance and many repeat putting-offs, the program has actually come about. If that gives you an idea that there was a certain amount of reluctance, it's true. Anytime I do anything anymore, there's a little bit of reluctance. So anyway, after about five different decisions, finally I got this little flier about the program, and when I got the flier after deciding and passing through my mind *well, maybe I just better not do it at all*—you know, which is not a comment, incidentally, on the format or anything—I thought *well I'll play some piano pieces and then play something else.* And then so as a consequence I came up with an interesting title. I don't ordinarily title programs, but I came up with a little title of my own: it's called *Death of the Piano.* Now I have very selective reasoning for saying that, though; I mean, after you hear me play you'll say *well, we can certainly see why you would like it to be dead.* Now there's another thing about this too, though; in my enormous amount of thoroughly American interest in getting just as rich as I possibly can over the course of the last six or seven months, as I've become increasingly aware of how expensive this is, I've found out something very interesting, and that is that I don't make piano music at all anymore—I haven't written a piano piece in ten years. And it reminded me, now this is one exclusion, some of you will know about that exclusion to that overwhelming statement, there's one exception to that. I made a small prepared piano piece a couple of years ago and it was written for one purpose only, and that was to be put into a museum collection—it was never played—except for those of you that happened to show up here, it was played the one time here. It will never be played again, at least in some ways I perhaps hope not, although I think it's as pleasant as almost any of this music that I've ever heard done for prepared piano. So you might think that in me talking about what killed the piano as a composing force, because that's specifically what I'm talking about and I'm well aware that there are people in this world—there are the Michael Tippetts and other people like that who do continue to make piano music. I'm also very well aware, incidentally, of the fact that in the recent Norlin Music survey, this is some nine months ago, the piano is still the largest-selling musical instrument in the world. There are more piano sales than any other instrument. So obviously I'm not talking about the death of *playing* the piano—which, of course, I mean, for me, perhaps that's coming sooner and faster and more furiously

than I had ever expected—but I am really talking about its death as a composing force. Because I think it's had an enormous dominance and so I thought it might be interesting to see some of the reactions of composers around the turn of the century as not such a polite preparation for doing all this.

Why did I choose the pieces I did? Well, because I make a parallel—you notice cigarettes on the piano, and since I'm still smoking, I make a really very interesting parallel, I think, between cigarettes and the piano. I see them in almost direct parallel. I've been smoking a long time and I've just built up the habit to the point that I can't keep from doing it anymore, and the same thing is true with the piano. I mean, I have one around and a couple of times I've thought, *I'm getting that monster out of my house, I'm getting that whale, I'm putting it on a flatbed truck and they're dragging it off.* Because so much money is tied up in it. You know how much money is tied up in a seven-foot piano? Seven thousand dollars I've got tied up in that devil. So I'm thinking to myself, *I won't just sell it outright, how will I get enough return?* You know, all these complicated financial problems. So I end up just with it, with the nineteen strings broken out. The parallel I make is, I've been doing it so long that I just can't imagine not going by [*strikes piano keys*] and hearing the sound that it makes. So one of the things that we'll talk about a little bit, and maybe we'll talk more and maybe we'll talk less, depending upon these subunits, is what it is about the piano that became so terribly fascinating. Well, the first thing that's so fascinating about a piano is the piano is the final result—it's a final technological result—of an instrument that's attached with keys, and that is at once its downfall and also its most magnificent property. Almost all piano music after the very earliest days—I had even thought about doing some illustrations—but, I mean, you all know that early keyboard music was all [*plays riff on piano*] things like this, et cetera, et cetera, et cetera. I mean, all the very little things that we regard as pianistic were really taking place in early keyboard literature. There's a lot of ambiguity in regard to: Was it being done for organ or was it being done for a real percussive kind of instrument, or a plucking kind of instrument that plucks its strings? What is the assembly? What is the structure that motivates the keyboard organization? The keyboard organization is the key to the whole thing about pianos. They are the—at the moment I would call them the albatross. Keyboards are the albatross of all electronic music production too; I mean, everybody's seen synthesizers hooked up to keyboards. And I've always said one of the greatest anomalies of the twentieth century—if it weren't for the fact that

I'm a keyboard player and I can trilly-poo and I can do all kinds of cuties on the keyboard that I couldn't normally do on a tactile sensor, like my face could be rigged and I could move my—[*audience laughs*]—it's quite true, I mean, there are composers who do this. You can take direct output from brainwaves. David Rosenboom does an extensive repertory of works analyzing brainwave patterns to control. So controller is very much one of the principal things about a piano which I think has killed it as a controlling force and as a composing force. And this contraption over here had very little to do with that aspect of the piece that I'm gonna do. And that is, the voice piece that I'll hope to be able to do for you today uses a certain kind of interval organization that doesn't exist on this instrument and that's one of the reasons for me being so interested in the voice. And the reason I've chosen to play the [Alexander] Scriabin work today is Scriabin—this is eccentric—Scriabin is I think one of the composers—everybody always says, *oh, well, John Cage was instrumental in killing the piano, [Arnold] Schoenberg was instrumental in killing the piano*—all of these composers, I think, did a lot towards killing piano music as a viable way to make music. But I think the thing that they didn't do really, I think the one thing they didn't do is that they didn't really look at the piano as a sounding instrument quite the same way that some composers have. Scriabin is one of these great examples. I started with contempt for Scriabin the composer and musician, and many kinds of stories about Scriabin, I think, come to mind. I mean, one of the funny ones, of course, is the thing—and it's really, really true—that when he was young he put copies of [Frédéric] Chopin's studies under his pillow in hopes, I suppose, that some magical element of infusion would come through. I tried and it didn't work for me, as you'll see today. I don't any longer regard myself as a pianist at all. I mean, I play well enough to get the chords out, you know? That's about the size of it, as far as I'm concerned anymore. It takes a certain kind of obsession, I think, with the mechanism.

The reason that I'm not choosing people like Schoenberg—I'll tell you the pieces that I'll play to illustrate this thing that I regard as a compositional death. Incidentally, I'm not saying that people shouldn't continue to write piano music. I know people who do write piano music. I'm just simply saying that of the community of the composers that I regard myself as being one of, the people that work in certain ways that I think are interesting, no one uses pianos anymore, and there are reasons for it, and I hope that this will reveal them a little bit. The three pieces that I choose to reveal this death that I think has happened since—God knows it's a slow

death, it's like everything in nature, nothing dies fast, it's a slow tortured death. These pieces are old. I know you like, for example, the work of [Igor] Stravinsky. I just can't abide Stravinsky. I even thought about playing some of it, but I just don't like it and it also doesn't as nicely illustrate my point. But what I really do like is this lovely Scriabin music.

Now, why do I like it? Well, Stravinsky remarked about Scriabin, he said that his music reminded him of the work of a neurotic dentist, and I think in some ways this particular work, *Vers La Flamme* (1914), that I owe Douglas Taylor, another musician friend, for introducing me to, I think this particular work in a lot of ways sums up more the situation than any other. Sometimes when I'm just sitting and thinking about the piece, I think, *well, this is music by a nut, for nuts.* This is really genuinely insane music; this is music for crazy people. The important thing is that by mystical delivery or whatever, he decided to make some very minor modifications to the harmonic system as we understand it, which is perfectly justifiable since none of the instruments are in tune correctly anyway, and he decided to look at higher harmonics and use these little peculiar added sounds. The result is to create a music which no longer uses melody, which of course is obviously impossible on the piano, you can't have melody—I mean, people are always saying [*plays figure on piano*] is a melody. Well, I defy you to prove to me and my sense of what melody is that that's melody. It doesn't strike me as melody at all. You're saying to yourself, *my God, when he does the voice piece what in heaven's name will come out?* You'll see what I mean by melody, hopefully, when we get to that point. What I do think they are is, I think they're modulation outlines. Scriabin is the only composer, and I think he's the source for what's really happened in music now. I think he's the source root for what's happening in music now. In a situation where we could actually do the piece. So I will, I'll play [*laughs and performs*].

I think at places a little unruly, getting through it. Thank you. There are a lot of unusual and very interesting things that take place in there. Scriabin was much more knowledgeable about what he was doing than probably that performance suggests. Scriabin was a pianist and primarily concerned with it, and I think he's instrumental in this thing I'm calling the death of the piano. Simply because of the fact that one thing is of paramount importance in the late Scriabin piano works and that is that the piano is just simply being used as a sounding instrument—a resonator. It's being used as a resonating contraption. Into that, stylistic artifacts are being

inserted. That's the first thing that Scriabin shares dramatically with every modern composer and with a whole tradition of world music, that music is not thought of as a beginning and ending statement in which everything is very highly architecturally sculpted. I hate to say I agree with Schoenberg about anything, but I agree with Schoenberg about one thing, and that is that composers don't need all of that junk. Schoenberg said that if he just has three different timbres and three voices, that that was enough to make music with, and I agree wholeheartedly. I don't think a wide range of timbres and a wide range of sound sources and an infinite array of things are important. What I do think is necessary for intelligible musical communication is an intelligible language, and I think that as long as piano music represented something that was a distillation and refinement of an existing compositional convention, where the resources of the piano were not really being brought into attention—and that's a very important difference, I mean, as long as the compositional resources of the piano itself were not being brought into attention, I think the piano is a viable vehicle.

I thought I'd mention that, and then another piece I thought it'd be interesting to mention, because it relates directly to *Banshee* (1925), before I do *Banshee*, and that is a piece that I like to do—it just amuses me to no end. Since the keyboard is already set up to do it, I thought it might be interesting to you. There's a work by Ichiyanagi, Toshi Ichiyanagi is the name. He is a Japanese composer, although he's trained in the United States. Originally, as I understand it, someone told me he used to compose like Aaron Copland before he changed because of contact with John Cage. It's a piece called *Music for Piano No. 4*, and I won't do all of it because it usually runs an hour, hour and a half, two hours. I mean, there's a psychological thing involved in this music. But it's interesting because it's an extension, a direct extension of this [*points to the piano's soundboard*]. Many people think that John Cage, for example, developed the thing of plucking and picking around inside the piano. Not so. Henry Cowell was responsible for making most of these innovations and frankly, I just can't get through a lot of his pieces; they're just too ugly to play for the piano. It's not true of a lot of his music—some of Cowell's music is very interesting—it's just the piano pieces, except for this and a couple of others. There are a couple of very interesting Cowell piano pieces and this is one of them, but it's kind of a sidestep. The piece is done in 1961 by Ichiyanagi and I didn't even know how to do it—this gives you an idea of what music was like in the '60s—until I heard the way David Tudor did the piece. It just says in the middle, "*Music for Piano No.*

4: use sustaining sounds only." It's right in the middle of the score, it's all you're told: "use sustaining sounds only." Well, I didn't know what to do. Well, I discovered that by communication between Tudor and Ichiyanagi they devised a way of doing it. And the way to make that sound, it's all done out here [*rubs his hand across the side of the piano to produce a squeaking noise*]. And then you hear the resonance from the piano. This piece of Henry Cowell's, a lot of people have made various things out of it. There is harmonic interest in it, incidentally. It uses a whole-tone scale entirely. I never knew that until I learned it, so I don't think that's the main property. Again, like these three composers today, all of them are still not making music which I think is solely concerned with just making music. *Banshee* is very clearly a kind of impressionist, in the Impressionist sense, piece. *Vers la Flamme* is definitely an Impressionist piece, in that sense. The interesting thing is that I think this tendency towards Impressionism is one of the things that ended up doing what I say has happened, to destroy this instrument as a composing force. Not because of anything really evil about the pieces or anything that they've done, except that they just explored areas of the piano in such a way as to make whole changes of thought, whole ways in which you think about a piano. It never occurred to me to think about a piano, when I was nineteen years old, in the way that Beethoven very obviously thought about the piano. It just never occurred to me, and it's because of these people. *Banshee* is played entirely on the strings of the piano and—enough said. I think you'll see how the piece works. Sadly, you'll have to see the backside of me. The first time I ever did this it was reported to me that someone out in the audience said, "Well, this is the first time that I have ever seen the rear end of a pianist for the entire concert." Because I never ever turned around. I just came out, I took the bow, and then I turned around like this and for the rest of the program I was like this [*turns around and hunches over the soundboard*], because I never did anything on the keyboard at all, it was all in here, you know. I beat the tar out of it, I'm telling you. There wasn't enough left of that piano, by the time I was through, to have swept up, and you know they forever held it against me, too; it was at a music school. So I'll do the Cowell *Banshee* [*leans into the piano and performs*].

Thank you—hard to double-time [*laughs*]. This piece of Cowell's ended up being the base material for a much later development in the case of John Cage and contact microphones where extremes are used—I mean really extremes—and using objects and things directly on the strings to get much more violent sounds. So the idea that a

lot of this interior piano is a late product—not at all. I don't think it's hard to see why he got sent to Russia for doing this, though; it's very unusual. I don't know if that's exactly quite the right way to put it; that may reveal the political content that shouldn't have been revealed. I mean, how many *Banshees* are possible? I mean, am I gonna do a *Banshee* up here [*rubs top of the soundboard*], or am I gonna do a *Banshee* down here [*rubs bottom of soundboard*]? You end up getting all kinds of very unusual methods of using it. Some of the innovations of Cage for example, the muting, hunting through the insides for sounds—I mean, it's the same thing all over again. It's people trying to use the piano no longer as [*plays melody on keyboard*] the communicator of that kind of vocabulary, and they're trying to explore it as a total sounding mechanism, and I think you can see what ended up being in the mind of Scriabin for making the change. In other words, all the mysticism and everything aside, I think there was a very honest and very clear and very conscious musical reason for making these changes. Similarly with Cowell, Cowell's a Californian and he's an inventor. I think he shares that with John Cage, and many made that observation but not the parallel, that both were Californians and both were basically inventors in music and I think you can make a case for the fact that Cage is an inventor in music, and a very interesting one at that. So that leads us to the final conclusion: Why am I doing the voice piece? Well, mostly because a lot of the people who I think would be here probably wouldn't be at a place where they might be able to hear the kind of music that I make. Since I no longer play pianos and since this is such a constant preoccupation, I thought it might be interesting. I have been doing a set of pieces called *Cantegral Segment* for at least six years, named after a street here in Dallas, Cantegral Street. I just couldn't come up with any other name—we were driving downtown to the post office and I thought, *Cantegral*, and so I wrote it down. "Canta," "negral," you know? "Integral," it's just great. Perfect excuse for a title of a series of pieces, and they finally started revolving around things that I regard as very important. Well one of the important things in my life was [*plays the chorus to Elvis Presley's "Don't Be Cruel" on the keyboard*], I'm sure you know this, and since he's just now died, I find it increasingly interesting to point out that all of my music for the past four years has been based on one Elvis Presley song. For those of you who remember the tune, you know it goes [*plays the melody with one hand*] and that's all there is to it, that's all. So, needless to say, that's been changed. And this is something else I've never ever done, and I thought it might be interesting today to take a look and see just exactly what

(196–212) Stills from Paul Bosner's *The Death of the Piano*, 1977, video, color, sound, 28 minutes.

it is. People always ask me after I've done these pieces, I use my cheater all together now, and they say, "What are you listening to on your cheater?" What I'm listening to is the information that I need to know about what note to sing next. My mother fortunately is not here today because she'd be running through the glass, she'd just crash through that glass. It's probably why she's not here. I just mentioned something about voice and she's heard me sing. Now it's true, my voice is not a beautiful one, we could talk a long time and I'd be more than, as you only too well know, willing to do just that, about how I feel about voice, but I don't like trained voice, for a variety of reasons—not the least of which is that it does something physical which I find objectionable, it puts an artificial formant . . . Needless to say, as I think you'll find out, this piece is not with any kind of accompaniment except an electronic percussion accompaniment. That's what works for the accompanimental pattern in the piece. There is no, in other words, melody and accompaniment as such, that doesn't exist. So that's what this machinery is for. It has the added side benefit, and I think the very happy side benefit, that it makes my voice, to my mind, attractive to hear, whereas if you were to hear it just flat-out I think you'd be pretty disturbed by the fact that it's not a strong-sounding voice. It's a weak voice, and with the machinery I don't have to use very much in terms of volume, so I take all my time working on one thing, and that is the notes and the rhythm. The other thing I think is interesting is that if you think a little bit about the tradition of singing, I think you're gonna find out that no other tradition of singing in the world has ever attempted to do this destructive thing: the introduction of the singing formant into the singing of music. The only case I know of is in the instance of certain varieties of Indian singing where there's an attempt to create a kind of nasality of style, and the reason for that, really, is to make the formant structure, the harmonics of the voice, more pronounced, so that the relationship to the drone is more comprehensible. I mean, it's the only reason for ever doing it. There are all kinds of mythological reasons but that's the real, practical, hard reason for doing it. You can actually hear whether you're in tune [*sings and electronically manipulates his voice; audience applauds*].

THE TRICKSTER
George Lewis

This text, written March 28, 1994, originally appeared as the first half of a piece called "Notes from John Bischoff and George Lewis" in "*. . . looking to the long shores": writings, reminiscences and ideas of and about Jerry Hunt*, a booklet published by the Inial Group that April on the occasion of a memorial concert for Hunt. George Lewis was the head of the dissertation committee for the group's founder, Stevan Key (now Paul Morris) in the department of music at the University of California San Diego. The text has been lightly edited for clarity.

My first encounter with Jerry Hunt took place at the Experimental Intermedia Foundation performance space (aka Phill Niblock's loft) in downtown Manhattan, circa 1980. I was still relatively new to "New Music" and to New York City, and I arrived for Hunt's concert a bit late, as is my wont. A loud, densely multilayered, intensely rhythmic sound complex greeted me as I opened the large, metal-clad, Fox-locked door to Phill's.

At this point a visitor to Niblock's space has two alternatives, based on what one hears at the door: walk straight ahead into the kitchen, where one finds refugees from performances of lesser merit or intrigue, or turn right and get a glass of wine and find a chair or an old couch in the performance space. The multi-rhythmic barrage, akin to Coltrane's experimentation with two, three, many drummers, obliged me to make that right turn, forgetting about the wine.

I was treated to the sight of a thin, somewhat disheveled man with thinly tousled hair, wearing an old, ill-fitting suit with a far-too-thin-for-fashion tie. The man was apparently in a frenzy, stamping about the room waving a long stick with small baubles on the end. Sometimes he would stamp on the floor, or smack it insistently with the end of his stick. Sometimes he would moan softly, a barely audible human sound just below the pounding polyrhythms. Or he would raise the stick high into the air, threatening the ceiling with it.

Frequently this apparently mad fellow, thinly tousled hair flying, would make a short, stabbing, spearing motion toward a large wooden box that stood to his right. These motions, made in the manner of Chaka's assegai, would produce an enormous whooshing sound, responding to the power and force of his gestures, an interactive melody of sorts, contrasting yet somehow in harmony with the non-repetitive yet circular rhythmic sounds.

Was this "electronic music," "computer music," as I had been informed? "New Music"? Up to that point, New Music for me was mostly people of various ages seated rather stiffly in chairs with pages of apparently difficult tasks, written in code, on their music stands. After the sounds stopped, somebody in a turtleneck and sport coat came out from the audience and took a bow.

Or there was the "alternative" brand of New Music: more people sitting around, making long, droning sounds, wearing open-necked "Western" shirts that one suspected really came from the Gap. In either case, there was never any dancing about or making any bodily or instrumental motion in the direction of ecstasy. Jerry anticipated the voguers and ravers by many years, even providing a version of the insistent four-on-the-floor beat characteristic of techno. Jerry's beat, however, was rather sixty-four-on-the-floor, coming from the large wooden box which contained eight eight-track tape players, a massively multichannel device, eroding the boundaries between low and high tech.

I was reminded of another southern Jerry: Jerry Lee Lewis, giving Europe's piano some transgressively disrespectful wallops, B'wana suddenly gone violently native. Our Jerry's long, baubled stick was like the whisk that African rulers once wielded, a symbol of authority, power, magic, and justice, now arrogantly appropriated by unjust, World Bank–supported usurpers.

Or I could flash back to Robert Farris Thompson's 1970s art classes at Yale, where if you were black and knew about dance and music you were, for once, at an advantage, as he danced around the lecture hall in a fashion which some of the children of privilege found either salacious or goofy, especially from one of their own tribe, and besides, "It's fun and an easy A."

To top the whole thing off, when the piece was over, Hunt was transformed into a rather soft-spoken person who announced the name of the piece as—I don't remember the name, but it sounded like the densest piece of New Music–type discourse, "Algorithms I" or something. The total effect was frankly disorienting, astonishing.

I read the baffling program notes and came away with the impression that Jerry Hunt had a powerful message for us, but it was coded in the fashion of the slave songs. This type of coding I recognized right away as a survival mechanism. You had to make the effort to train yourself to understand the message; less interested parties would pass right by, hearing it as noise, gibberish, "bar-bar"—nothing to worry about, no need to impose sanctions. For me, Jerry's work exemplified his assumption of the mantle of the trickster, Elegua, bringing us uncomfortable truths about ourselves and our world, reminding us of Fate's cruelties and ironies.

STOMPIN' AND BEATIN' AND SCREAMIN'
Gordon Monahan in Conversation with Jerry Hunt

This interview was conducted by Gordon Monahan during Hunt's visit to the 1986 Newfoundland Sound Symposium. It was originally published in the fall 1987 issue of the Canadian avant-garde magazine *Musicworks*, which included a cassette titled *Music Affecting Music*, featuring a compilation of artist statements, compositions, and recording excerpts from Wende Bartley, Michael Snow, and Michel Tétreault, among others. The cassette includes a short segment of Hunt and Monahan's conversation and a performance of Hunt's *Fludd: (Volta): Jal (MUSIC)* (ca. 1986). The version here has been lightly edited for clarity and is accompanied by a new introduction from Monahan.

(219–40)

In July 1984, Jim Tenney and I drove my 1969 Chevy Impala from Toronto to Hartford, Connecticut, to perform in his work *Bridge* (1982–84) at the New Music America Festival. Upon arrival we were greeted by festival director Joe Celli, and over the course of our welcoming dinner, Jim asked Joe what performances he would recommend seeing during the festival. Joe mentioned several concerts and performers, but he made an emphatic point not to miss the incredible and indescribable Jerry Hunt. I had never heard of Jerry; several people with whom I talked that week also spoke highly of him, but no one could actually describe what he did, aside from loose descriptions of "sound-based performance art using interactive technology," which in those days was considered "cutting edge."

Not knowing what to expect, I was immediately struck by Jerry's unorthodox stage presence, his sense of seeming (or pretending, as I would later ascertain) not to play to the audience. Jerry walked haphazardly on and off the stage, mumbling, then shouting nonsensical sounds, sometimes toward the rear wall (and obviously "projecting" away from the audience). Then he might pick up and shake his homemade sticks and "pointers," or grab a suitcase from offstage, which he would proceed to bang with a broomstick while stalking an invisible spirit across the stage, all the while causing a loud, droning sound to resonate throughout the theater. The music, on its own, was not that unusual or particularly sensational, but when combined with Jerry's indescribable stage persona and riveting charisma, the entirety of the performance was mind-blowing. Seeing Jerry for the first time left an indelible impression on me and remains perhaps the most amazing performance I've seen in my life.

I don't recall if Don Wherry, the Newfoundland Sound Symposium artistic director and cofounder, also saw Jerry's performance at the Hartford festival, but when Don invited me to perform at the 1986 Sound Symposium in St. John's, he agreed to invite Jerry to perform as well. Since all participants at the symposium are asked to stay for the full two-week festival, Jerry and I spent a lot of time together. He did an amazing performance at the Cornerstone bar, a historic building that at one time was a Catholic church. A day or two after the event, I sat down with Jerry to record an approximately four-hour interview. Jerry loved to talk, and it was almost like pushing a play button once you asked him a question. After I pushed the record button on my tape recorder, I could barely get a word in, until he might suddenly say, after monologuing for a half hour or so, "Do you want me to keep going or do you think you have enough?" I would chuckle and attempt to ask another question, which would set him off again.

—Gordon Monahan, Meaford, Ontario, March 2021

STOMPIN'
AND BEATIN'
AND SCREAMIN'

**AN INTERVIEW WITH
JERRY HUNT**

THE WORLD IS NOT A SYMPHONY

Jerry Hunt: Everybody's always talking about new sounds. I haven't heard any yet. I haven't heard any new sounds. I'm not saying I've heard all sounds; I'm saying that if you say "new sounds" what you're really talking about is the reborn experience. In other words, *I've been reborn to sound*. And then there are these absurd excesses. Once we were at some program someplace and we were outside, and Cage had been there and he'd been giving a lecture and this woman was coming out and she even had her fingers on her earlobes and she was saying, "All the world is a symphony!" You know, I mean, it's not. It's just not a symphony. It may be a lot of things, but it's just not a symphony. And this raises something that I think is a critical issue and gets to a very serious problem: I don't think Cage really believes what he says himself, because he needs his jobs; and I don't want to say that I believe it myself because I need my jobs, too. And I don't understand why it's the only thing that interests me to do. I have no understanding of that at all. But, in fact, you don't need concerts. There's really no reason to listen to music at all, particularly in the world that we have now. The real reason for music is as a way for exchanging money. That's its real source. It has nothing to do with sound or technology or new resources or anything else that I honestly can see.

Now, I can see how you can specialize your vision and then all of these games work. If you just specialize your vision here or here or here, then all of these questions of new resources or new sounds, new technologies, new concert attitudes, can work. Yet it looks to me like people have gone into a kind of relooping. People are continuing to reloop around the same old stuff all the time, and as a consequence the real avant-garde part has totally broken down. The money structure that supports music has shifted. The avant-garde has been redefined in a completely different avenue, and that's in commercial, technically sophisticated dealings with masses of people in Top 40 global rock. In other words, where the real innovation is, is with Prince. Prince is a real innovator because he is utilizing ideas and life patterns. He has a profound influence on global culture. Stevie Wonder. I'm not trying to isolate individuals. Cyndi Lauper. They cease to be individuals as soon as they're powerful. They're now institutional forces. You can use a conspiratorial or consumerist-dominant or monopolistic theory to explain it, but the fact is that they are truly innovators. And it's not sound innovation that they're doing. It's social engineering in a kind of funny way.

Music has taken on a powerful importance in modern times. I think music has been more important since 1960 than it ever has been. In the US, for example, music wasn't that important when I was growing up. In 1955, music wasn't that important. Music was a kind of a special thing you went and did. You know, you didn't have to have your music *with you*. When I first got to Philadelphia [en route to Sound Symposium in Newfoundland], the woman who took my tickets off of my baggage before I got onto the thing to go over to the right terminal to stand there in eighty-seven-degree air-conditionless heat and claw at a metal grate to try to get air—took my ticket and I went out and was waiting for the bus, and then she came out. She'd gotten off work. I saw the biggest boom box I'd ever seen in my life. I swear the thing was as big as . . . it was enormous. It had two speakers; it didn't look like it was terribly heavy. It didn't look like her arm was about to be disjointed. I've never seen such a big one, you know. So you're thinking, *Is this a consumerist conspiracy?* In other words, the more of those machines that we can provide for people—the more Walkmans, the more CDs, the more PeeWees that people can come up with—the more product can be sifted and shifted and manipulated.

HUNT GOES HEAVY

JH: Then there's the reality of independent distribution. You come to one of these festivals and everybody's made forty records. Where are they all? It seems like there are about twenty-five distributors around the world that'll even piddle with the stuff. I nearly fell over dead when I saw Tower Records carries Irida. So I'm sitting there and I'm thinking, *Why is Tower carrying Irida?* PR. They don't make any money off of carrying those things, but it's good public relations to be able to say in your advertising, in your literature, in your four-color glossies, "Most complete record store on Earth." And you walk in and you say, "Do you have blah?" "No, but look over there." And so you go over there to look, and an entire wall, which doesn't take up very much space in their overall stores—and you see up on that wall are about 250 to 300 independent labels, a few records from each. And you think, *They don't have what I want, but they do have a lot, don't they?* I was impressed myself. They

do carry a lot of independent stuff for one of those clenched-fist-type record stores. But it's obvious they don't have my picture in a relief punch-out, holding one of my wands out, up in the front of a stand-up sign: "Get 'Em While They're Hot, Hunt Goes Heavy." And a picture of me on the front of *Newsweek* magazine?

POUNDING HIGHER AND MORE FURIOUSLY

JH: The only piano music I really enjoy playing anymore is late romantic music, from Chopin on. I like to play Chopin, Rachmaninoff, and Scriabin. I love Scriabin's piano music; I think it's just a joy to play because it's like a nut, it's like the music of a nut. Like this thing "Toward the Flame" I love playing that because it's just this incessant pounding, rising by augmented fourths, and you just pound, and you go up a little higher, and you pound faster and more furiously, and you pound even more furiously and higher—you pound even more furiously and higher and you just keep pounding higher and more furiously, and finally you just stop pounding, because you're tired more than anything else. I mean, it's just like he spent himself at the piano. And I've never forgotten that at the movies. When I was a child I went to the 25th Street Theatre in Waco and saw some movie. To this day I don't know what it involved, but something had happened between this man and woman and the man was, I think, blind. He sat down to the piano in this kind of purple velvet room and he began just beating furiously on this piano, playing this pounding manic music. A lot of Hollywood composers picked up on this

JERRY HUNT IN PERFORMANCE AT THE CORNER STONE DISCO, ST. JOHN'S, NEWFOUNDLAND.

Schillinger-Scriabin harmonic language where there would be these—what I think of as cocktail lounge chords, just pounded straight to the bone. And he sat and he did that. He pounded these slightly dissonant things and from underneath the dark glasses, tears were streaming down, and the camera kept moving in closer. Scriabin is a fulfillment of that. He's the ultimate fulfillment of just spent passion at the keyboard. But those slightly luscious things use the twelve-tone intonation, particularly with the piano, marvelously. He really understood piano resonance, like most pianists do. Rachmaninoff was a great one for that. Even Chopin was a great one for understanding how this mechanism that took so long to build up can

I despise sustained sounds. I think sustained sounds are repulsive, they're pseudoreligious . . .

really be made to work, and to make it sound for its own sake.

I don't think I could have ever had a career as a pianist because I never ever wanted to play the notes the way they were written. I was too sloppy to learn them quite right. And I've found that a few pieces I can never, ever memorize because of the way Rachmaninoff, for example, composed: First he wrote the pop song, the tune with chord changes. Then he slithered around a lot up and down, and after he got the slithers in, then he'd put accent marks over a few of the slithered big notes and scrape some of the other slithers out and voilà! "Sonata No. 1," "Sonata No. 2." Which is the thing I like, it's kind of an aesthete and degenerative cocktail music. He's just more sophisticated than your regular cocktail player because it's crisper, it's more highly defined. But I could never memorize these works because the note choices are so completely arbitrary. I don't think I would ever have been able to make it as a pianist.

I've got a feeling now that I was an arrogant child. When I was young, I felt like I didn't need any training. But I don't feel apologetic about it, like a Schoenberg, and yet I'm not proud of it. I don't make a cult of stupidity and ignorance, but I think I'm sloppy and self-indulgent and then I also know that I am just personally afraid. In other words, the reason I've stayed in Texas is because it's always been relatively comfortable and I've just been sort of generally afraid to go anyplace else. And you hear all of these interviews with composers and artists and read in their bios, *then I went to blah-blah* . . . and you realize that what they've done is, over the course of a few years they've written a fantasy about themselves which becomes part of their work. So you read these long discussions, you know, in the European tradition particularly: *And then I created . . . in the middle of the night I woke up and a vision appeared to me* . . . Like, what's happening to Stockhausen? Apparently the music is being sent here from Jupiter? Is that where it is? I'm trying to get the planet right. He thinks he's from some planet now. You would think that these people never ever had to shit, that all they ever did was just work on their next work and there was no time for shitting. You know, *Pardon me, I'm composing this symphony and, oh, seal the bathroom up. I don't need it, I'm not through with my work yet.* And to me, what's most important about life is the need to shit. That's the really significant detail about it.

A 100 POUND SHOW

Gordon Monahan: When did you start to really get going with your current work?

JH: It really started happening, I think, in the middle of the '70s. By that time the National Endowment for the Arts and other federal government

Some of the children of some of my friends like what I do, sort of . . . in the sense that *My parents know this strange person*.

programs were beginning to get pretty well organized, and there was a move towards decentralization of funding, giving more to the so-called regions. But the nice thing for me was that a lot of people all over the US, I think, knew what I did; there were people in Europe who knew about my work, people even in Asia who knew about it, but only by word and reputation and, I think, curiosity. You know, *Why would someone whose name is J-e-r-r-y, who lives in Texas, be doing things like this without moving?* I think that was the only novelty about me at all. But then I think I came to be of service—that there was a need to show decentralization of funding.

I've always thought of myself as a New Music novelty act, socially, in that if you call me, you can guarantee that I don't cause a lot of technical problems; I don't require a lot of complicated technical setup, because I just don't believe in it. So for instance, you've got no lights? I carry my own: four or five 15- to 35-watt bulbs, a few sockets. I have a few pieces that use interactive dimmers, but it's still my own stuff. Uh, sound system? Mono, up. The reflections are bad in this room? So the sound reflects. I re-equalize, or I change what I do. I get there and I think, *This is awful, I'll X.*

So the way that I think I benefited from this need to decentralize funding was that people had always heard about me, I was an easy act to install. Also, I'm guaranteed to be different from everybody else—I mean, I'm just absolutely

guaranteed. I'm not saying that it's so original, it's just that I think a lot of people aren't willing to do anything that awful in such an unstudied way. I don't work at being bad. So I'm guaranteed to be enough of a novelty act that I don't slop off into other peoples' areas; I'm extremely flexible, and so I was a natural. I'm pretty cheap to travel, too. I don't come with seventy-five thousand pounds of equipment because I gauge my weight depending upon what I think I can afford. I have over 150 light poles, some with dimmers; I have five different dimmer subsystems. I've got at least five hundred stage objects that David McManaway and I have worked on over the years—some quite large, some quite small, some as big as this room. If it's practical to use, I use it. If it's not practical, I don't. I judge everything on the basis of weight and cost. So this was a hundred-pound show. That's basically how I think about it. It was one hundred pounds. And that's mostly because my power supplies are old and heavy.

So that's what entered me into this pattern of this concert network. And when I started meeting the people involved and getting to know them personally more, I got to thinking, *I like them. Almost everybody I've ever met in this business I actually personally like.*

A GREAT BIG HAPPY EASY ACCIDENT

JH: I've been listening to the people here who are in the ages twelve to eighteen, who are kind of hanging around this festival because they have to, because their parents are working there. I've talked to some about what they think of this stuff, and it's flat. They are neither enthusiastic about it nor are they bored. It's a flat response, uniformly. *It's OK. It's kinda interesting.* That's the peak enthusiasm: it's OK. It's an experience they're not sorry they've had, but one that has not moved them in any way whatsoever. They are going to go out and eat the same food, go to the same stores, buy the same clothes, have the same conversations, raise the same families that they would have before they came to the concert. And that's got to concern you in some way. I can't understand how people are not concerned by that. It isn't even that I want them to like it. It isn't "like." They don't dislike it.

Some of the children of some of my friends like what I do, sort of. They sort of like it. But they like it in the sense that, *My parents know this strange person.* The other thing that's odd to me: I'm getting old enough now that I'm developing a following of a kind that I don't completely understand. I attract boys in the age from nineteen to twenty-seven. I'd say that's about the age. I can't touch a boy under eighteen. They have no interest in me at all. After I do a concert, usually, if I go to an alternative space thing, these boys come to me after the concert is over and I'm sitting there and I'm looking at them and they're looking at me kind of funny. And I'm looking at them funny and we're both sitting there looking at one another and they're kind of in a ring around me and I'm thinking, *Why are you here looking at me? What's interesting about me?*

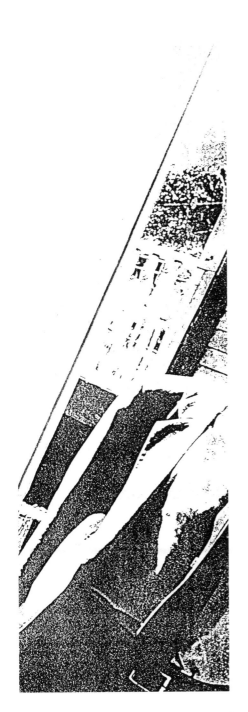

My friend says he thinks that what it is, is that they are at a point in their lives when, very soon, they're going to have to go to school, select a career, something like that. And most people offer them rather extreme choices: that they must either take drugs and live in the street and maybe end up a bum in a drug rehabilitation center if they freak out too far at one end, or that they're going to have to use the missionary position, produce two children, three cars, and a mortgage in the other extreme. And they can look at me and they can think, *Well look at that old fart. He's just kind of buggerin' on along. He hasn't lost all his marbles and yet he seems like he's kinda having a good time. There are options in life.*

I don't attract girls and I'm not sure why. I do attract a few, but not as many as boys. The girls I attract are in the same age period, and I think it's because maybe these girls have had less sex indoctrination, or they are genetically or chemically disposed in a slightly different way, and so they also have that feeling of independence to make a choice. But I think for many women, still one of the easiest choices is just to socially relax, and that will result in a house and a life and a washing machine. Just by relaxing a little. It's still very endemic to US culture. A girl really has to work very hard to stop being a girl. They don't have any choice. Am I glad that I'm a white male? You better believe it. Because I've never had to make any of these choices. I didn't have to do it. It's been very easy for me. My whole life has been one great big happy easy accident in which all of my stresses and neurotic reactions and unhappinesses have been complete luxury items which

I can indulge to whatever degree I find satisfying. In a way I wish everyone could have that choice.

BOOGIEING

JH: I find the level of craft and competency in music one of the most serious threats to your salability as a musician. When I was in college for a year and a half, I was probably one of the best pianists around. If I entered that college today, I would probably be one of about two hundred, and we'd all be equally good. It's because if a child is two months old and there are these things hanging over the crib and it goes *boo-dappy-boo-da-boo-padoo*, immediately it's ripped up out of the crib and carried to the conservatory and put on bongos. I mean, there's no chance to not have every possible talent exploited by anybody who is anywhere from the middle class up.

CAKE DECORATING, WITH SOUND

JH: I've always felt like it was boring to me to go to a music concert and see people work the mechanism of their instruments. And I just can't understand why, when you talk to non-musicians, they say, *Oh, well I just think it's fascinating.* I'm sitting there thinking, *In what way? How is it fascinating?* And then I think, *Well, I can understand it a little bit.* Like, you'll be walking down the street and you'll see somebody doing some kind of a very careful spray-painting or lettering of a sign; it's a manifestation of a virtuoso skill and you can think, *Oh that's fascinating. Look how beautifully that person's doing that.* It's a refined

skill. It's fascinating to watch a pastry cook, for example, who is very good, do the finishing. Like, I've only seen it once, this exquisite Italian sugar lace-work that started in Sicily. It's almost like in Belgium, where they do that very fine lacework and go blind doing it. But they do this cake decoration, and it's fasci-nating to watch once or twice—but then to spend thirty-five years of your life on subscription series? You know, *What are you doing tonight? I'm going to go watch cake decorating for two and a half hours tonight, with sound.* In other words, I don't understand how continuing to see the exercise of a skill remains interesting more than for just a few minutes.

THE GREEN SLIME DRIPPING OUT

JH: I taught myself to play the piano. I've always been able to play, the minute I could get my hands up. I've always wanted to play the piano. It's the only instrument I've ever really liked, and it's the only one that's ever interested me. I have no interest in things you blow through. They seem dirty to me. I mean, the idea of putting my mouth on some-thing, you know. And all that spit and they get slimy and—have you ever smelled a reed? They're dirty. I don't like winds. And drums, they're fascinating. I like beating on things, but drums are very frustrating to me. I see people beat real fast and I think, *I oughta learn to hold long, hard sticks and flamadiddle.* Then I think, *Why should I learn to flamadiddle? If I get small enough sticks, if I get tiny sticks, I can play like the best of 'em.* The only reason that the drums are hard for a pianist to play is because they're too big and spread out and you have to use these sticks. If you can get those sticks down so that you don't have to deal with weight and everything, you can just go to town. I can't do anything with a normal trap set. Your shins start aching, you know. But you get these real fancy foot pedals that are three or five hundred dollars for the thumper, that makes the thing work, and you can just go to town like this: *Look, no hands.* So, it's just if you can afford high enough equipment, you don't need any technique.

I always loathed the organ. It's not the keyboard I like. I loathe the organ. I think it makes one of the ugliest sounds known to man. I despise sustained sounds. I think sustained sounds are repulsive—they're pseudoreligious, first of all. Ninety-five percent of this drone crap is pseudoreligion. It is. It's to play on some kind of peculiar afterimage of some phony religious experience that people have had, and I think it's a fake. I think the whole thing is a fake and it makes me feel creepy when I'm sitting there. And then the rest of it sounds like science fiction music to me. Like that piece that I

heard the other night. It was "The Attack of . . ." I had the whole scenario worked out . . . the monster . . . and it's hairy here, there are little globs that come out and there's this ugly kind of hair and then two hooks like steel, and there's green slime dripping out of here . . . *uuuuuhhhh, uuuuuuuuuuhhh*, lot of echo . . . a lot of sustain . . . *uuuuuuuuuhhh*, it's for the movies, isn't it? All electronic music to me, just about, as practiced by convention before it went DX7-disco, all sounds like the movies. Like Tangerine Dream, they started playing chords and rhythms outright and not using electronic music as anything but kind of souped-up organs. Then they got klinkier and then they DX7-ed everything and now it's real pert and snappy. But it seems to me that's what it's really for. It's either pseudo-religious or it's science fiction music. And I'd have never thought that fifteen years ago. If I'd said that, you would have thought, *Why, you crude son of a bitch, you don't understand what we're doing here.* And the trouble is, I did it myself

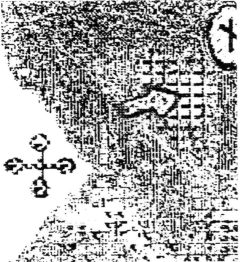
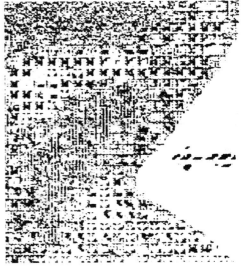

and didn't feel that way about it—I didn't feel that way about it at the time.

GM: But what you're saying about pseudoreligion and sci-fi describes your work, too.

JH: I know that, yes. The reason I don't mind talking this way now is because I realize I don't mind holding myself to the same standards. I'm not saying I've found a way around it. I feel the same way. The other day for my workshop here at the festival, I had provided a piece; they wanted an example of something and it had to be nine minutes long. So I thought, *Well, what I can do is that I can set up some of the recordings and a small program and run into the recording studio and plug directly into the gadgets and run 'em through some Yamaha reverbs, and make a nine-minute version.* So, first pass, nothing. It didn't work. I mean, it was still going *bhuhmlam-lablubbladldaddleiliddledliddle* . . . and it was nine minutes, and it wasn't getting anywhere. So we turned it all off and we goosed it again, and the second time it ran 8:54. I think it stopped reasonably at 8:54, and then there was this long sound at the end that trailed on out. It went *duuuuuuuuuuuuu* . . . and it trailed on out and I said, *That's what we'll do, we'll cut duuuuuuuuuu out. We just quick—snip it out. And when that last drum clunks, you just cut it. Cut the tape.* And so when it runs through the Yamaha it'll bonk and it'll just die away in a nice eight-tenths of a second delay. Sounds great, you know? So when I was listening to it the other day I thought, *That's a piece of shit. That's a piece of shit.* And yet I liked it when I heard it. I carried it home and I thought, *This is a wonderful little Eva-Tone* [a flexi disc]. But then I sit and listen to it and I think, *Under the circumstances this is the best I can do.* And I know everybody else is doing the same thing. The trouble is, nobody's talking about it. But the fact is, everybody is saying that. The people in the audiences that are not practitioners of the cult are feeling and saying the same way. And they're being nice to you when they tell you otherwise. I've been walking around in the audiences. I know what they're saying here. I know what they're saying at other festivals. It's interesting to me. In fact, that is the focus of what my interest is now: given that situation, what are you going to do about it? That's an interesting thought. Earlier this year I thought, *I'm sick of this shit.* Very real. I thought, *I'm sick of this shit. I don't care about hearing any of it. I don't care about doing it. I don't like my work, I don't like anybody else's.* And yet that's not true. I mean, I've been here now for two weeks. I've genuinely enjoyed hearing some of the things here. Even the pieces I didn't like, I enjoyed. But then I got to thinking, *The reason you're in a position to appreciate it is because everything has been set up to accommodate you that luxury.* Back home in Canton [Texas], would I ever go see a piece like what was on last night? The chances are absolutely, I can tell you, pure *zeeero.* It is the purest kind of pure. I could write a five-hundred-page dissertation on the purity of that zero. I'd never go see it. And yet it is the logical consequence of me being here, the whole conditioning. It's *them* against *us.*

THE TECHNICAL SETUP

GM: Could you explain your technical setup?

JH: Yes, I can, but there's a history to it. Because of some of the general feelings I've had about what performance

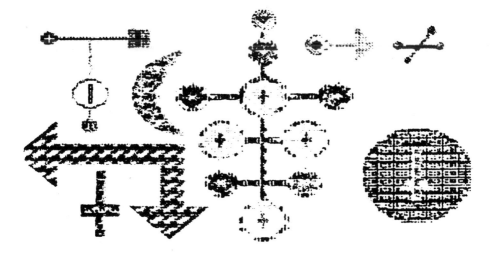

means *live*, to be with a group and to be in front of them, I never felt satisfied about using musical instruments, even electronic ones; or, playing tapes in halls never satisfied me, and I've never done that. I've always avoided it. I've never put a tape up and played it in a darkened hall, for example. So I was looking for some alternatives and also something which I could travel with. Now, this is before computers. Recording seemed to me in a way to be the most powerful thing because it's just basically memory, and there's a psychological aspect of music I'm interested in, which is memory. So, by accident, one day I happened to be going through a used equipment place. By the middle of the '70s the idea of cartridge recorders had pretty well died out, and Sanyo had dumped these things. There was a period where everybody thought they'd go from two speakers to four, and the eight-track stereo cartridge had caught on and was popular. And Sanyo thought, *Well, I'll make a higher fidelity eight-track, but it'll be a sixteen-*. In

other words, it'd be a four track four-track. And I happened to see one of these and I bought it and kept it for two or three months. Then the first use of it was in some concert somewhere. The way it was used was that there were sensors around on the stage and they just had triggers on them, and when I hit a trigger, that would turn on whatever happened to be on whatever track and the thing would just cycle through. That was, I think, about '75 or '76. Well, by 1978 it had changed entirely. I just kept working on the interface to the thing and added electronic and electromechanical switching to the tape transports. So I have electronic switching between tracks on the same channel and slower electromechanical transitions between channels of sets of four tracks. I prerecord material onto the cartridge along with a timecode track. I record the stuff a group at a time and play the timecode on by hand. It's very time consuming and very labor-intensive for twenty minutes of potential material that might be heard by an audience.

There's almost 850 minutes of actual recording for every twenty minutes of possible performance that anyone might ever hear, in some combination. But every part must be worked on efficiently because you never know what part might be heard.

I went to timecode so that I could go fast-forward and back and locate relatively arbitrary places in the tapes. In other words, there's logic in it so that a single digital word will cause it to try to find one of these places. Then I designed it so that I can electronically listen to everything that's happening on every track and I can, at the same time, preselect. I can select backwards by listening to tone code off of it. That tone code is sent into a very simple frequency detector. So with tone code I can locate what kind of material I've got. I'm up to eight different tones for eight different kinds of material. The tones are different and they have different logic significance on each of the tape transports. They're just arbitrarily wired up differently. I have no idea how I hooked them up. There was a group of wires and they came out. I never put numbers on them, so when I hooked them up, I said, *Well, I'll hook one to this pole and I'll hook two to this*

and three to this. There was no order at all, no effort in straightening them out—they're just hooked up. The machine has built into it a certain priority.

The machine is, to my mind, system transparent in the sense that any kind of compositional algorithm or any kind of idea about synthesis or any philosophy of music production is available to the instrument. It can sound totally electronic just by producing these recordings entirely with electronic sources; it can be just a noise generator, it can be huge volumes of distorted noise, it can be human speech, it can be birdsong, it can be environmental sound. It makes no difference. I can do a thousand different qualities out of it, even conventional rock music. I've even appeared with jazz and rock bands using this system.

The serial nature of the machine is what's bothering me the most, combined with the occasional serendipity of the whole operation. So the unfortunate part is the serialism, that once that place is past [on the tape], you can only rewind to get back to it at a speed of four times; and you must go all the way back around, so it is, by nature, serial. That's a bit of a problem. Then, because of the nature of the circuitry,

there's some delay, which is absolutely essential in making choices. By about 1980 I started getting very strong ideas about how a tree always has its roots down in the ground—the trunk goes up and the leaves are up. You never see in nature a tree with the roots up in the air, the stem down and the leaves on the ground, reversed. So I thought, *At this level it's nice to play the game of natural orientation*. There is a bottom to the picture frame and there is a top and I would prefer the representation where the head is pointing up and not hanging down only because it's the convention. So my pieces are not really concerts or performances but conventions. They're convention exercises because I accept the convention arbitrarily. One of the things that I've accepted in this is the serial or sequential nature. I'm really getting tired of that now, so I'll be using exactly the same system next year except that I'm transferring over to disc. I'm changing to a disc-based system for audio and, I hope, video.

Every piece I've ever done has involved what I regard as a rational translation of something that's happening in the space [picked up through sensors] into a consistent rational schedule of changes. I don't do direct translation, which I think is vulgar after three minutes. It's fascinating to watch somebody go like this [*waves arm*] and hear a sound connected with it for a minute or two, but then it becomes compositionally appalling after a while. It's like watching Etch A Sketch, you know—it's wonderful for a few minutes and then it limits itself. It becomes so self-limiting that no matter what you do in the way of effects, it just gets increasingly self-defining until it just keeps getting tighter and tighter, and after thirty minutes you're almost ready to scream, because you say, *I got the idea. Oh hey, he did a new sound. I got the idea. Oh hey, he did a new sound. I got the idea. . . .* That's all you can think of at a certain point. So, I wanted to stay away from that.

Now, decoding. That's one last thing and then I'll stop for a second. I've used a lot of different methods. The most interesting to me in some ways involved a video scanner, where I used a black-and-white television camera and I analyzed a sixty-four-square grid out of a television camera space, whatever it saw, and translated it into data that controlled the machine. The interpretations that I've used through microphones have been different ones. I tried to get complicated in the early ones by doing almost vocoder-like analysis of a couple of microphones. But they've all involved some kind of system along this line.

I like this idea of modeling, in a Renaissance sense, and I've always been a fancier of Rosicrucian chess, which is a kind of three-dimensional chess. So one day a friend of mine handed me a bag of IC game chips— Chess Challenger and the like. They play kind of interesting games, so I've got two of them in the machine now. A certain change in the space [picked up through the sensors, such as microphones or video camera or microwave detector] is always translated as a certain move in the chess game [e.g. Q-R4]. That game might start anywhere. I don't work at controlling it, I just preset and start it up. And then there are little triggers that are arbitrary that start it, depending upon the piece it is. If it's a piece in which I don't want to finger-start then I have a way of starting it

Every piece I've ever done has involved what I regard as a rational translation of something that's happening in the space into a consistent rational schedule of changes. I don't do direct translation, which I think is vulgar after three minutes . . . it becomes compositionally appalling after a while.

via some challenge which sometimes is extraordinarily simple, sometimes very obscure.

GM: For instance, the other night you had a phonograph needle on the stage that you had to hit to start it?

JH: Yeah. I was using it on the lip of the stage. Because of the room and because they kept fiddling around and I didn't have time to work on placement and I didn't know who might be up on the stage, I thought, *Well, the only way to solve this problem is just the best way that I know how: I'll use a crystal cartridge on the door to the stage and I'll just pound the performance up.* That cartridge is translating the material which tells the machine whether to start or stop and whether to preset or reset. That pattern is usually read off of a microwave detector which scans the room, but I thought, *This is no good, there's too much happening in this room, I can't have it constantly turning on and off throughout the whole performance. That won't do at all.* The space was so uncontrolled. But my first idea was that I would put it in a secure area of the room so that I could go over there, still be in focus with the microphones, and I could go over and pound and thump and get

the audience kinda worked up, and we'd really get to going with some poles and some beatin' and screamin' and by that time that would build up enough material and it would get me started on my little playlets. There are specific scenarios for each of these works that involve certain relationships with objects—what objects I carry, what is available. I have a list of strategies and a list of goals and interests and pursuits and exercises and desires that I'd like to work out with the audience. Some very personal, some confrontational and violent, some overtly sexual, some pretentious, some apologetic, some friendly. They're all just interpersonal games with tools.

GM: With a lot of religious references?

JH: Yes. There is a lot of religious stuff, which I think has become increasingly overt in recent years because I realize that it allows people's imagination to relax into things that are understood, and it allows a kind of casual conversation that is nonverbal and yet clear. The use of the cross, the use of the egg, the use of the hand, and the use of the pole are, I think, basically very strong, simple ways of gesturing that are a little larger than just the hand. When I started doing this, I didn't use

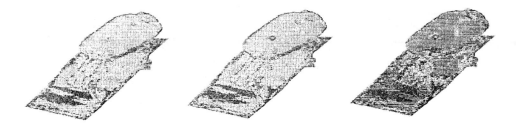

any gadgets or props or anything. All my stuff was just with the hands. Everything was just hand jive. That works for a while, but it doesn't give you very much to work with. The other problem is that it requires a special knowledge of me as a personality. It works in Indian dance beautifully because the language is extremely well-known to the audience, so the tiniest little gesture immediately gets a level of communication out of the way so that you can deal only with inflection and interpersonal relation. That's the power of a deeply convention-based thing. For a typical audience I only have one shot at a lifetime. Someone may only see me once every five years. So I thought, *I've got to be more brutal. I also must be more overt and specific, and yet I must be sufficiently general.* But these are mimetic transactional exercises. That is what I call them and that's exactly what I mean them to be. These objects are not symbols, they're seeders that seed the attention. *This is what this is about. This is the seed. Now we can get on to the transaction of why I'm here: Why am I displaying for you? Why are you allowing yourself to watch me? What are you getting out of me? What can I extract from you? How can we do this with the convention of the music being made to go on?* Because one thing is true of all of my equipment: the sound

will finally stop if I stop moving around and beating. It'll finally stop.

So in general, that's how everything I've ever done works. What I'm headed to is the exact same process of performance, but I'm changing physically what happens on the stage. In other words, in the way that I deal with people. I'm changing the way the machine works in that I want very high speed, precise access so that literally this twist of the hand can just, within a millisecond, bang, and it's on the appropriate cue. And I'm hoping that I can do that with video, too.

The audience is probably thinking, *Oh, this is just a tape recorder.* But it behaves in ways, sometimes, that I have no understanding of at all. I did a concert in New Jersey several years ago, and I set the system up and we were having trouble with the basic access system. It was so strange. I was just working along and I was thumping poles or scraping something or I was using lights, because I think it had an optical interface. I've done about twenty different interface gizmos to plug into it and about twenty different ways of translating these gizmos, including different hookups of Chess Challenger to retranslate information into different patterns and ways that seemed ultimately more interesting. All of a sudden I was aware of wild mechanical chattering offstage where all the electronic gear and the sensors were. Since it was very dark offstage I happened to glance over there and I could just see electrical fire coming out of the top of my box, and yet sound was still coming out but the sound was CHRRRRRRRRRRRRRRRRRRR . . . coming out of the loudspeakers and I thought, *Good God, how am I gonna get out of this?*, because I was only about halfway through the performance, you know. And so I just kept on a-stompin' and a-beatin' and a-screamin' and trying everything I could think of, because I know it's particularly sensitive to certain combinations of movements of very-high frequency, or short transients. Low thuds on the floor or low thuds like a drum or my suitcase that I use some-times tend also to introduce kind of global changes.

So most of the time I don't even know what's going on. What difference does it make how it's working? It is systematically working in some way.

THE FIRST CHURCH

GM: When did you start your first church?

JH: Well, I've always been interested in religion, although I've never been a member of any church. I have never been to any religious service by compulsion. I don't know what happened to me. I think it's genetic. My genes just say "of a reli-gious nature." I was disposed to it from the time I was just a small child, just from origin. I used to stare at light bulbs when I was a baby, and it worried my mother so much that she carried me to the doctor and she said, *Is it going to hurt his eyes?* and he said, *When it begins to bother his eyes he'll close them or look away.*

And it may be that that's got something to do with it, that it's just a neurological disposition that is partly chemical, partly genetic. But the fact is I've always been interested in religiosity in some way. I've always been drawn to meditation prac-tice, and in the town where I was born [Waco] and where I was raised until I was eleven, the library there had a very, very large collection of books on Vedanta. I got interested in yoga, and so I just started practicing yoga and meditation at a very early age. It was just some-thing that made sense to me and was a delight to me. And then when you're ten or eleven years old, there's *the club, the cult*, and I started getting interested in all of these other religious groups and move-ments. So at one point, when I was twelve or thirteen years old, I was a member of every Rosicrucian organization in the world. There were about seven or eight at that time and it was complicated, because I was underage, to join several of them. But in the course of all this, somehow I also felt like I had to teach. So when I was twelve, a friend of mine's mother had access to a lithograph offset device, and his mother was extremely indulgent with him. Anything that this boy wanted, she'd do for him. If he had said, *Momma, kill that man*, she'd have pulled a gun out and shot him without any ques-tion at all. I've never seen a mother this indulgent, and it ruined his life, too. Bill has just recently, in the last year or two, gotten himself pulled out of that.

Anyway, we had access to a press that way and so I began writing reli-gious exercises and sermons culled from different sources. Some would be lectures on alchemical exercises, partly intellectual, partly physical. Some were just basic yoga that I had simpli-fied. Some were devotional exercises;

some were just plain old, good old common-sense advice. Other things were different Western magical ritual traditions, like the ritual of the pentagram and the hexagram and the like, that had been compiled at the time. This was my pre-Crowleyian period. But out of all of this came this desire to start a church. So I just began putting notices up, "All Truthseekers, Write to Post Office blah-blah and Receive Further Information." And I would carry them around and put them in libraries and community centers and stuff like that, and pretty soon I had a mail-order church going. I had a group of people who were sending me between five and fifteen dollars a month to receive these things. It ended up being quite a complicated thing because here I was, thirteen years old, living in the suburbs of Dallas, Texas, with my mother and father out in the front on the weekends in Bermuda shorts doing the lawn, while I was in the back in my bedroom at my typewriter, answering letters from the devotees. And the funny thing was, I think I was of help to people. I took it very seriously. It wasn't a joke. It wasn't a scam. That's what I'm sorry about now. We wouldn't be talking here now. I would be living in, I don't know, Paris? Rome? Madrid? I don't know where I'd be living, but I'd be living comfortable with a couple of Rolls-Royces harnessed out in front of the house, and a servant and somebody cooking up something. Nothing but the best coffee and the best Sauternes, and life would be fancy and it would be beautiful and it would be nice in a lot of ways that I now realize are not so bad after all [*laughs*].

But I was so serious about it all, and the crisis came when there was a couple in their eighties who had been dying to meet me, and I'd kept it very obscure where I lived. They just desired to meet me really furiously and I kept putting them off. I'd write them and try to keep them from meeting me because I thought, *This is terrible. I can't let them find out that I'm thirteen*. They were quite persistent, because one of the topics in their letter was that they wanted to arrange to leave all of their money to me in their will. And that's when I learned how true it is, you know. Aleister Crowley writes in his *The Book of Lies*, there's one thing called "The Truthseeker," and this man keeps coming back to the guru saying, *Tell me the true secret of life*, and he keeps saying, *You have to give me five hundred pounds in gold*. So he gives him five hundred pounds, and the man comes back a little later, *You must tell me the true, true secret*, and The Truthseeker says, *Give me five hundred more pounds worth and I'll tell you*, and the man works for years and brings back the gold and he keeps asking. Finally The Truthseeker says, *If you just give me one more payment of five hundred pounds worth of gold, I'll give you the ultimate secret of the universe*. So the man goes and he gets five hundred pounds worth of gold and he brings it to him and The Truthseeker says, *A sucker is born every day*. I mean, this is in a religious text of Crowley's. I think that's the lesson I really learned there, and that we were both suckers; this couple, they were suckers, and I was too, but we both received satisfaction from it. It made me understand things about myself, about the world and about human nature, and it seemed to please other people. They got satisfaction, they got strength, and I think it helped them.

GM: What happened with the old couple?

JH: They wanted to leave me the money so badly that they went to the post office and found a way to trace the box number to my street address. I never did figure out how they traced that. And it was Sunday afternoon, and my mother and father truly were out working in the yard and I was back preparing lessons for the next week. I had a heavy schedule. I was going to school, practicing the piano all the time, working nightclubs on weekends, and writing meditation exercises during the week. So I had a busy life when I was thirteen, but I was also very hyper. I only slept about three hours a night when I was a child, so I had more time than I do now. Now I'm up to five and a half, six hours sometimes. So I was there in the house and I heard this screaming in the front door, and I ran to the front and I could hear my father screaming, *If you don't get off my property in a minute, I'm going to call the police, you goddamned bunch o' weirdos!* It was this man and his wife and some friend of theirs who had come to meet the master. So they drove off and I never heard from them again.

The desire to believe is so very strong, because you do have to have it. You've got to have some form of belief to go down the steps, to know when you need to go to the bathroom, that you need to go. Belief is not something that you can do without, or that you can cut on and off like a tap, or that you can rationalize yourself out of. I'm not belittling these people, it's just amazing to me how deep it is. That it is so strong. I feel certain now that if I had written a letter to this couple and just gone right on as if I didn't even know what they were talking about, that they would have thought, *Well, it was all a mistake. We misunderstood. This is a test. This is a test of our faith.*

I got interested in Crowleyianism when I was about seventeen. I really went full speed, full blast for a couple of years on magical practice of the arcane kind, where you do the ritual of the pentagram, you cut the pentagram in blood. I used to make beetle cakes, compounds of ground wheat and raw honey and butter and just choking spices. I used to do invocations to planetary intelligences, for example—stuff like that. There was a period there in my life when I got sufficiently disturbed. It came about when I was between the time of sixteen and seventeen, I guess. A lot of things came together at that time and my parents decided that there was something wrong with me mentally. So I did spend a short time in a mental institution [*laughs*]. But it was not for treatment, it was just for observation.

IT WOULD BE GREAT TO BE REGARDED AS THE WORLD'S GREATEST MERINGUEIST

Jerry Hunt Interviewed by Guy De Bièvre

This interview was conducted in English and translated into Dutch for the September 1988 issue of *Logos-blad*, the monthly newsletter of the Logos Foundation, an experimental music organization based in Ghent, Belgium, where Guy De Bièvre worked. The limited-run publication was distributed primarily to members of the foundation, which hosted a performance by Hunt in spring 1988, around the same time as the interview took place. While Hunt was touring Europe—performing in Cologne, Berlin, and Ghent—he made stops in the Dutch cities of Middelburg and Eindhoven, where he presented his where he presented two installations, *Birome (ZONE): Cube*, 1986, and *BIROME (Zone): CUBE (Frame)*, 1988. The version of the text published here includes De Bièvre's new English translation of his original introduction (which had also been translated into German and republished in the January 1994 issue of *MusikTexte*); it has been retranscribed from the original audio tape and includes material omitted from the Dutch publication. The transcription has been edited for clarity and length.

Three objects are assembled to form an arrow perpendicular to a little stick. Jerry Hunt follows the arrow to the wall, illuminating the trajectory with a tiny, trembling flashlight. The beam of light becomes one more in a web of immaterial lines that will be spun throughout the performance. The audience follows the arrow, or follows Hunt, or follows the images that appear now and then on the video monitors. Hunt plays two autonomous subjects: the equipment, which reacts to his actions and movements, and the audience (or rather, as he would specify, its conventions). He has to distribute his act in a balanced way to keep what he might call the "system" working.

Whether and how Hunt's actions trigger images on the screens can seem obvious, but the functional relationship between image and sound is elusive. They do not seem to have any direct relation; they are, as Hunt would say, more like the concentric circles used in the Renaissance to depict heaven and hell. Heaven and hell run parallel to each other: the angels are in one circle and the demons in the other without the groups ever interacting. This dynamic contrasts with the traditionally direct association between the visual and auditory actions of the performer. His hands shake from beginning to end: they shake lights and an amazing collection of bells, rattles, and other simple but often very suggestive objects. Associating what one sees and hears, and what causes what, is left to the spectator's discretion, to their personal "agreements."

In a shamanistic ritual, one probably also often questions whether little events should be attributed to chance, to the shaman, or to the invoked "spirits." Part of it depends on how the shaman controls their "technology" and their audience. Hunt has several traits in common with Fred Astaire, not least his appearance and idiosyncratic limb movements, even if Hunt's tap dance is more intense. (During his first visit to the hall of the Palais des Beaux-Arts in Brussels, where he was to perform, Hunt was very enthusiastic about the wooden floor: "I can beat dynamite out of this floor," he said, a statement emphasized by the size of his quite heavy shoes.) Astaire would draw an arch with a stick in his left hand, beginning with a tap on the floor to his left and ending with a tap on his right, and then walk under this imaginary arch; there, we witness, in a simple way, a very complex geometrical construction. Similarly, Hunt not only suggests a lot of things, he also suggests the suggestion itself.

Hunt's work should only be interpreted in a literal fashion. As soon as you go looking for more than what is there, you are lost. This starts with the titles of his works; many of them, often the most intriguing, happen to be names of Texan locales, while several others are literal descriptions of the work's relevant objects or processes. Some titles include both aspects: Texas sites and reflexive descriptors. The installation he presented in Middelburg and Eindhoven had as its title *BIROME (Zone): CUBE (Frame)*. It was literally a cube formed by a frame containing an interactive (or, as he described it, "transactive") zone. Birome is a small town in Texas (about twenty miles north of Waco); the inhabitants themselves ignore the name's origin. A similarly literal approach is also required to grapple with the sixteenth-century memory patterns that Hunt applies to his work: this interactive system, both in concerts and installations, uses chess computers hacked in such a way that they allow for some kind of Rosicrucian variation on the game (it is three-dimensional, with one chess board perpendicular to another). The hack causes the computer to not respond automatically to each move, but rather to memorize a number of moves and, from that collection, deduce a pattern of repeated moves and then react with its own move. This way of working avoids the phenomenon of one action causing a single reaction (e.g., *I push button A and the red light switches on; I push button B and the blue light switches on; and this is what I should always expect*). As Hunt said, this is not how life works—with him, button A should be able to switch on both lights, or none, or to alternate them.

Hunt's work is never obviously predictable, and explaining things is never simple. What is remarkable is that Hunt manages, with the weirdest attributes (often referring to religious symbols) and technology (though without any techy aspect or feeling), to allow us to choose between a number of agreements with ourselves, his actions, and the audiovisual events within a social environment (concert or performance) in which we are present. Within Jerry Hunt's work we experience the rare luxury of having our intelligence directly addressed and our conventions continuously questioned without any submissive attitude toward a performer, who, in this case, does nothing but propose to us a number of possibilities.

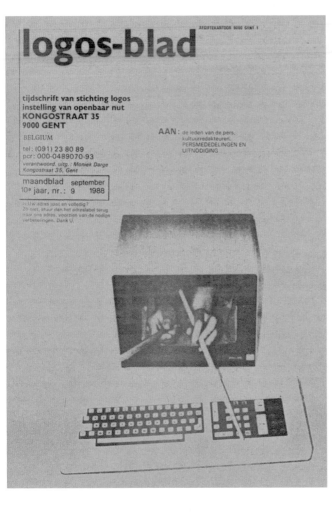

logos-blad

AFGIFTEKANTOOR 9000 GENT 1

tijdschrift van stichting logos
instelling van openbaar nut
KONGOSTRAAT 35
9000 GENT

BELGIUM

tel: (091) 23 80 89
pcr: 000-0489070-93
verantwoord. uitg.: Moniek Darge
Kongostraat 35, Gent

maandblad september
10ᵉ **jaar, nr.: 9** 1988

Is Uw adres juist en volledig?
Zo niet, stuur dan het adreslabel terug
naar ons adres, voorzien van de nodige
verbeteringen. Dank U.

AAN: de leden van de pers,
kultuurredakteuren.
PERSMEDEDELINGEN EN
UITNODIGING

Cover of *Logos-blad*, September 9, 1988.

Hunt in Eindhoven, Netherlands, ca. 1988. Photos: Maria Blondeel.

Has anything weird happened during one of your concerts—something that would be provoked by the shamanic gestures?

JERRY HUNT

I've had unusual audience reactions, but not so much to what I do now as to what I used to do. I have had people who behave strangely. I did a concert in Houston where someone in the audience, at a gallery, crashed their arm through the wall, and we never figured out why. It was a thin wall, like what we're sitting against now—maybe half an inch. The audience member was very nice about it and he said that my performance had gotten him all excited and said, "I'll repair it tomorrow." He offered to come back and repair the hole. But it's more occasional that there are unusual reactions. And, in a lot of these programs now, I feel strange—because I haven't been here [in Europe] in a long time, it's been ten years since I've been away from American or Canadian audiences—sometimes I feel like time has stopped in a sense, and that the audience reactions are more the kinds that I associate with an earlier time in my own career, when people were more surprised by what [I was] doing. Occasionally I'll get feelings very reminiscent of earlier times because in the States, the audiences have changed, and I don't think it's all entirely good—but good in the sense that they are very mixed. In other words, there's no longer a special interest community following you. It's just a mixture of people off of the streets, there out of curiosity, or they may have never seen anything like it before—and then there are the specialists and your friends, and then there are the musicians and composers. But it's almost an equal mixture of these kinds of sources for an audience. And so I think that makes a different sensation because you get very graded reactions to what you do, from really not liking it at all to being very enthusiastic about it. There's a wide spectrum. Here, I feel like there's a little bit more of a tendency to be polarized: people either don't like it at all or they're very enthusiastic about it.

There's the background that has a lot to do with it. I did a concert in Philadelphia a couple of years ago, and the particular work had a lot more Christian kitsch in it. I mean, there was a lot more of the Roman Catholic tradition—things that I later realized could be read as specifically about the Roman tradition. At the time I was doing it, I really didn't have that much in mind. It just had to do with the Rosicrucian myth of the box—it's a resurrection thing, and there's material about God. The action is very loosely based on that, like the floating down—the thing involves a certain kind of movement in the space. There are no literal allusions to any of this at all, but there were enough little symbolic references to it that a more mixed audience would have, I think, just dismissed it and seen it as part of the visual activity of the evening. In Philadelphia, oddly, it seemed like I got a very strong Catholic audience. Most people in the audience were either Catholic or ex-Catholic. And so they saw it, in a strange way, as a parody of the mass. I mean, they kept seeing it, and they just translated it completely into a parody of the mass, but that can happen to you. I mean, you can give a program for an audience, all of whom are specialized in some way, and it's like performing at a festival, too. I mean, the perceptions of other people who work in the same field you do, and when you have an audience that is mostly other people who do the same kind of work, that's a very unusual reaction that you get because it's very highly specific, and it's very highly specialized, and they have all kinds of—to my mind—eccentric questions or very particular technical questions, or they'll isolate a certain aspect of what you do because it's interesting to them or it feeds their ideas.

So it's the same thing in a way, when you're doing a performance for a bunch of specialists, and then you accidentally get groups of people, all of whom have some cultural or racial characteristic, but of course I don't get invitations usually to do things for the kind of audience that would be particularly knowledgeable in something like Voodoo. Voodoo is unlike many of the unique things that I have experienced. But it would be very curious to me to see how people reacted to me, say, in Haiti now, particularly given the political situation and the political implications of Voodoo, because most of my interest in it is nonpolitical. I know nothing about the politics of Haiti, but [Voodoo] was very politically charged there. I mean, it was associated with the dictatorial regime and was used as an instrument of manipulation. To do a work in which there was some reference to Voodoo in a place like that, it'd be sending an unintended message that you didn't know you were sending.

I've looked at it myself and thought, *this is an interesting thing to use and, why, I'll use one little aspect of it.* After a while, it contains its origin, but in its eventual working out its origin is deeply embedded and only specialists can see that. You never know exactly what your audience is going to be. It might be people with expertise in one area or special cultural backgrounds. And sometimes I think it'd be interesting to sequence, to see what that is like, to see what the experience is to put it into a culturally foreign environment where you don't share a lot in terms of ideas or language or tradition or culture or architecture—all those things—and then see what happens.

I think it would be interesting to do a concert in what clearly would be kind of a hostile environment, because none of the basic preparations are there, because a lot of the music and performance that I do is based a little bit upon a knowledge of the convention of the performance—because I really don't do so much music as I do what I myself even see as convention manipulation. And when you have an audience whose whole idea of those conventions is totally foreign, then what they receive is, in a way, purely foreign and exotic experiences. So I suspect that an African audience, for example, would look at me and say, this is what Westerners do. So it would just be taken as an exotic experience to them, and that would be interesting to see how they respond.

GB   I liked the idea of considering a concert as a social event. And taking into account that fact, I always wondered, when you organize a concert, you have people coming—what is your relation to these people? I know you bring them there—what do you give them, or how do you treat them, and how do you hold their attention? When you were still a pianist, did that aspect of audience versus performer occur to you?

JH It was always annoying to me in a way. One of the things that I think changed my attitude about it was when you perform that way and it's as if there is a glass shield between you and the audience—it's a conditional glass shield, and you can lift it or lower it by modulating it in little funny ways because every-body knows [the conventions of the performance] so well. If you disarm people by letting them know this gate is going to go up and down, and it's not going to stay up all the time but it's not going to be down all the time either, then I think that puts their attention there. And the first time I ever noticed how that worked was when I used to do a lot of piano playing in different ways to make a living.

I used to do a lot of solo club work where I just sat at the piano—and at the back top of the bar was the piano and people would sit around. It was interesting there because it wasn't so much a glass as it was a little sheer curtain that was between you and the people in the back where you could talk and visit, but there was this other convention of distance between you so that it wasn't rude for them to sit and have intimate conversations with one another while you were in earshot because this invisible plane was between you, and yet at any time either of us could open it. I could make some remark to them about what they had been talking about, or they could pull this curtain back and say something to me personally. It was also very helpful to me to get over a very difficult problem that I had with performance itself, as I used to be terrified to perform; it was very frightening to me. I think working in bars got me over that. In fact, I have more trouble even today dealing with an audience when the space is very large and the physical distance between audience and performer is very great—that's always a little frightening to me at first, and it's slightly disarming because I think I can't really see them, as they're too far away and too many of them. Sometimes when I've done large concerts where there's a large audience and I'm at a platform kind of above them and at a distance, that's also strange to deal with to me now, but it still doesn't bother me as much as it did when I was a child, when I started to play. It's not that same frightening goal that it once was.

GB   That's also the nice thing about it—the fact that you, on one hand, had that audience relation, but on the other hand you can't rely completely on that while you've got to get the thing working. Many religious manipulators only have the audience to manipulate.

JH They're also driven by the program of the ritual. There is an interesting parallel with the Catholic mass, for example, in that mass is always addressed to the congregation and yet there's also a magical operation taking place, too. There are moments when the attention of the priest and all the assistants is very directly focused to the audience, the congregants. At the same time, you have a shift to the specifics of the mass, and there are moments in which the concentration is always completely on the operation going on at the given time. [This two-way focus] exists in all kinds of social occasions—in bars and public spaces. We're doing it all the time, which is something that's interesting to me. If you're going to break away from the tradition of Western art, there's nothing to break away from—that's all over.

So what's left? David Tudor said once, when I asked him what kind of music he was doing, "I'm just finishing up what's left." I think at the time I thought, *that's very ironic, a kind of desperate and sad thing to say.* But in the last few years I thought, no, it really isn't all that desperate or sad because in fact there really is a lot left. One of them is just to do a very simple thing, to pay attention to what everyone had been doing for the last forty or fifty years—and to not assume that it is anything more than an arbitrary structure. And then examining sources, and endless fields of information start to become available when you start asking questions. One of the things that was the most amazing thing to me—and it's this very simple thing, because it's almost more important than the music that's being produced, in ways—is the Liszt decision to change the orientation of the piano, keyboard, and performance supposedly because of his idea about his vanity. Clearly it changed not only instrument design, but it also changed the whole character of the presentation. The idea that you're addressed to an audience as lateral and not direct—or your back is not to them. You're not facing them. You have your side to them and you see that even the instruments have all been designed to provide that kind of presentation. And it's just an odd connection of things, any one of which has a perfectly reasonable explanation if you look back at a distance that's not too long. But if you look at a longer distance, you see how arbitrary these things are. They're funny side products of how cultural habits accumulate. And the side effects are things about the demeanor in the manner of concert presentation, how concert time is spent, the sense of expectation starting and stopping, ideas about continuity, and all those things. It just seems it's a rich mine to dig in.

I think I finished this business when I stopped looking at the immediate circumstances of concerts and presentations and got interested historically, because a few years back I decided that rather than even use modern ideas about this, I would use a historical period that had been well researched, the English period in the 1600s, because there were some ideas about memory and the idea of theater and the theater of memory that you can look at now as just a historical exercise. You can look at it and say, *I want to learn more about this,* and a lot of research has been done by Frances Yates and others— she's written a lot about it. I thought, *that's a fascinating way to use this model of the world—quite arbitrarily but very consistently.* In other words, I don't use it just as coloration of what I do, but I use it consistently and, in fact, I think that's the one thing you would probably never suspect from seeing it—that it had anything to do with sixteenth-century conceptions about time and memory. And what's fascinating is, even though it's arbitrary, it is a closed system but it's as workable as a modern idea about memory and about time and about the representation of events and the layering of different patterns of memory, whether it has to do with musical sound or whether it has to do with images. It's very much the same. So, I don't know whether that's more of an answer than you had wanted: three questions for the price of one.

GB   I want to come back to the idea of manipulation. Do you know about the Pentecostal church in the nineteenth century in Europe? I think they had those big fireworks to impress people. That movement has continued in America. The very first time I saw Jimmy Swaggart on television it was a shock to me, because it was in a big football stadium. That was an extreme example of manipulation because you really could see in the football stadium the effect of the preacher on the people. This is something, to me, that doesn't exist anymore in Europe, not on that scale. So do you think there's something American about it that works there and doesn't exist here any longer?

JH Well, I think one of the reasons that it works in the States is there's been some writing about it, about why now at this time in history, particularly the last ten years in American history, there is such a reinvigoration of the interest in evangelical religion? Because interest in evangelism has gone in cycles, I mean, since the late 1800s. And it's always been pretty much the tent and screaming style, but the point is that it has come back now. It's kind of interesting. And I think it's very much the same reason it's always historically come back: because the United States essentially is a country without any kind of cultural foundation except ones that are invented, in a sense.

And I think now, more than any time probably in recent memory, people have gone through periods of relatively higher affluence, in which no one is particularly without anything and no one has a very clear memory anymore of what it was like to not have very basic things, for the most part. This doesn't include the very unfortunately increasing band of people who had virtually nothing at all in the beginning and who now are truly deprived—the numbers are growing, and the level of their poverty is growing. But for a large part of the last fifteen years, a middle spectrum of Americans came to a point where for most of the things, if they wanted something, there was a consumer society that produced a gratification for it—not necessarily a real satisfaction, but a gratification because consumerism is based on that. I mean, there isn't any ultimate product in consumerism, there's no need, you don't need anything as you just keep buying. I mean, there are a few things you must have. Most of consumerism is based not really on the artificial but on the manipulation of real needs so that there's a constant necessity to buy.

And if you live that way for a while, I think it's something very easy to exploit, the sensation that nothing has any inherent value or meaning. And for people who live that way for a while, the idea that they could have an experience brought up by someone in a large stadium that makes life seem very vividly real for a moment, it's just natural for the evangelical preacher to exploit that. There are also technical reasons why it's possible, too—the proliferation of radio and television, because it has a new form. I mean, it's different now from what it was thirty years ago, when there was a big wave of it, or forty years ago, and there was the biggest wave in the past. And there's no doubt that some of the things that I do and some of the ways that I behave and perform, and some of the ideas that I have during my performance, have come from that tradition because I was born in it and I've always been around it. I'm not Christian, oddly enough. My parents were both raised as Christians, but they always let me be totally free about things like that. They're very unusual parents in almost every way that I can imagine—very ordinary in some senses for their place and time, but extraordinary in others. I've always had complete personal freedom, complete intellectual freedom, and complete religious and aesthetic freedom from them. I was the only child, and I was very indulgent in a funny way. And I was surrounded by a lot of indulgent parents, and I was a bright one too. That connection of the bright and only child, coming also toward the end of the war when there weren't a lot of men around and there were not a lot of children, too, at that moment. I think I ended up being indulged in certain kinds of ways that form you in odd ways.

de Vleeshal

UITNODIGING

JERRY HUNT

BIROME (Zone): CUBE (Frame)

1.4 t/m 1.5.1988

OPENINGSCONCERT: vrijdag 1.4: 20.00 uur in de Vleeshal, gelegen in het centrum aan de Markt.

Deze uitnodiging dient tevens als bewijs van toegang.

Openingstijden: di t/m zo: 13.00-17.00 uur, informatie 01180-26251/428.

Middelburg

Announcement for Hunt's installation *BIROME (Zone): CUBE (Frame)*, de Vleeshal, Middelburg, Netherlands, April 1–May 1, 1988.

I've been a few times—maybe ten, eleven, twelve times—to different kinds of services to see what they're like, but I've only been in Christian services probably ten or eleven times in my life, of different denominations. But you're always aware of it, even though it wasn't taught to me. Particularly in Texas and that part of the South, it's everywhere, it's a very common religious alternative. The cultural and economically predominant faiths are the more ordinary Protestant denominations, but there's a rich tradition of Pentecostal and Evangelical kinds and particularly the kinds that are concerned with the coming end of the world.

When you do have extreme religious movements, sometimes they can be quite strange, until you reach the West Coast, where it's like a cafeteria, a smorgasbord of religion. In the '50s, California was regarded as the religious weirdo capital of the world, because anything you wanted, from sex magic to snake worship to Rosicrucianism, astrology, Vedanta, animism, totemism: everything was available in California. You could just go out there and you can find a little cult or community of people who were practicing, preaching, teaching, publishing. But that's changed. California is not that way anymore. There's still a few diehards, but at one time, oddly enough, I was a member of four different Rosicrucian organizations at once; I never visited any of them at the time that I was a member. And then, when I was doing a tour in California a couple of years ago, I was doing it by car, and I thought it'd be nice to go see one of these places, the Rosicrucian Fellowship in Oceanside. I went there, and it was the strangest experience I've ever had because the place still looks like it was built in the '20s, which it was—it was built in the late '20s by its founder, who came from Germany and set up this community there—and it was preserved precisely. That's one odd part. It has this kind of look of late-'20s movies. It looks like, if you're going to make a movie about a religious cult in the late '20s, this is how it would look. But when you go to the meditation garden in the back—as you walk further back into the meditation garden—you look off this kind of hill and it drops off, and below this hill, all around there are, just as far the eye could see, these apartment complexes, these multistory apartment complexes with cars and parking lots and honking horns and lights, and everything just down there in this pit. So it's kind of like standing up here and looking down into hell.

It was a strange experience to go visit that place after all those years of being involved in the letters and everything. I was quite serious when I was young. You can get so involved, and it gives you an interesting insight about reality when you can read books about philosophy for hours and study religious practices in life. But until you've had the experience and then come through it and changed your ideas, it really truly changes you profoundly to practice an invocation to the god Mercury, for example, in the Roman style and to, in every reasonable sense, in a nonpsychiatric and nonhallucinatory way, see him and know that's possible and yet not have any religious faith. It enriches your sense about what reality is—that reality really, in a way, is also a convention of manipulation that only by the destruction of brain cells, in some ways, is possible to not be able to manipulate. That's the ultimate manipulation: when those cells are lost and they are no longer available to you. They may be available to others, but that's one convention that isn't manipulated any longer, it's permanent manipulation. But it changes your ideas about time, and it changes your ideas about space.

I guess when people got interested in meditation and religion in music in the '70s in the States, it was because one of the first things when you throw out traditions—about how you're going to divide time, that you're going to put time markers down by conventions which are symbolized by changes in the way notes and tone colors shift that—when you give that up, it's as if time is stopped in a way. I used to always think about it the other way around, that people had religious experiences and then went to so-called meditation music. I think it was really the other way around, they just found that that [meditation music] was the only thing to do. There wasn't anything else left, at first, because you think it's like *I'm floating* because there's no articulation of the time or the space anymore, because all the conventions are gone. I feel like I was really seeing it the wrong way. I used to read it as if it was a response to meditation practice. Now I think it was just a natural consequence of doing what was left—and not much is left. And what *is* left tends to go in a certain direction because it's an art of elimination, in which you've eliminated certain kinds of conventions. What's the next nearest one? Eventually I think the label "meditation" was put onto it because it is, in a way, in a phony sense, religious, because it has slow tones, big sound, long decay.

GB It's funny, that approach that you have, of being nonreligious while there's some experience of religion. It's also funny to me that here the main religion is Roman Catholicism, which is how I was raised. I went to church every Sunday until I was an adolescent. I went through communion and all these things. It never had any effect upon me—or, it had some effect, somewhere in my brain, but it was never convincing. I considered it more as a social activity that everyone has to go through, like military service. Nothing more transcendental than that. Well, I think if they would use more efficient manipulating means they would have much more power on the people. Sunday Mass is a very boring thing. So where experience is nothing, the only divine presence is just a little red flame that burns. I think very few people are convinced by that.

JH In Western art, at least in the last forty or fifty years, until recently, I think a lot of that has changed, because I think in a way the United States is the true postmodernist country. And if there ever was anything there, now everything is gone. There's just really nothing left at all in terms of ideas, in terms of the future or concept. I don't mean that in a desperate sense. Though it could become desperate. It's just that it is a special kind of vacuum that I can't trace all the causes for—but I can trace a few. One of the things that sometimes I am disappointed by is that people don't find, in a kind of pre-Christian sense, that the world is extraordinary without divine mediation and without the instrumentation of a priest. It's always a little surprising to me that they don't find the world as it is about as good as it's going to get and good enough from time to time. But clearly that's not completely how the world works. I mean, it doesn't work just on the basis of no mediation and everyone being able to do it, so it serves a lot of functions for people. It used to amaze me. I had a very close friend who was not, I think, in any sense at all religious, but she was crippled badly. And I realized at one point in my relationship with her that there was a component of modified religious conviction that I could have never have any experience of, that she had developed over the years in connection with her disability, and that it was invigorating to her. She was one of the liveliest and most energetic and outgoing people I've ever met.

Even though religion just serves as a kind of symbolic mechanism for a lot of people, it does sort of exist there, rotating, so I can see how people can turn to it. If the convention of a religious activity brings that kind of reinforcement to people in places where they feel the need for it, as long as it's not terribly destructive—which is what you sometimes see with religious zeal, you see religious zeal become very socially destructive—I think it's fine. And particularly in [the US], there usually has been a controlling force. I was getting very alarmed six years ago, I guess. It was getting to be a strange coalition between evangelical faith and political power. And in the last year, it's been very clear that it was a coalition of expediency at best—it's not lasting, it's not enduring, because it was an artificial coupling in the first place, just a coupling of convenience. Two things passing in the night, and then after a while they've serviced one another, and that coupling comes apart. I don't see that as an example of what I'm talking about—but in a personal, very private way, I could see how, no matter what my objections are to some of the activity and particularly the social direction that a lot of religious experience wants to push on people, that it can be of very powerful use to people. For me it's informed a whole worldview, in an interesting way, of being a disembodied observer, almost, of religious activity. It's almost as if I am neither faithful nor a nonbeliever because sometimes you get people who are deep believers and then at some point they pass a critical test and they think it isn't true. And then they spend the rest of their lives reacting to the knowledge that they've acquired—that in some funny way, it isn't true. I don't know what any of that means, if it's true or not. That's crazy, I've never had that reaction to it. It's not distance and it's not disinvolvement exactly; in some ways you might say that I am really extremely religious, but certainly in a completely unreligious way because the model of reality, for example, that it's based on are odd ideas: a lot of them have been transplants from the 1800s.

It's like the idea of the contrast between science and art, where you see this gulf between them and you could think *this is crazy*, because people are talking about an idea of sounds which isn't even from the twentieth century, it isn't from the sixteenth or seventeenth century. It's like the 1860s. Most of our ideas about physical reality, somehow, in casual and common culture, have frozen and stabilized around 1860–1880, when a lot of the early experimentation took place. And the results of those unusual experiments, which were interesting in themselves, have really created a tradition in education so that people have the idea of scientific demonstration, for example, something that has nothing to do with contemporary physics at all—that has something to do with Victorian experiments by English gentlemen who wrote books—and that imagination has moved forward. When I'm hearing people talk about the contrast between science and art or science and religion, you have to realize that they're based on these ideas that were part of the educational system. And it has nothing to do with the reality of the disciplines or the interest or the ways in which they've never related in reality in modern times. I mean, certainly the modern physical, conceptual, and theoretical groundwork and the articles of faith that modern physics is based on—because it's based on articles of faith, very much like any other kinds of coherent system—are all totally different from the ones that people conventionally think of as being scientific. That's always a little bit of a starting point for me, to get people beyond that, so you mustn't just keep using these ideas. They were interesting for what they are, and I've even seen some interesting art in modern times.

A lot of this stuff I see—sound art pieces and sound events and sound installations—it strikes me that they're Victorian scientific experiments that are displaced, that have been brought forward and updated slightly with modern electronics and put into a gallery setting instead of a well-to-do gentleman's backyard in his country estate. In the summertime, when the duties of state and my position are over, I have four months to kill. I think I'll work on this thing called static electricity. So you have these whole sets of works between 1970 and '88 that deal with static electricity or something, and you can find precedent for them in the writings of these Victorian dabblers, these amateur scientists, so-called—in the moderate sense—amateurs.

GB   Here in Europe, to my mind, religion has very little emotional impact on people. It does for some people, but I think they could gain more power or whatever by adapting—by updating—their means. Most churches still have stained glass, but that's no longer effective; people have color TV.

JH Clearly that's what's happened in the States. The church updated in the sense that it became a consumerist mass media operation, and it ultimately found its most successful manifestation in those who had no physical church at all—even in the case of the fellow [Robert Schuller] who started with a drive-in theater for the church, now he has this thing called the Crystal Cathedral. It's kind of beautiful and it's so grotesque, with all this glass. The interesting thing about it, it's almost as if it were designed with the TV camera in mind. Even when churches do have imposing physical presences for their operations, it's either close to an amusement park, a drive-in theater, or a television studio. The two great examples are Jim and Tammy Bakker and Swaggart; the two most successful evangelists, really, have no church at all. They have business offices, they have business holdings, and they have—*did* have (things are not so good now)—a very extensive public relations campaign.

GB   Here "technical" means not to *get to* the people, but to impress people. I would expect that any church with stained glass will be replaced by holograms, which are a little bit more impressive than stained glass. People don't understand high tech, so you can still impress them with it.

JH But you've got a problem there as long as the means deal with just the conveying of the message. One of the only things that religion as it's popularly thought of has going for it—and this is its most powerful thing, and this is true of the occult tradition in the West and the East as much as it is in the non-occult and the overt and manifest version of religions—is that they all promise or pretend to have a special connection, not only with deepest essential reality, but a deep essential reality which is also hidden deeply in the past. When the attendance at churches was dropping in the '60s, there were thousands of happenings in churches all over America, with rock and roll, throwing paint and eggs, and screaming, and every once in a while, they'd say the word "Jesus," so that's what that made it Christian. The funny thing was that they didn't take on anybody. In other words, it didn't work; it didn't help things. People came to the happenings, but they didn't ever come to the church again, except when they put on one of these extravaganzas.

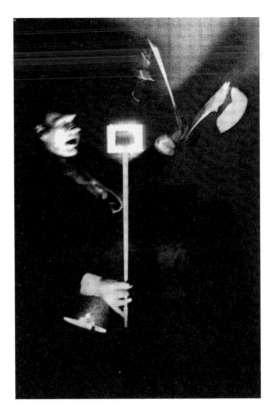

JERRY HUNT

vrijdag 23 december 1988
21.00 uur, ƒ 7,50

In de concerten van Jerry Hunt (1943, Texas) gaat live
performance samen met het gebruik van electronische
media. De bewegingen en gebaren van Hunt, èn de
materialen en de symbolische voorwerpen die hij als
instrumenten hanteert, vormen een ritueel.
De bewegingen en acties van de performer sturen
tegelijkertijd zijn computermuziek.
Jerry Hunt provoceert het gevoel voor samenhang van
zijn publiek. Het is aan de toeschouwer om uit te maken
wat het verband is tussen beeld en geluid, performer en
instrumenten.

programma:
Transform (stream): pounding (reflex) (1977, 1978,
1985, 1986)
Volta (Birome) (1984, 1986)
Mask (Window [Des Arc]: SOYGA) (DIOM) (1986)

Dit concert is tot stand gekomen met financiële steun van de
provincie Noord-Brabant.

foto: Paul van den Nieuwenhof

Postcard for Hunt performance at Het Apollohuis, Eindhoven, Netherlands, December 23, 1988.

There are many people coming along trying new religions. Scientology, for example, was an interesting effort in that direction to create a modern religion, a new one. It was not based on old ideas and it didn't succeed properly. It's been pretty successful financially, but it has not succeeded in that it's really, truly the most insignificant minority cult in the world—very minimal impact. Then, the world has changed so much now, too, that you have layers of information. You no longer have massive catastrophes or ways in which large groups of people can be as successfully brought together to work on a single project because our idea of individuality, for example, works against that. Every place in the world, virtually, it's almost as if the way you even define "emerging third world" is how much of a concept of the idea of the individual they have. If they have a concept of the individual, then you say, "They're somewhat more progressive." If they don't have a modern idea, which again is an 1800s idea—if they don't have the idea of the individual so much, you say, "They're not progressive." In places like that, the idea of the individual is not yet formed. The idea that you and I have separate, distinct entities and concepts and feelings that are equally important in any sense for the democratic or even social unit: it's just not something that makes sense to them.

Unless some kind of event took place in Western culture of a massive proportion, which I think would have to be some kind of global devastation, I don't think you'll ever see a new religion catch hold because when I was young, I used to be very interested in some of these and none of them have succeeded. Of course, the reason they haven't is that the only way they can get inheritance in the first place is to make connections with the past. And that's why I use it. One of the reasons why I find a lot of these things that are somewhat religious in their character is because they're so widely shared by so many different cultures, even non-Christian and non-Western. I've never had the experience of being in front of completely untrained audiences for whom your behavior is completely foreign, but I would suspect that even there, more than just pulling out, like we were talking about earlier, layers of content that would be intimate to them—there would be a lot of layers of content available to them, because we do have relatively similar nervous systems and we have basically the same modalities of perception, so that there's not anything you can do that's so novel that they would not bear information of some kind that at some level that wouldn't essentially be the same. I'm not a Universalist in that I don't think that all human beings, because of their nervous systems, perceive exactly the same way, but the nervous system's organization is the thing in itself. It's not this object—which is the observing thing that's animated by the mind—and if it were, then I could see how it would be possible that there would be universals and that some brain stems do as good a job as others. But since the world itself is the brainstem for all practical purposes, the real physical meat of your ability to sense at all, then there are bound to be things that we all share. And the question to me, and I think it is a legitimate criticism, is: are those basic identifiable elements so low-level that they don't communicate enough information to be artistically satisfying?

I never had the experience with an audience like this. But I have a feeling that that's probably true, that things that you regard as an art, and I mean this not in the sense of sophistication or sublimation but in a sense of complexity of organization, that already involves the higher parts of language and not the lower. In other words, the lower is just the topological, the basis of language or whatever means of communication. But I just came from a very interesting experience about human language—spoken language—that has been insightful to me. I've spent a week trying to communicate with people in which there are only about nine or ten words that were usable in communication. And it's amazing how deep communication is possible without using language and by not using signs or numbers or pictures at all. Communication with language is very powerful because of its efficiency. But it also is colored by an extraordinarily powerful mechanism because, again, I think we share common neurological systems. It isn't as if we're that separate. I may be wrong about that. It may be that they might perceive much higher than that I suspect. And then you do things that you know are just tricks—this is for one person in a thousand. *I know this is there,* and I'm not opposed to that. I used to think that was charming in Bach. When I first started learning about him, I learned that there would be this little thing in a Bach work, and some scholar would dig and dig and dig and finally find out that he really put it in as a little trick for that one person in ten thousand. And probably at the time that the music was being performed, one in a hundred or one in five hundred would notice it. Two hundred years pass, and it's one in fifty million; only scholars now can find it. I think that's pleasant: it's like cooking a good meal and knowing a certain guest is coming and thinking, *I'll put that little special piece of something in this dish and they will be the one to sense it.* No one else will know that it's there, but it'll please this one person.

GB   We've talked about convention manipulation and its religious aspects. Where does the music fit in?

JH   The music fits in the fact that I've actually been talking about music all of this time. I really haven't been thinking about the visual, and it's interesting because it's suddenly stunned me into the thought that you think I've been talking about the television images and the objects of manipulation in the way I perform. People say: Do you regard yourself as a musician? And I regard myself as ninety-nine point nine percent music and one tenth of a percent everything else, and it's partly because of my training. It's the way I see everything, as musical activity. I know from audiences that, lots of times, that's not the first thing they notice. The first thing they notice is my manner of performance, my presentation, my physical presence. How much is it the evangelical preacher in me that makes the performance bearable and how much is it the content? There's always that question, but the music is in fact almost always the source of all of the other images. One of the reasons for that is—I started composing again pretty directly because of John Cage. When I was a child, I used to compose because I could play by ear and all that. I started learning how to write notes. It was really terrible: it all sounded like terrible Chopin and Rachmaninoff. Then I went modern briefly before I quit. I got fascinated by Bartók—all that early music sounded pretty much like Bartók.

And then I just quit composing, because I had the idea that I could have a career as a pianist. I got very interested in performing and started working in clubs and bars, started doing some jazz playing. So, suddenly I was going off in a lot of different directions, and none of them really were composing music anymore. And I never really thought I would do it again until I was about seventeen years old. I got to thinking, one day, I don't want to live as a musician like this. This is not interesting enough—because basically you're supplying a product of entertainment. It would be like going to pastry cooking school and learning how to do a certain kind of meringue work. And then for the rest of your life, for twenty-five years, every morning, you'd get up and do meringue until sunset. I thought, yeah, it's wonderful to have the skill, and it would be great to be regarded as the world's greatest meringueist, but probably that won't happen to me. I'm very good, but I won't be the greatest pianist in the world. The idea of repetition of something that didn't seem musical to me was really not very pleasant. And then at the time, I was overly serious as a kid, I guess, and I thought music was not meaningful enough. It's too much of a form of entertainment. It has to have the ability to be a philosophic tool of inquiry, a scientific tool of inquiry—it has to be an art again, in a way, in the old-world sense of art and the other cultural sense of art, of something that is vitally important to human activity.

That's when I came upon John Cage and the work of John Cage; all of a sudden, I thought, here is somebody who, even if I don't like his work particularly, he's not talking about music as entertainment or as product, or as fulfilling a certain consumer location in the exchange of goods and services and the repetition of an experience. But he's talking about music again quite clearly as a religious, philosophic, scientific, and artistic tool of inquiry, where there was an exchange between people and audiences. It was eye-opening, not in the sense of new sounds or new timbres or new anything, but just the experience was very vivid and very special and very real for me at the time. I thought, this is fascinating because it allows me to do what I used to like to do, which was to make up music—but without copying a pattern or a model from any half-learned style. Instead, like a lot of Americans, I think what we have to do is self-invention: I'll just invent myself as a composer and I'll use music in this way as this mechanism for inquiry of various kinds—sometimes turned in on yourself, which I think is a tendency in American art, to just spend your entire life figuring yourself out, as if the world cares.

Is there a way, like semaphoric signs, to begin signing music so that it isn't just a visual experience? Because one of the things that's always bored me to death is to watch people make sound. It's not very interesting to me. It's nothing like Phill Niblock's films of people working, silent. I find that much more interesting than watching the fiddle player fiddle a fiddle, and it isn't even because I know how a fiddle works. I don't. I don't play the fiddle well enough to really, truly know how they sound. And it's true: I watch them play sometimes and I'm amazed that the sound comes out given the physical gesture, but that's not enough to satisfy me. So I began thinking: What would be visually interesting?

I had a background as a child, a curiosity about electronics, because when I was eleven years old, my step-grandfather took one of these mail-order courses in electronics—like, you cut out the coupon on the back of the magazine. He took about four lessons and became bored, but he took it just long enough to get a box of components. And I went out there and began playing with it one day and I thought, *this is interesting. I can build something that works, and I can learn how it works and build variations of it.* He saw I was playing with it and he said, "I don't want to take the course, but I'll keep taking it if it interests you." So I took the national radio course when I was eleven years old because my grandfather was willing to keep it coming. It was this little house in the back, and in the summertime I'd go there and play with it. So I've always had that interest. And then I got interested in television for reasons that I can't honestly tell you. And sometimes I'm very sad because television is quite ugly. I have no illusions about it being an attractive visual medium, and yet it's something you can't leave alone. Once you start, it's almost like an addiction to cigarettes or coffee or addiction to drugs. I mean, once you get started on it, it becomes an irresistible lure.

There's not much serious criticism of this kind of work—it's glib and a little silly usually. I think you could just really go to town on me. In a certain way, I think you could attack me very carefully along the line of this extremely complicated house that I have constructed, which is pretty well nailed up and has a good roof on it and it's got nice windows. It's got a nice yard and good trees, nice flowers, good entranceway, two cars in the garage—they all work. But there is a question about who lives inside the house. In other words, is this system doing any more than just shaking in people's faces, and then they trace these almost cobweblike lines to it and they think, *well, that was kind of interesting*? Because this could be the only reason that I'm tolerated as an act. You could hardly say I'm successful, but the way I'm tolerated as an act is that in the world that we have now, none of these conventions has much meaning. And that leaves a lot of open space for things where people are sort of shopping. I think a lot of the audiences at home now, they're a little larger and they're more varied, maybe, because people really are experience-shopping. They

Above and overleaf: Hunt performing at Het Apollohuis, Eindhoven, Netherlands, ca. 1988. Photos: Paul van den Nieuwenhof.

are at a loss for what kind of experiences mean anything to them or have any connections to their lives. It could be that after they've tried me a few times that they think, *well, no, the left shoe doesn't fit*, or *it's a nice house, but it's not my style.*

There is that problem with every kind of music now, in a way, outside of this monolithic global rock music, which communicates at a level which I find at once exhilarating and amazing and also mysterious. I don't understand why teenagers in Thailand, when they hear Madonna sing, are able to receive something from it with such apparent depth because, for a long time, I thought, well, this music is connected with very specific kinds of Western and very uniquely American kinds of social phenomena, problems. The whole foundation of the blues, for example: you can't understand how, globally, it's been as successful as it has because it's based on such highly specialized kinds of relationships—not only musically speaking, but socially, culturally, the thematic emphasis. I mean, the idea of sexual anguish, for example: I don't see how that would work in cultures that are not based on certain kinds of sexual tensions. And yet it *is* successful—and how that is, I don't know. It's really quite fascinating to me. And so, as a consequence, I look at people like Prince and I think they're the real modern musicians. They have succeeded in a strange way, in a way in which I haven't exactly, because I look at what they do and I think it's not as sophisticated as what I'm doing in a sense, or it's not as deep—it doesn't explore as lovingly all the connections and roots. Yet, when you see twenty-five thousand people in the stadium responding to him and you hear what he does and you find the sound so intriguing, and you look at the persona that has been generated on the screen, and the film, and the video, and the print, the text image, and you say, here is someone who as an American has completely from scratch invented himself, a theology in which he fits. I mean, Prince is quite peculiar. I think in that respect, he's created a kind of a religion, which is this bizarre mixture of almost Hollywood glitz, sex, and middle-American puritanical religion mixed together in this incredible combination with this very basic rhythm and blues foundation down at the bottom and an extraordinary musical personality and a strong musical presence.

In a way, I have very funny feelings about it. Yet, do I like to listen to this music for a long period of time? I don't. It's not a sustainingly attractive music to me. I'll see one of the things that he's done, and if I don't see it very often—like, if I see or hear one of these things that last no more than thirty or forty minutes about once a year, when he makes something new, when he does a new record or a new video work or new album or something—it's a delight to hear it when it comes out. But then I don't really want to hear it much again for a year or two. So it's also funny in that sense. But it could be because he's much more directly connected with the world in which everything is disposable. I was born close enough to the war; I know some of the older musicians and artists that I've talked to here since I've been here visiting, because I talk a lot—but I do listen some, because I speak only English. One of the things that I've been sensing is that people who are about the age I am, or five to ten years older, particularly here, more pointedly can identify very clearly a sense of loss: that something forty years ago died in some important cultural direction. I think I've got a little bit of that in me too, that there is a little point in me where I'm still reminiscing about how the good old days were, where art was directed and vivid and continuous and not a disposable commodity, and that maybe that's the reason that I can't listen to Prince more than once a year, is because I cannot give up this built-in idea.

I'm demanding that to be classified as art, it has to be repeatable—that the experience has to be re-investable, that you can continue to invest attention in it over and over and over, and that it will continue to yield new kinds of inter-relationships. Whereas a lot of this work is based on one, two, maybe three, maybe four, very intense repetitious experiences that I'm also not familiar with. Kids are deeply involved in it, just for the moment. So they become more deeply involved for shorter amounts of time but, when finished, it gets dismissed and something else is going on because they're not looking for roots.

I think at one point, maybe early on, that infatuation is connected with a much more emotional view of what I'm talking about. And then eventually that's replaced by the habit of consumerism. I don't mean it in a simple way of a thrill for today. I mean it in the sense that there must be new products supplied continuously, because there must be continuous consumption, because you're not fulfilling a need. I know even when I describe it, you can hear the contempt in my voice. You're not supplying needs, you're just exchanging. I think sometimes, if there's anything you can find at fault with me, it's in that area. I have no positive sense about the value of what I do at all. I couldn't begin to tell you whether it fits into the category of good, bad, entertaining. I don't have any clear sense of that. I know that everything that I've ever done in my life leads me to the next work, and then I'm not interested in doing anything else. And that's my full-time business for practical purposes.

I mean, occasionally I do things to make more money that are disconnected, that explore those kinds of talents of the music business that I've always had and I still have, and that use old associations—friends from over the years. I can do commercial work of various kinds: practically, for no reason except to do work. Twenty years ago, it bothered me that I could so easily go into a studio and work dedicatedly and completely freely on a commercial product and never do anything that you could even vaguely call New Music or avant-garde or bizarre, and be perfectly satisfied and work to achieve that product aim, and then turn around and do the other work. It used to bother me a little bit that I could do that, and I was slightly ashamed of the fact I could do it. Now I'm not. Now it doesn't bother me. And that's one change in how I see myself in my own work, that it's no longer shocking to me. I think, *well, naturally you'd be able to do that.* I mean, it's the exercise of the skill, using imagination—and the standards are quite high there too. It's a very high-relief art exercise. You go in knowing what the parameters are—they're absolutely predefined by the user. The user says, I want a thing that has to be one foot this way, and this far deep, and it must consist of thirty-five notes, it must have a fiddle, and it must have a flute, and it must never go high, and it must never go low. Now make it for me. I'm not all that good at it. It's a challenge. One of the most serious challenges for me is to produce that kind of very transient, high-impact, high-contrast work. So it may be that that's the goal: to turn into a so-called commercial artist.

If I did it all the time, I don't think I'd feel that way. I don't have a career doing it. I mean, I don't call them. They always call me—it's friends, and the way I live, I can get by that way. I don't have to have these jobs all the time. If I can get one job a year that pretty well is enough. It's a little bit like the sense of patting yourself on the back. You can think, I am an *artiste*, and at the same time I can go and do these jobs and knock them out. I've heard the work of a couple of commercial arrangers and composers who do work that I think is just extraordinary. It's extraordinarily inventive, and I don't think I've ever really done it. Of course, I think one of the reasons is that they do it all the time. I don't. It's very much a sideline for me, and it's very much not with them. So they get up in the morning thinking, *what new high-contrast, high-relief material can I create today?* And I get up in the morning thinking about my life and all this work and the monitors and the new objects and new sounds and new triggering mechanisms and new memory products and new ways to process. You live in this world, again, of your own invention—so completely that these other things, they're like silver fish that are very attractive in a certain light. They swim through your life and you think, *Oh, what a beautiful thing.* But you know it'll leave—it won't be there forever—and that you won't every day have that same fish coming through that you've got to respond to with equal fascination and vigor and integrity and interest.

GB And another thing about commercial music: First, you've got the power. You've got twenty-five thousand people, which is a powerful experience, versus the involvement with New Music, with sound, with all these things. A rock song works with all these very basic harmonies, these basic rhythms, and somehow, although they can be very vulgar, a lot of basic harmonies can sound pleasant—

JH That's the thing that I know people were always appalled and shocked by: I have never had any problem at all with the tone and harmonics system, but I have also never had any problem with understanding that twelve-tone tuning was, in a sense, a commercial decision that had to do with a very temporary solution. I think it froze a lot of invention in pitch. I think the price most Western music paid for twelve tones is invention and novelty. Melody ceased to be, and so you get this ornate overdeveloped timbre and dynamics. I don't think dynamics would have ever come into musical performance, because they're nowhere near the loudness and softness of other world musics that still have tuning systems that are manipulable, or nowhere near as important as they were in a lot of Western music once that pitch system was assumed to be in practice. But you know, the reality is that even in twelve-tone music, with very few exceptions, only instruments which are of a certain design come anywhere near that temperament. And even then, they don't really come into it very truly, because pianos are never truly tuned to twelve-tone. They're all stretched and pulled to make them sound a little brighter or more dramatic—you'll change the tuning to make the Mozart work sound a little better, even though it's being done on the wrong instrument with the wrong orchestra in the wrong hall. There's a modern assumption about how Mozart and others sound even now, it's true. So they changed the tunings for that. They'll brighten and stretch the octaves a little for Liszt and Rachmaninoff.

The thing that I found out about tuning and what got me fascinated in it very early on is that I realize that in order to have melody and harmony, which I think are very important, you must absolutely have flexible pitch. It is absolutely essential. There is no way to be able to do this job without inflection because of the piano's mechanism. I did one work for the piano, and I'm happy with it in some ways. But it clearly exploits only one capacity of the piano to respond, as a resonating instrument. And that's the only way without manipulating it in funny and mechanical ways that you can escape its inherent pitch stability, but it is escapable because the strings, restrung, begin to behave as free resonators. The kind of pitch relationship ceases to be so important. But even in that work, I realized that the convention of the piano sonata was more important in that piece, *Lattice* (1979), than pitch—that it's a parody of the piano sonata in a sense. It's the great romantic piano sonata in that it uses all of the piano sonata mechanisms, but it uses them as if they were just compositional tools. And that's the only way I've ever been able to come to terms with, with a piano. It's very funny because I was trained as a pianist, and the early concerts I did were all these contemporary music piano works, like with amplified keys, and all the amps in the guts and all the Cage works and the [George] Brecht and taking pictures and burning them and trying to make it eat. We used to do the La Monte Young—feed the piano hay and, if it eats it, give it water. We went through all those. I just never burned one like Annea Lockwood because nobody ever gave me a piano to burn.

The problem there was I just had to get away from the piano entirely because I couldn't bend notes. I think it's important to establish tonal relations in music over a note or two. I think that bending is absolutely essential in making music have a life.

JH   Yes, I expect it's my favorite keyboard instrument. I have a
work for clavichord, which tries to explore that capability a
little bit—but it also has a problem. It doesn't have the dynamic
resources of a piano to cover for some of the clavichord's
inflexibility in terms of pitch, because the pitch variation is
always connected with rate of change. You can't have slow
areas because that string dies away; you can't have continuous
vibrato. Also, the key has to be engaged before the variation of
pitch can occur. One of the wonderful things about electronic
instruments, like the human voice, is that they can be in stable
pitch positions and can come on and off. I mean, the gating,
the timbre change—because I think ultimately almost all of
your ideas about how music ought to operate in some way are
connected with the voice.

   Although, I don't think the voice was necessarily the
original musical instrument. I have a terrible feeling that it
might've been percussion. I don't know if that's true, but I
know that there used to be an argument, was it voice-based
or percussion? I think clicking and counting might've been
the first music, really, in a way, but I don't know, I don't have
enough sense of the history or the ideas about the archeol-
ogy of music to understand that clearly. But for me, at least,
there is some component of song in all music that I think
is indispensable, and that ability to manipulate pitch in that
way is very important. And the only way you can have the
manipulation of pitch and high relief is to establish a tonal
basis of some kind. I've never written a twelve-tone piece in my
life, even as a student exercise. I never did it because I went to
a kind of conservative school, and they were never interested
in having us learn the twelve tone. They thought, *well, that's a
waste of time; he could do that at home with a little hand calculator
or something, or an abacus, but he certainly shouldn't have to do it
here. What we want him to learn is sixteenth- to eighteenth-century
counterpoint and harmony.* Those rules never made a lot of sense
to me because it seemed like they were conventions that had
outlived the 1890s ideas of science—that's my sense about that.

   There's another thing about using pitch and using melody
and using tonal relationships. It allows people to conceptually
and perceptually relax. One of the things I find particularly
annoying about New Music is you can't hear new sounds. Other
people have asked me about this and say, "I do not believe in

new sounds"—and in a way that's really quite true. In fact, you do hear new sounds from time to time, sounds that you've never heard before, because your experience is not closed . . . I mean, what is it that human beings are perceiving that keeps their perception clued and keyed to the next upcoming event so that they don't get century fatigue and feel like time is moving slowly? If you have that, then you might be able to write very simple and very efficient and hence very complex signatures in electronic music instruments to produce really startling and truly unusual music, maybe, and that might really be a significant departure because at the moment there's nothing like it at all. Ninety-five percent of the electronic music that is being produced today consists of copy and paste—which is what I do, because you can paste arbitrarily and it's transparent, it's a lot like memory in that it's transparent, there's no inherent system to my synthesis, it's just paste and change—there is the philosophy of synthesis of one kind or another. And again, they're all based on these late 1800s ideas. There are dramatic movements away from that now, pushed away because of better information about how the eye and ear operate, more flexible models that produce new ways of attacking the problem—but still there's nothing as amazing as, say, the revolution of ideas about gravity and ideas of speed and the like in the 1600s and 1700s. I mean, so far nothing radical like that, even in modern physics, has emerged about perception. We're still really very much in the dark about it, as far as I know, despite all these kinds of promising things. Because, I think, again, the idea of development is still tied to this late eighteenth-century idea. You're going to have to get a wave or two of scientists who are so far away from that eighteenth-century model that they can just approach it from another kind of mechanism.

GB   You see that with visuals, too. I mean, there's no new visual images. If you have all these people who will come up with synthesized and digitized images and they say, look, this computer will make the most extraordinary drawings—it will grow trees that men have never seen. And you see all these stupid drawings that no one would ever even think to make because they are so stupid and so silly.

JH   One of the things you realize immediately when you work in computer art is you can either work very expensively—where

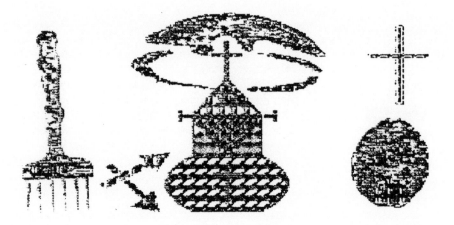

JERRY HUNT
Birome (ZONE): Cube; een installatie

22.4-22.5.1988
Opening vrijdag 22 april vanaf 20.30 uur
Openingstijden: dinsdag t/m zondag van 2-5 uur
concert
zaterdag 23 april: concert/performance
21.00 uur, ƒ 7,50

Jerry Hunt (1943, Waco, Texas) is pianist, componist, beeldend kunstenaar en maakt in zijn werk gebruik van de verworvenheden van de huidige technische mogelijkheden op het gebied van het beeld en het geluid (video en interactieve computertechnieken).
"Birome (ZONE): Cube" is een installatie bestaande uit een besloten ruimte in de tentoonstellingszaal, waarin zich een soort pop (homunculus) bevindt. Wanneer iemand naar binnen gaat zijn geluiden te horen en verschijnen tekens op een aantal beeldschermen; een situatie waarop de bezoeker moet reageren en waardoor er verandering optreedt. Wat de bezoeker doet en de tijd die hij in de ruimte doorbrengt, zijn van invloed op wat bezoekers die na hem komen er zullen meemaken. De installatie accumuleert informatie gedurende een bepaalde tijd die bepalend is voor wat de machinerie mogelijk later op de dag zal gaan doen. Elke activiteit van de bezoeker wordt geregistreerd en vertaald in het systeem.

HET APOLLOHUIS
TONGELRESESTRAAT 81 EINDHOVEN
5613 DB. H O L L A N D
TELEFOON 040-440393

Birome (ZONE): Plane (1986)

Announcement for Hunt's installation *Birome (ZONE): Cube*, Het Apollohuis, Eindhoven, Netherlands April 22–May 22, 1988.

you create things that are exotic because they violate conventions and perspective; that's the thing that characterizes expensive computer-generated images—then you have the mid-range stuff, which is where I work, which is fuzzy and which just barely gets an image on the screen. For me, I work entirely with image cliché. They're novel in the sense of the timing and of the presentation, but they're all cliché images right down to even the conventions of moving through the screen. They're very controlled all the time, in the sense that I never move on alternate axes. I never move beyond the center of the screen. Everything goes rectilinear up and down, left and right; rotations are always consistent and cyclic, they never ever do anything bizarre. I never go for anthropomorphic movement; things just twitter. I never go for real animation because all that would happen is that people would point to the technical deficiencies and say, *well, this is vulgar, I've seen better than this*. It wouldn't do any good. It would be a futile effort. And in fact, that's what fascinated me about it since I first saw it. I thought, well, this is a simpler way of what I wanted to do in the first place. It's more efficient in a funny sense, and it's much less efficient in another. And then the whole argument about efficiency—that's a complication, too. What is it that you are trying to achieve by this greater efficiency? Are you trying to create more product, or are you trying to create higher-contrast product, or are you trying to make the product better?

If you're trying to make it better, in what sense are you trying to make it better? Are you trying to convert more to reality so it's more difficult to tell that it's artificial, or are you trying to make it more artificial seeming, because it's very easy to make it seem artificial? Or are you trying to create, again, this mock Surrealism? That's the thing that is the most devastating about most of the very sophisticated digital work that I've seen in imaging in three dimensions, and now this color image laser display as well. It all looks like it's been run through once already in the Surrealist period, suggesting that the Surrealists have already done it all. And so now you're just looking at it with all these funny limitations, but it's back on a two-dimensional flat screen, or it's being projected on smoke in a space. It's almost like the same old show, but in a new space, and again, I think it's not because of the talents or the imagination or the resources of the people, but I think it's just worldview, period. To my mind it is a prison, this 1800s worldview. I've really gotten wound up over it over the last three or four months because when you start seeing it around you, you see that it's everywhere—that all of these things, which are passing as modern and developed since the '60s, are actually people saying, finally, we're getting a payoff from those Victorian experiments. And we don't have to have long beards and funny-looking coats to do it. I mean, it's almost as silly as that. You have a strange feeling that it's a cosmetic improvement in the last hundred years in science, but what's really needed is something other than cosmetic improvement. You need a new avenue.

SOME APPROACH STRATEGIES USING THE DEE ENOCHIAN TABLET STRUCTURES

Jerry Hunt

This essay, written in 1993, was originally printed in *". . . looking to the long shores": writings, reminiscences and ideas of and about Jerry Hunt*, a memorial booklet printed by the loosely University of California San Diego–affiliated Inial Group in April 1994. Hunt's posthumously published text, originally intended for inclusion in the *Inial Journal*, offers a rare elucidation of certain procedures and materials rooted in the mystical Enochian system, developed by sixteenth-century philosopher John Dee, that are central to Hunt's compositional practice. A slightly expanded version of this piece appeared in the anthology *Arcana III: Musicians on Music* (Hips Road/Tzadik, 2008). The version here combines the more-complete body text found in *Arcana* with original epigraphs drawn from Hunt's letters to Inial Group founder Paul Morris (formerly known as Stevan Key).

There are no articles which deal with the specific mechanisms I've used since 1978: no one has ever asked about this directly, and the few written materials published deal with general approaches. I don't use direct translations of the tablets or other material, but I do use, as isolated objects, a selected and fixed set of mechanisms of operation of the watchtowers and angelic names. All of the process strategies use isolated sets of closed system extractions of historical models using a systematic approach of content neutral derivation. The model arrays are distributed to feature translation and derivation according to their principal characteristics. I do have some material which describes some of the individual processes involving the watchtowers, geomantic processes, skrying actions, and Rosicrucian chess operators . . .

I hope this is of some interest and amusement—one small warning: the attempt to read any of my "writing" aloud can result in mumbling and loss of breath.

> —from letters Hunt wrote to Stevan Key concerning "Some
> Approach Strategies Using the Dee Enochian Tablet
> Structures," 1993

The Enochian tablets are magical patterns using letter, word, sign, and number combinations within a system of grids received through the vision experience of Edward Kelley and transcribed by John Dee during a stay in Bohemia (c. 1582–89). These visions provided a group of materials which included some indications for the translation and utilization of the tablets. The principal tablet source is *Liber Mysteriorum Sextus et Sanctus*; this material has been the foundation for my transformational and translative uses of the Dee Enochian system in my work. My copies were provided by Douglas Taylor; they are photocopy reproductions from the originals in the British Museum. Specific information about the tablets, angelic and telesmatic names and sigils, Rosicrucian chess, geomancy, and associated topics may be found in a compact format in Israel Regardie's *The Complete Golden Dawn System of Magic* (Falcon Press, 1984).

All of the production strategies I've developed have employed the tablet structures as mechanism formalities; each strategy employed always uses some specific implementation of one or more aspects of the root generative procedure of the tablet systems. In my applications, the target operator or mechanism takes one of three forms, depending upon the definition requirements of eventual application and structure: *translative*, *generative*, and *transformational*. The procedures of application are always derivative and root-active: element substitution, parameter cross-mapping, or other direct substitution methods have never been used. The earliest formulation of these tablet strategies was first implemented in 1978 in the forms suggested here.

Translation

For purposes of application to procedure, translation involves a configuration of one or more of the generative mechanisms associated with the tablet result; this relation is achieved by reversing the system of attribution of element layers of the tablets to provide action or action sequence sources which produce patterned key layer associations which, when used in concordant confluence, generate strings of transformational gestures, weights, keys, changes, or element processes. The source roots are:

> (1) geomantic derivatives,
> (2) tablet-based translation mechanisms implemented as layered template modulation either serially or globally, and
> (3) sigil root derivatives, which always involve sequential temporal streams of layer elements.

1. Geomantic Source

The geomantic trace definitions are translated by convention assignments derived from the extraction processes of geomantic interpretation with weighted associations: each association provides incremental and/or defining access to a contiguous string of action operators; the action operators are negotiated through translation to a performance system gloss of goal, target, and strategy strings or directly implemented in a specific system of string-action sign translations to performance.

2. Tablet Source

Tablet sources use multiple layer tablets configured according to the rules of tablet structure, using fixed assignments (column-row blocks, elemental groups). The (angelic) letter strings are translated as operator calls to an assignment list of functions. Signatures of names are produced by connected strings of letter-elements: the resultant sigil operator is a dynamic function subject to orientation variables and can be used either as a template reading reference (into the tablet layers by reference orientation variation or other strategic modification) or a derivative series (by tablet correlation between compounded layers): each sigil operates as a decisional weighted key or matrix extraction process. [A parallel definition uses tablet element configurations with sigil weight associations as one of several compound layers of ruled motion for the action of Rosicrucian chess: the operator elements have assignments from the tablet ruler assignment system and function; the assignments are incrementally accessed as decoding or defining conditional series which are evaluated by the weighted tablet and ruler assignment as state process actions.] Element assignments, as extensions of each positional element, carry point-assignments into compounds of evoked match material. An emulation of the ruler operators and weighted tablet rules in compound arrangements creates multiple-depth weights for evaluation of a history of state transitions translated from action or action-sequence models (obtained through detection-block input-streams).

3.   Sigil Source

The sigil patterns are produced as tablet-referenced configurations: the sigil patterns are used as template weights to evaluate successive and accumulative tablet configurations produced by translation of serially received time-frame formatted transition events (obtained through presence-source detection-block input streams). Sigil pattern matches evoke successively engaged rule strings for accumulations of material and its modulation characteristics.

Generation

For generative applications, strings of material within variable interrelation must be produced within layers of successive definition ranges to provide high specificity of parameter and control characteristics, and include combinative and interrelational rules and variants to produce string sequences for multiple strand synchronous sources. Tablet and sigil source bases have been used for these configurational extensions and development. Most of these translations have produced base constellations of material which are utilized in the production of the generative model or mechanism, but in some applications the translations have been directly implemented as the root generative mechanism, as memory element, program or technical arrangement, and procedural definition.

1. Tablet Source

The generative application uses tablet source translations in two modes:

> 1) a direct source mode in which the tablet sources are translated to functional equivalents for the calling of action strings which result in the production of rooted action, gesture or pattern strings, and
> 2) an indirect source model in which the tablet sources are translated to functional equivalents for the calling of transformational or modulative action strings.

The translation in both cases is always based in procedural translation, not item or object replacement: each source element from a tablet represents an entry to a series of actions which in operation results in the selection of an action element which in turn calls the action or modulation string. The tablet elements are always used as active operators: this corresponds to the natural mode of the element basis of these tablets: the configurations of elements represent angelic signatures, roots, and sources, all of which become available as event processes rather than object isolations. The tablet sources are always presented as block templates. Weighted translations of the tablet elements, with their associated conditional locations within the tablet, are serially scanned for pattern weight strings. The weight strings are accumulated; the accumulation result, which conforms in one or more mode models to the sigil extractions, is used in serial evaluation with layered test pattern-structures (each carrying a unique weight). In electronic or mechanic implementation, a match-translation serial approach, through programmable strategies or fixed system extension with appropriate interface, is used: this procedure has been followed in almost all practical applications.

2. Sigil Source

The sigil source procedures work directly from sigil comparisons and form a simpler approach to the tablet implementation: model strings for the generation of action strings are confined to predicted structure weights and associations (each motion from or into a sigil node point is always weighted). The sigil sequence weight structure predicts associations of action, gesture, or modulation strings: successive passes through these weights create dispositions to dominant and subdominant structure correspondences. As a generative process, this approach of translation is always used with a categoric isolation of a group of correlated input action-gestures or process strings, and corresponds in an inverse way to the extraction of sigil structures from tablets using angelic name translations.

Transformation

The transformational mode of utilization involves the active translation of tablet or sigil source weighted pattern sources to action, gesture or action strings. The resultant process lists are applied through interface to a procedure which modulates or transforms layers of interassociated action strings. The transformational mode is often used in combination with generative and translative procedures as high-level priority control, modulation, or convergence exercises to isolate increasingly small details of an action string or process.

1. Tablet Source

The tablet sources are translated to produce associative strings: the weighted associative strings are applied by test categories to one or more layers of incremental variables (at once for every element or node). The tablet bases are always correlated to the subordinate strings which they affect. Because the subsets of variables are very large, the tablet source is always used at lower levels of predictive correspondence and correlation.

2. Sigil Source

The sigil source procedures work directly from arranged sigil sequence comparisons and form a simpler approach to the tablet implementation. Sigil extractions and the orientational variants produce weighted associations of elements and nodes which through successive correlation and correspondence tests produce strings of transformational action, gesture or action sequence strings. The sigil weights are compounded and evaluated sequentially in incremental association with decisional nodes throughout the subordinate layers.

A *tablet* consists of a patterned structure of signs, usually rectilinear, sometimes square, using a finite set of signs, each element of which carries a specific and interrelational significance.

Enochian is an invented language consisting of a series of signs (and associated sounding) and a system of inherent syntactical and grammatical rules; Enochian, as presented by the Dee-Kelley material, is similar to the Hebrew and Greek Cabala; combined words and sentences in special text configurations produce subordinate and interconnective meanings and associations through systematic procedures of number and pattern extraction within the tablet arrangements and some other text and text-number organizations.

Geomancy is a procedure of divination which uses earth as its focal source and is operationally similar to rod and pole divining; the modem variation of geomantic divination uses a combinative form of action which involves automatic writing and earth skrying.

Skrying is a vision procedure, originally using crystals as a focal source.

A *sigil* is a sign-form, usually two dimensional, which results from the connective trace of a group of associated elements from a tablet.

Rosicrucian chess is a form of chess action involving an immobile embedded rule tablet base (board) and variably powered mobile elements (pieces); *three-dimensional Rosicrucian chess* uses multiple layers of hierarchically arranged immobile embedded rule tablets (boards) and multiple variably powered mobile elements (pieces): multiple rule interrelationships produce an eventual series of weighted isolated outcomes.

—Jerry Hunt, 1993

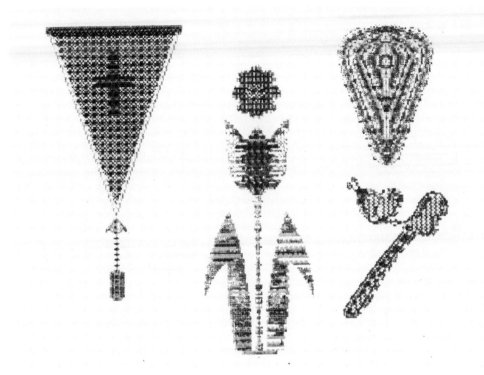

Above and following pages: Computer- and video-generated symbols from the handout for Hunt's installation *BIROME (Zone): CUBE (Frame)* at de Vleeshal, Middelburg, and Het Apollohuis, Eindhoven, Netherlands, April–May 1988.

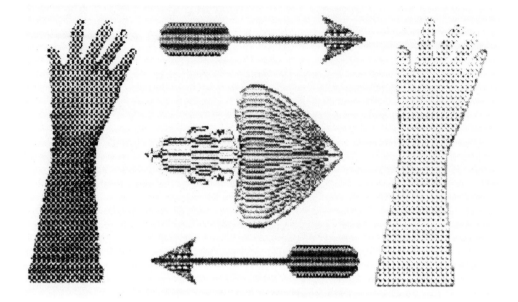

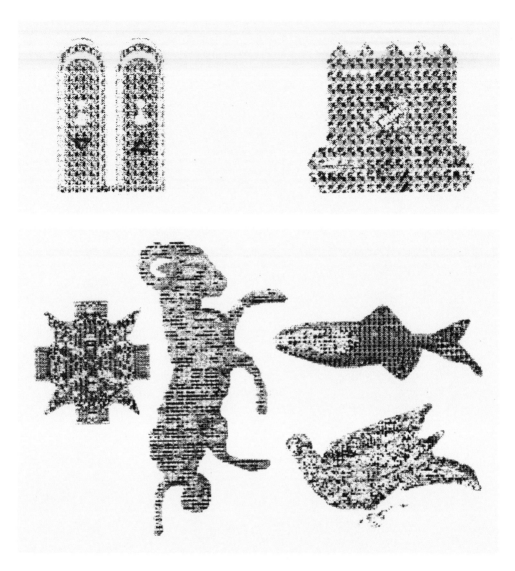

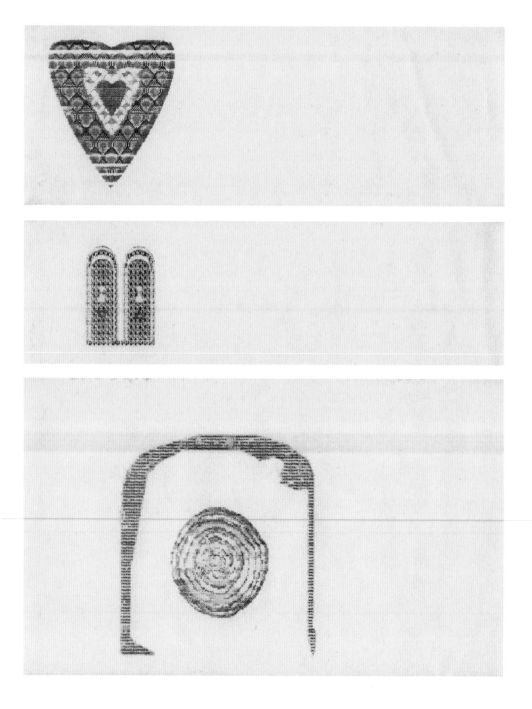

Jerry Hunt, untitled computer- and video-generated sigils, ca. 1986–89, ink on paper, various sizes. Hunt created these symbols for use in his "Birome (ZONE)" series.

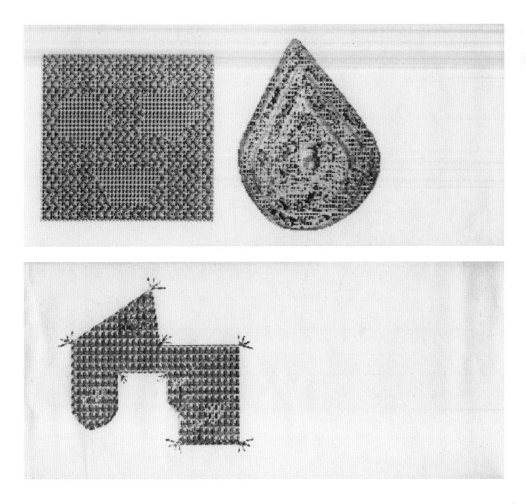

"DROP LINE . . . I KNOW I DON'T KNOW"
David Rosenboom

In this new essay, David Rosenboom reflects on his experiences with the person and musical art of Jerry Hunt. The author explores Hunt's very early, rare scores foreshadowing the evolution of his later work blending the physical and electrical, and his means of making distinctions in complex adaptive systems. He concludes with philosophical discussion of Hunt's practice.

(293–320)

Significantly deep discerning skills seem to be necessary to enable knowing when you *don't know*, and recognizing you don't know is an essential imperative and prerequisite for establishing an effective individual discipline.[1] In a personally revealing 1989 interview conducted by composer–sound artist Ellen Band, Jerry Hunt says, "The one thing I'm absolutely certain of at this point in my life is that I have no idea whether what I'm doing in my life is worthwhile. And *that* I'm really very sure of. I know I don't know."[2] For Hunt, this was firmly tied to the notion that "in addition to not really understanding the motivation [for his artistic practice] I also don't see any way out of doing it." This sufficient raison d'être for Hunt's musical art unfolds in a complexity-simplicity-mind-body-information-memory practice. We'll try to unpack a little bit of that in what follows, focusing particularly on relatively unknown early scores.

Jerry Hunt was one among a few rare individuals I've known whom I refer to as virtuoso talkers. Another was Anne Wehrer, the centerpiece of Robert Ashley's opera *The Trial of Anne Opie Wehrer and Unknown Accomplices for Crimes Against Humanity* (1968), in which her astonishing improvisatory philosophe-psycho-art-life verbal output drove the engine of extraordinary performances. Hunt was another, a very different sort, whose endless output, when ignited by friendly surroundings, could jump listeners around unexpectedly among landscapes of personal philosophy, sociocultural economies, musical practice, technology, spontaneous choice-making, instruments, paradigms of interactivity, performance presence, the nature of audiences, fluidly modulating personae, and more. His mental multiplexing might have seemed, to the uninitiated, stream-of-consciousness disjunctions, but for those ready to energetically engage in finding connecting threads among arrays of ideas, inspiring lightning bolts flashed all around.

1   The *don't know* imperative is well described in relation to Zen practice in Seung Sahn, *The Compass of Zen* (Boston: Shambhala, 1997). At a very young age, Hunt developed an interest in Vedanta, Buddhism, and processes of meditation.

2   Jerry Hunt, interview by Ellen Band, January 27, 1989, transcript. This interview, shared by Band, is part of a project she calls *The Motivation Interviews* (1986–91), conversations with music artists pushing the edges of definable practice, not about their music but about why they do what they do. The language and sentence structures in quotations here reflect the verbatim transcription of Hunt's speech as recorded on tape.

I was privileged to meet Hunt and live-video maker Houston Higgins for the first time during the 1972 International Carnival of Experimental Sound at the Roundhouse in London. This was a wild carnival, to be sure, with performances happening all around, hour after hour.[3] I watched Hunt and Higgins's performance, with onlookers coming and going, in which items of furniture were manipulated high in the air with a tangle of ropes ending in Hunt's hands, accompanied with extraordinary sounds and video images showing on monitors. I especially remember long, wonderful conversations around the Carnival environment traversing an uncountable array of fascinating subjects: futurist thinking, sociocultural-political matters, high-technology evolution, aesthetics and econo-philosophy, experimental music communities, and more. Apparently, there were a few onlookers who expressed some angst about the image of these American performers—no doubt others may have triggered it as well—because the Vietnam War was still raging.[4]

In early 2001, with my musical colleagues Ron Kuivila, Vicki Ray, and Mark Trayle, I prepared several concert performances to be presented as part of a collaborative production by the Getty Research Institute in Los Angeles and the California Institute of the Arts School of Music entitled *The Art of David Tudor: Indeterminacy and Performance in Postwar Culture*. This was both a conference and a festival celebrating the spirit of the newly established David Tudor archives at the Getty. The process included going through the archives and looking for inspiring discoveries with which to construct our programs. I discovered many relatively unknown nuggets of creative history in them. Among these were several score manuscripts that Hunt had sent to Tudor: *Helix 2, Helix 3 for Variable Sound-Producing Means, Helix 4, Helix 5 [for Variable Sound-producing Means], Stabile w/ Continuous Plane*, and *Stabile w/*

---

3   For more on this, see Dave Thompson, *The Avant-Garde Woodstock: The International Carnival of Experimental Sound, 1972* (self-published, CreateSpace, 2017).

4   After this first encounter with Hunt, we crossed paths during various musical gatherings in the 1970s and 1980s. Two highlights include bringing Hunt and David Dowe for a residency at York University in Toronto in 1975 and again in the Center for Contemporary Music at Mills College, Oakland, CA, in 1986. These residencies included performances, visits to classes, and social events replete with continuous, broad-ranging conversations that continued for as long as everyone's stamina could hold out. In the Mills concert on November 7, 1986, Hunt had taken up using the Synclavier digital instrument, which I remember being present on stage, and which he used in delightfully unconventional ways.

Cylindrical Surface.[5] All of them are signed "Jerry E. Hunt, Dallas, Texas" with various dates, all in 1964. Several instruction pages are also included. In an accompanying letter to Tudor,[6] Hunt also mentions the score for *Stabile w/ Continuous Sphere*, about which he says, "I've held *Sphere* back since he is not notated as simply as I'd like, since there's a mental juggling with it and I don't think people will like that."[7]

For the Tudor fest, having known Hunt for a couple of decades, during which I developed a deep appreciation for his work, I endeavored to develop a performance interpretation of his *Helix 5 [for Variable Sound-producing Means]*. I used a piano; a variety of light percussion instruments, some of which I strapped to my legs and arms; and a pair of oscillators with transducers, normally used as alarms, attached to long wires that I swung around in space as if they were lariat ropes. The instructions for *Helix 5* refer to conditions when the piano is employed. This, along with Hunt's having sent the score to Tudor, reinforced my choice to include the piano. I am a pianist as well, with great admiration for Hunt's own piano playing in his extraordinary work *Lattice* (1979). Some influence from that work may be detected in my realization of *Helix 5*. I attempted to invoke and honor at least a hint of Hunt's extraordinary spirit.

Curiously, a website devoted to Hunt's work and life includes a page titled "Jerry Hunt: Work Listing," featuring a list that Hunt is presumed to have compiled early in 1993. Of course, Hunt decided to leave the universe later that year. In the instruction text for *Stabiles*, he refers to nine sequentially numbered Helix works. The online list includes only eight such works, though the word "helix" appears in the titles of some other pieces—for example, *Sequential Helix* (1971), for electronic sounds and magnetic tape, which appeared on an Ocean Records release as part of their Composers Cassettes series (ca. 1977). On the website, all the Helix pieces are given different dates from those Hunt wrote on the manuscripts that I found, and

---

5   These titles are listed as they appear on the manuscripts except for *Helix 5*, where Hunt occasionally used a hyphen to connect the word and the number.

6   This letter is undated, though it was likely written around the same time.

7   The punctuation found in Hunt's letter to David Tudor, and in the instructions accompanying his scores that follow, has been maintained as it appears in the manuscripts.

the performance resources are often listed differently.[8] *Helix 5* is listed there as a solo for contrabass, with a date of 1969 instead of "5-17-64," which is inscribed on the manuscript. The Stabile works, which are truly very interesting compositions, are not listed at all. Nevertheless, I pushed on.

I would like to get into the weeds with some of Hunt's very early scores to explore how these overtly incomprehensible documents might reveal relations among emergent forms, complex adaptivity, modular musical structures, and other related paradigms. How might these early score documents hint at what was to come with Hunt's complex interactive electronic instrumentation systems, especially as typified by his Haramand Plane?

First, we'll examine the score titled *Helix 5* (fig. 1).[9] The title specifies "(for variable sound producing means)" and the text instructs to "employ any instruments/ and/or electronic devices." The instructions for interpreting it are, to say the least, difficult to unravel. As Hunt says in the letter to Tudor, "*Helix 5* with all its inside-going on is so difficult a problem I'm wondering about it. As usual the instructions may be a little terse. Talking to yourself is always easy though."

At first glance, the score looks complex. Or is it simple, like a texture? Maybe it's a continuous gestalt, like a forest or a field. Images of tangled strings or ropes or the cloud chamber traces of particle interactions emerge in these fields of lines. Questions abound. How do these fields of lines interact? Are they drawn freely, or, given Hunt's deep understanding of the nature of waves and electrical phenomena, do they originate as waveforms? Are they signals for gestures to be freely realized? Are they, counterintuitively, complex versions of simplicity? How are the intersections among lines to be interpreted?

Six fields of lines, waves, dots, arrows, and circles labeled A through F comprise the score for *Helix 5*. Hunt calls them "six notational complexes." Accompanying instructions include specific texts related to each complex. They must be read over and over to extract the intended meanings. One particular instructional phrase appears again and again: "Drop line." If one views the notational complexes as initially timeless fields, "drop line" invokes the

---

8   The list on the Jerry Hunt Home Page, maintained by Michael Schell and Hunt's estate, contains some titles and dates that are inconsistent with other documents and score manuscripts.

9   The documents I found reference five Helix works, all with dates in 1964. I've examined numbers two through five. I have not seen a *Helix 1*.

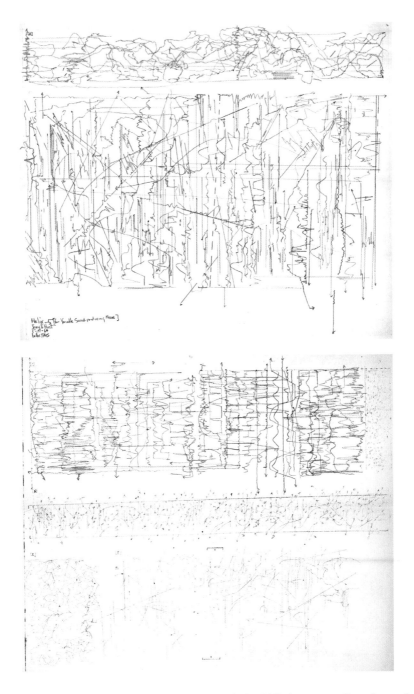

Figure 1. Two score pages from Jerry Hunt's *Helix 5* (1964), David Tudor papers, Getty Research Archives. Complex A is on the upper and B on the lower part of the first page. Complex C is on the upper, D in the center, E on the lower left, and F on the lower right part of the second page. Courtesy Getty Research Institute, Los Angeles (980039).

injection of moments into the field—moments of definition that eventually lead to linkages among events emerging among all six fields in interaction. "Drop line" is a way of making intersections that delineate ways of making distinctions in the fields. Temporal differentiations, or moments, then emerge. Complex A acts as a kind of master of emerging flow. Its vertical axis codes physical speeds, from "slow as possible" to "rapidly as possible." When an interpreter drops a line through the complex, they delineate intersections in the field of lines. These become simultaneously active entities. The interpreter is then instructed: "Select a convenient mode of calculation. Each moment from the complex may be freely associated in any way with the moments from the other five complexes."

Complex B is about "the extent of harmonic conditions from physically slowest (bottom) to fastest (top)." Some of the lines in this complex begin to invoke images of waves, though they mostly appear vertically or on some oblique angle. Long arrows, mostly slanted, course through the field as well. These indicate "modes of procedure to harmonic conditions beyond the determinations." They can have varying degrees of relevance according to "their angle and speed of departure," which allow for a "change of determination at any event altering the condition of the sound-process." Hunt reveals in later instructions that the arrows can also offer means to escape Complex B. The instructions for this complex are the most intricate. They include allowing for the influence of "predetermined eventualities," such as instruments used, acoustics, and environmental conditions. They discuss horizontally represented changes in "harmonic potentiality and activity," and proportions of used and unused determinations. Again, dropping a straight line through the complex will determine a given moment. Finally, after all this, Hunt asserts, "Instruments should in no case in a given performance use the same notation twice."

Complex C is about the "timbral condition for each tone in a moment." The lines in this field are the most evocative of waves, though, again, they are mostly vertical. The instructions leave lots of room for interpretation according to the instruments or sound-producing means in use and "whatever scalar condition is part of their nature." A rectangular box appears at the far right of this complex. It is filled with small arrows that are meant to "indicate directions of harmonic intensity in overtone structure, and are particularly relevant when piano or electronic devices are employed." The instructions for this complex are the ones revealing that, in general, interpenetrating arrows offer means of escape, as in Complex B.

A narrow, horizontal rectangle filled with arrows and vertical lines makes up Complex D. Like Complex A, Complex D influences the overall structure of a performance. It addresses density: the quantity of determinations, from whatever complexes they emerge, that can be engaged simultaneously. Dropped lines, bottom to top, track least to most activity. In addition, vertical lines drawn in the score indicate density, and arrows inscribe a "process of relation between points of occurrence." Performers, especially soloists, are directed to assess the practicality of the maximum determinations that can be simultaneously activated and to ensure that each one maintains a kind of individuality with "a separate flow, harmonic, timbral, intensity, and attack determination."

Complex E appears to the left of Complex F. It is intended to address amplitude or loudness in given situations. This instruction is very brief, and the interpreter is reminded that dropped lines delineating determinations at intersections are multidirectional.

Finally, Complex F addresses what Hunt calls "attack quanta."[10] The vertical axis maps lowest at the bottom to highest at the top. As markings approach being vertical, they invoke maximum simultaneity. This is to be contextualized by metrical situations that are determined by horizontal distances in Complex B. This is tricky to understand, because that complex focuses on *harmonic conditions*. The clues lie in these statements from Complex B: "All areas not containing notations are potential areas of harmonic inactivity. All determinations are related to the smallest length taken horizontally between the caesura and employed moment." A possible interpretation is that metrical influences should be drawn from the horizontal distances between interruptions of harmonic activity in Complex B and adjacent moments delineated by dropped lines. Further, curvilinear and straight deflections in the field of lines of Complex F can modulate maximum simultaneity among attack quanta. Lastly, in Complex F, a few circles appear. These reference "points of accumulation" and give the performer license to "employ any mode determined from any recent (performance process) event." Here, memory is implied, which becomes critically important in Hunt's later electronic work, in which prerecorded cartridge tapes and other means of audio storage are integrated inside the electronic networks of his instrumentation.

---

10 By "attack quanta," I believe Hunt is referring to the number of sound attacks occurring within a timeframe. A kind of granular density measure seems to be invoked.

Two final paragraphs in the instructions for *Helix 5* lay out conditions for interpreting it with groups of instruments at various levels of "density." Interestingly, these paragraphs indicate how *moments* may be determined by a cueing system, by environmental circumstances, or by employing the Stabiles. This linking of Helix scores with Stabile scores is very interesting, pointing to a kind of modular thinking that may tie all these pieces together. Hunt goes on to say that even "events of a theatrical nature" can emerge from using the Stabiles or his *Theaterfunction 1–8* in conjunction with Complex A; the former can also be used "for distribution of sound."[11]

In this super complex—though only two-page—document, three more paragraphs are provided about *Helix 2*, *Helix 3*, and *Helix 4*. These instructions are simpler, draw on those for *Helix 5*, discuss performances by small groups, and suggest ways of using these scores in a modular, interchangeable manner, in which determinations from any one might influence determinations in others. For instance, performers might use the drop line method in a particular complex of one score to determine conditions for selected musical parameters to be applied to moments in another: time, harmony, timbre, density, loudness, attack quanta, or other parameters. Hunt elucidates this further by describing how specific, whole complexes may be interchanged or superimposed among scores. For example, Complex A of *Helix 3* may be interchanged or superimposed with Complex A of *Helix 5*. He even describes how, in an ensemble of up to five performers, each player could each use a separate Helix piece altogether. He includes a few specific details for interpreting combinations of Helix scores depending on which ones are being used together.

Not all of Hunt's later work is modular in this fashion. However, in his solo electronic pieces, he no doubt drew very freely from the reservoir of materials he developed over time in whatever manner seemed to fit particular performance circumstances. Perhaps he also viewed the complexes in these scores as collections of building blocks that could be assembled according to certain minimal guidelines in a myriad of ways.

---

11 On the Jerry Hunt Home Page these are titled "theater functions" (two words, all lowercase), dated 1960–61, and identified as being for "various performer and ensembles, arrangements."

One wonders, why are these pieces named after helices?[12] What does the helix form reveal when applied to the geometries in the scores and the complexes? What was Hunt's original vision in concocting these structures? This is very tricky and hard to discern. Are the rectangular complexes meant to wrap around a cylinder? Are the fields of lines already the result of some such wrapping? If the complexes are rotated ninety degrees, some of the lines, especially in Complex B, look like they could have resulted from a continuously rising cylindrical wrapping. If some of the complexes were rolled into tubes, one might imagine the lines, especially the wavelike ones, coming from some gyrating inscription of waveforms, almost like wax cylinders unrolled and laid out as rotated horizontal rectangles. Who knows for sure? Again, we don't know what we don't know.

And what of the Stabiles? Is Hunt using this term in the manner of Jean Arp's appellation for Alexander Calder's nonmobile, fixed-position sculptures?[13] Maybe. Hunt wrote an instruction page for the three Stabiles. They are extremely complex and obtuse, necessitating multiple readings to even speculate on their intended meanings. There are references to "alterations within a stabile planal immobility producing or not producing movement." In the case of *Stabile w/ Cylindrical Surface*, the titular surface is described as "planally static." Perhaps the Helices are to be observed as constantly mobile in contrast to the Stabiles, which may require the points of view to move for the pieces to become dynamic. Clearly, one must work carefully to extract meaning from all the instructions for both series in trying to understand them. Figure 2 shows how I highlighted various elements in *Helix 5* to guide my realization of it.

I found a separate instruction sheet in the Tudor archive titled "*HELIX 2* (1–4 performers/sound-sources)," dated January 16, 1964. In the center of the score sheet for *Helix 2* (fig. 3), there is

12 A helix is, of course, a spiral shape, like a corkscrew or gyre that has a left- or right-handedness in its geometry, like a 3D, stretched-out and twisted, sinelike object. The most common helix is also known as a cylindrical helix, the parametric representation of which is easily written down. There are also conical helices that are a bit trickier and spherical helices, also known as loxodromic spirals, which are involved in making map projections.

13 Jean Arp is reported to have coined the term "stabiles" while visiting Alexander Calder in Paris shortly before a showing of his work arranged by Marcel Duchamp at Galerie Vignon that ran for a week in 1932. Duchamp had suggested the term "mobiles" for Calder's work in a show at Galerie Percier in 1931. See Seymour I. Toll, "My Way: Calder in Paris," *The Sewanee Review* 118, no. 4 (Fall 2010): 589–602.

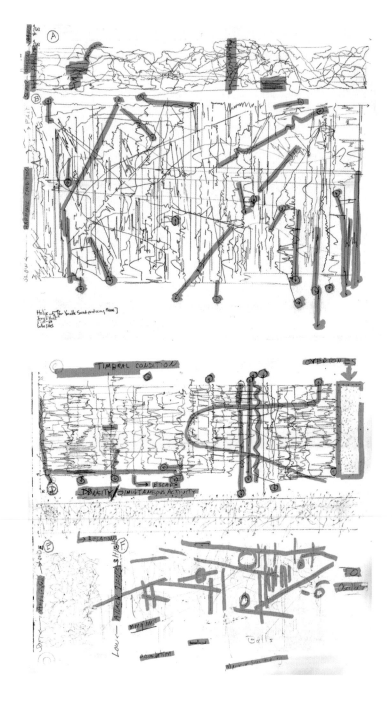

Figure 2. Copies of two score pages for *Helix 5* with various figures highlighted, part of Rosenboom's performance preparation process. Courtesy Getty Research Institute, Los Angeles (980039).

a field of mostly wavy lines arrayed horizontally. Hunt lists four categories of notation contained in this field, described here in a simplified manner: 1) relatively rough squiggly lines for "noise or discrete sound processes whose components occur of their own nature," 2) more wavelike lines for "noise processes which are articulated through agency of performer or control-device," 3) dashed lines for "controlled process whose nature is determined by any other notation horizontally," and 4) two brackets framing a central group of lines for "band accumulations employing total chromatic block/ internal articulation determined by time-flow coordinate." Around the central complex of lines there are fields of dots, short lines with arrowheads pointing in many directions, and other lines and curves. Most of these are for controlling "attack process" and "points of alteration in time flow." A dense cluster of longer arrows appears in the lower left corner, enclosed by two horizontal brackets. Understanding the precise purpose of this requires more study. Again, lines are to be dropped to determine intersections, delineating distinct programs for players in a group. Symbols for guiding the "direction of reading within a determination" are also scattered around. Hunt also indicates that the other Helices—*1, 3, 4,* and *5*—may be employed simultaneously. What I have provided here is a cursory overview of *Helix 2*, meant to give a taste of these instructions, which in total are much more complex and detailed.

The score for *Stabile w/ Continuous Plane* (fig. 4) evokes a kind of visual topography articulated by a field of curled lines. It is meant to be initially undifferentiated, unless employed simultaneously with the Helices, reminding us of the modularity with which these pieces may be combined. Again, dropping a line through the field produces distinctions at intersection points. The field also contains circles with arrows extending from them in various directions. Selecting one leads to discontinuities representing "alterations within a stabile planal immobility producing or not producing movement." A band of symbols like those appearing in *Helix 2* is associated with alteration of time flow, which, I believe, is referred to in the instructions as a "time flow glyph." An underscored instruction asserts that in all Helices and Stabiles, players may "perform any moment in any amount at any time changing any time and returning in any way." However, no directive must ever be performed more than once.

It is easy to imagine the score for *Stabile w/ Cylindrical Surface* (fig. 5) being wrapped around the surface of a vertical cylinder, which Hunt describes as "*planally static*" (emphasis added). It shows three clearly identifiable regions. A central field of curved arrows

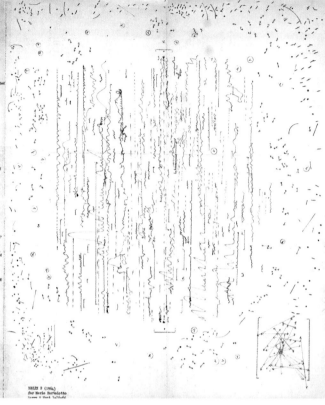

Figure 3. Score page for *Helix 2*. Courtesy Getty Research Institute, Los Angeles (980039).

Figure 4. Score page for *Stabile w/ Continuous Plane*. Courtesy Getty Research Institute, Los Angeles (980039).

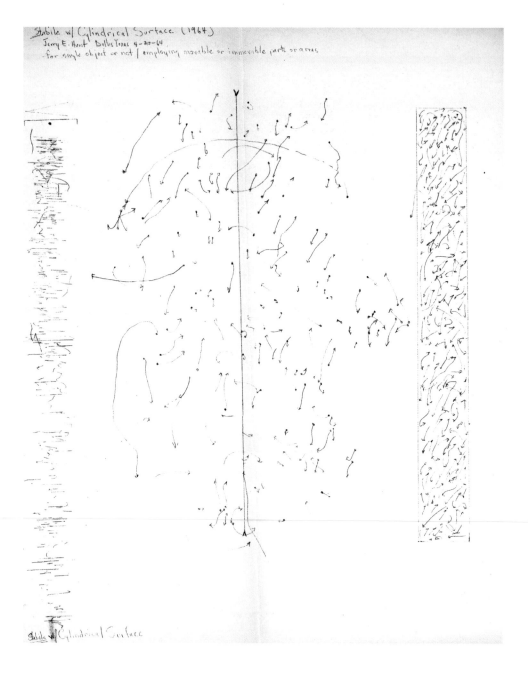

Figure 5. Score page for *Stabile w/ Cylindrical Surface*. Courtesy Getty Research Institute, Los Angeles (980039).

through which a line is to be dropped to create intersections that delineate "a condition of alteration in a static condition." These are considered to be moments, the condition of alteration of which is determined by association with the physical position of other intersection moments in a rectangle to the right of the central area containing more curved arrows. Dance or stage movements may also be invoked by freely associating them with "moments from continuous plane events." To the left of the central area is shown what is referred to as a "time flow graph," tracing "physically slowest to immobility to fastest to immobility." This graph is also meant to be used when performing *Stabile w/ Continuous Sphere*, though I haven't found that score. In general, time in these pieces is flexible. Hunt refers to speeds as "conditions"—moving at particular rates with respect to particular space-time references—and directs the performer to "establish some useable mode for time."

In summary, we can ask, do these works anticipate a further evolutionary pathway in Hunt's later work? I believe they do. I can imagine how the intricate complexities inherent in the verdant jungles of symbols these scores contain may have found other materializations in the interactive, complex adaptive circuit networks that were to emerge, particularly within the Haramand Plane system.

Hunt's Music and Complex Adaptive Systems

I have found it interesting to look at the scores we have examined as foreshadowing Hunt's later, more well-known work with electronic information complexes and examine them through a lens borrowed from theories of Complex Adaptive Systems (CAS). CAS is not a singular theory; rather, it is a broad field of research that in the last half-century or so has illuminated rich new landscapes of inquiry in the arts, sciences, design, engineering, aesthetics, philosophy, and other fields. I feel that drawing from certain CAS perspectives might offer insight into this investigation of Hunt's work.

On January 31, 1975, Jerry Hunt and David Dowe presented a concert in the Instructional Display Area and Foyer of the Fine Arts Center at York University that included three named works: *Haramand Plane: Parallel/Regenerative* (1973), *Video Unit(s) 1, 2 (. . . . .)* (ca. 1975), and *Cantegral Segment(s) (transverse)* (ca. 1975). Dowe, who had a position at Southern Methodist University in Dallas and was director of the Video Research Center, had taken up collaborative projects with Hunt, presenting video work displayed on color monitors. Encountering Hunt's *Haramand Plane* in this event was particularly enlightening, as I began to understand the depth of his technical acumen and to regard *Haramand Plane* not as a musical piece or crystalized composition but rather as an always evolving *complex adaptive musical system*, something even beyond what we might have presumptively thought of as an *instrument*. The Haramand Plane system was to become increasingly rich in its scope and adaptive nature throughout much of Hunt's subsequent work. In the program notes for this York concert, he wrote that *Haramand Plane* includes "an interactive prediction-control system. For the performance, processors, consisting of recirculative storage elements, are designated to operate over structure and interrelationships of control hierarchies, dynamically as compositional process." And later, in his biographical statement, we read, "Since his composition *Sur. Dr. John Dee* (1963) which utilizes changes in the performance environment, Mr. Hunt has been concerned with adaptive and interactive processes in musical composition and performance. His current work involves various systems for predicting and selectively altering the histories of performance processes as composition and their specific application in audio and video generating systems."[14] These are some of the most clear and succinct statements of musical intention we have.

Can the scores we have examined also be considered complex adaptive systems? It seems very natural to me now to ask this question, because these scores can look like interacting living matrices. They are adaptive in how their forests of lines—initially frozen by a hand drawing on paper—can grow variable manifestations via a framework of instructions for interpretation, which present a mixture of specificity, openness, modularity, navigational tools, and formulas for emergence. The simplicity or complexity of the results depends upon the observer's viewing perspective and cognitive context. I also draw from personal experiences in many long discussions with Hunt, some of which explored highly technical territories, that his intuitive insight into the nature of what we now call emergent systems was profound and formative in the way he framed his practice. Because these investigations are pertinent to the evolution of music, art, and culture today, it is possible to regard Hunt's approach as prescient, and a potential source of ideas and inspiration for further developments to be made by artists, artist-philosophers, and artscientists now and in future generations.

---

14 Program notes distributed at the concert "Jerry Hunt and David Dowe" at York University, Toronto, January 31, 1975.

Measuring complexity in the multisensory environments of music and multimedia that include interactivity and adaptivity among performative agents—the essence of any CAS—and including both organic and artificial agents presents significant challenges. Among the many brilliant complex systems researchers whose ideas may be pertinent, I find frameworks proposed by one of the field's foundational theorists, John H. Holland, to offer significant potential. Holland was a key theorist at the Santa Fe Institute, for many years a leading center devoted to complexity science. He outlined a set of requirements for something to be considered a Complex Adaptive System in his book *Signals and Boundaries*.[15] I list them here with brief comments about their applicability to the Hunt scores discussed above.

> Requirement 1: "Signals and boundaries, and all things employing them, should be defined with the help of a *formal grammar* that specifies allowable combinations of building blocks."[16]

As inscrutable as the instructions for these early pieces may be, they do contain clearly formalized operations. Hunt's "drop line" instruction, seen again and again, is a method for drawing distinctions and differentiating boundaries separating moments, conditions, actions, and alterations. These become the building blocks that are combined to manifest a performance.

> Requirement 2: "Each generator used by the signal/boundary grammar should have a location in an underlying *geometry*, and combinations of generators should be mobile within that geometry."[17]

"Every piece I've ever done has involved what I regard as a rational translation of something that's happening in the space (picked up through sensors) into a consistent rational schedule of changes."[18] Hunt's translation systems correspond to these generators, and they

15 John H. Holland, *Signals and Boundaries: Building Blocks for Complex Adaptive Systems* (Cambridge, MA: MIT Press, 2012).

16 Holland, *Signals and Boundaries*, 51.

17 Holland, *Signals and Boundaries*, 53.

18 In this volume: "Stompin' and Beatin' and Screamin': Gordon Monahan in Conversation with Jerry Hunt," 235. Originally printed in *Musicworks* no. 39 (1987): 6–11.

are mobile within the geometry/topography of fields of symbols in each score. Additionally, in multiple places, Hunt suggests ways that all the scores may be drawn on in modular fashion to generate relationships for actions to meet given performance conditions.

> Requirement 3: "The grammar should be capable of generating *programmable agents*—bounded conglomerates that can execute arbitrary signal-processing programs."[19]

In these scores, instructional units interact with each other according to delineated conditions—drop line, again—in particular fields. Conditions differentiated in a given field determine alterations to conditions in other fields. This is a kind of programming. In Hunt's later electronic works, programmable agents clearly course through his systems.

> Requirement 4: "The signal/boundary grammar must provide for *reproduction by collecting resources*, whereby an agent-conglomerate reproduces by collecting copies of the generators that define its structure."[20]

Forms of memory and reproduction were critical components in Hunt's later electronic works. I think early manifestations of this do appear in these scores. *Helix 5* contains circles meant to be points of accumulation in which modes from recent performance process events are employed. This is an important function, in spite of repeated assertions in the instructions that no determination—a condition delineated in the notation fields, usually involving the drop line action—should be activated more than once.

Later, in discussing the preparation of tapes used in his electronic systems—for him these are memory materials—he says of visual objects and "the manipulation of a group of symbols or objects" that each is

> tied up with a scenario that consists of its sound and the kind of melody or timbre development or whatever that is just one single string of material, and each of these strings is made uniquely on its own. They are attempts to create a particular fulfillment of that thing just in itself. Once

19 Holland, *Signals and Boundaries*, 53.

20 Holland, *Signals and Boundaries*, 55.

that principal type has been done, I make many different versions of it.[21]

A kind of reproduction is involved here. We can also recall the statements quoted earlier from Hunt's biography for the 1975 York University performance that refer to adaptive interactivity and selectively altering the histories of performance processes as musical composition.

I conclude, then, that these pieces, and certainly later work, meet the requirements to be considered complex adaptive systems. "So my pieces are not really concerts or performances," Hunt once said, "but they're conventions."[22]

Physicality and Reality

Profoundly palpable, Jerry Hunt's performance practice critically involved an arresting physical presence—in the moment, in interaction, or even in confrontation with audiences. "More and more, I try to make the physical presence and the implied information of that physical presence . . . interchangeable, the same, equivalent."[23] Physicality in performance has long remained a complex issue in electronic music. Hunt addressed it uniquely and with powerful affect.

In thinking about Hunt's physicality, I find it interesting to review his criticisms of some of the impulses driving early developments in virtual reality technology: "Virtual reality has recently started. The test of it is how well do they trick you into thinking that it's real. But there is no new space, no new reality. Time and space become malleable in art. Virtual reality slavishly copies time and space."[24] To twist things more—today, this subject lies in deeply theoretical territory where art and science meet—the real is malleable.

In his profoundly presaging 1991 book *Virtual Reality*, Howard Rheingold quotes legendary computer scientist Frederick P. Brooks

21 "Interview between Leon van Noorden and Jerry Hunt," in *Birome (ZONE)* (Eindhoven: Middelburg Bureau of Culture and Het Apollohuis, 1988), 7.

22 "Stompin' and Beatin' and Screamin'," 234.

23 "Interview between Leon van Noorden and Jerry Hunt," 5.

24 René van Peer, "Common Ground: Jerry Hunt and Paul Panhuysen in Conversation," 1993. Jerry Hunt Home Page, http://www.jerryhunt.org/van_peer.htm.

Jr. in the title of the first chapter, "Grasping Reality Through Illusion."[25] Wielding the powerful tools of illusion—and I regard illusion to be at the root of the sometimes-overwhelming problems in human cultures now—in whatever sphere of human activity they emerge from calls for deep thinking about responsibility. Hunt was keenly aware of this perplexing philosophical arena, which predates the emergence of the technological infosphere by several millennia.

For Hunt, these considerations brought up the notion of modeling. He once said, "I like this idea of modeling, in a renais-sance sense."[26] He was probably thinking of sixteenth-century Enochian matters, but still, I think it applies here.[27] Modeling is one of the ways we make things happen, but it's easy to fall into the trap of equating the model with the real. That leads to rigid, though materially effective, classical engineering—in machines, economies, social structures, health systems, and more. Today we can think of adaptable models and an emergent engineering approach for systems that change according to circumstances. In Hunt's case, we should not regard his systems, whether in the drawings and instructions for scores or in electronic instrumentation, as containing models *of* something. Here, the model is not purported to be of something real, and the score is not a map of some other territory. The instrumentation systems and the scores are the real in themselves, and the performer activates performances with them as pre-contextual creative stimuli. Rather than being *of* something other, the models are entities unto themselves. They are there to be played. This view has also fueled my work with models as instruments in what I call propositional music, a point of view about composing that addresses the activity of model-building as one of process, inviting

25 See Frederick P. Brooks Jr., "Grasping Reality through Illusion, Interactive Graphics Serving Science" in *CHI '88: Proceedings of the SIGCHI Conference on Human Factors in Computing Systems* (Chapel Hill, NC: Department of Computer Science, University of North Carolina, 1988), 1–11; and Howard Rheingold, *Virtual Reality: The Revolutionary Technology of Computer-Generated Artificial Worlds—and How It Promises and Threatens to Transform Business and Society* (New York: Summit Books, 1991).

26 "Stompin' and Beatin' and Screamin'," 235.

27 Hunt references the Enochian magical systems of John Dee and Edward Kelley from the *Liber Mysteriorum Sextus et Sanctus* book of mysteries in some of his compositional systems, for example in his 1993 essay "Gesture Modulation of Templates." He devised deterministic, goal-oriented strategies that were partic-ularly useful in coding electronic translation systems. He also described them as extending to "all levels of mechanical, electronic and social performance or production operations." See Jerry Hunt, "Gesture Modulation of Templates," 1993. Jerry Hunt Home Page, http://www.jerryhunt.org/mw_39.htm.

engagement in exploration and discovery inside propositional worlds that may emanate from whole domains of thought and life.[28] I believe Hunt's scores can be thought of as models, not in the sense of determinist, mechanical generators, but rather in the sense of providing dynamical graphic-music ecosystems.

Consequently, all this music is emergent in the actions of physically present moments. Each activation is equitably valid. Hunt's music is not the music of predetermined forms to be mastered in advance. He said, "There was a time when I was more interested in being a composer, in having people play. It hasn't worked out that well. My music is not about rehearsing."[29]

Hunt's scores are clearly not about rehearsing in the sense of perfecting the delivery in performance of fixed musical architectures. They invite engagement. They suggest means for delineating sonic entities with which performers are intended to engage and interact. They successfully avoid predetermination. Outcomes cannot be prestated. All engagement with them produces emergent forms. It just so happens that in some circumstances audiences of ideally imaginative listeners may also be present to engage with what emerges and we call those circumstances performances.

The scores themselves, as hand-drawn physical objects, do not evolve—at least until the paper on which they are drawn eventually deteriorates—but their contents are endlessly adaptable to unforeseeable performance situations. They preset fields of possibilities while remaining imbued with the vision of the artist that created them. Of course, we could take a position regarding all scores this way. Perhaps Hunt's scores are a reminder that our perspective is generated by the way we choose to perceive them. Then how does this choice-making relate to Hunt's views on the matter of free will?

---

28 See David Rosenboom, "Propositional Music: On Emergent Properties in Morphogenesis and the Evolution of Music; Essays, Propositions, Commentaries, Imponderable Forms and Compositional Methods," in *Arcana: Musicians on Music*, ed. John Zorn (New York: Granary Books/Hips Road, 2000), 203–32; Rosenboom, "Propositional Music of Many Nows," in *Tradition and Synthesis, Multiple Modernities for Composer-Performers*, eds. Dušan Bogdanović and Xavier Bouvier (Lévis, Québec, Canada: Doberman-Yppan, 2018), 121–42; and Rosenboom, "Illusions of Form," in *Sound Work: Composition as Critical Technical Practice*, ed. Jonathan Impett (Leuven, Belgium: Leuven University Press, 2021).

29 Peer, "Common Ground."

Free Will

In his extraordinary interview with Ellen Band, Hunt talks exten-sively about the question of free will. By this time, he seems to have come to view free will as illusory. Hunt was a person full of what I would call meaningful contradictions, all of which are well worth pondering deeply. These meaningful contradictions popped up, I think, because he was incredibly perceptive and sensitive to the cracks and holes riddling cultures, societies, models, languages, arts economies, and general presumptions about the way things seem to be. He says to Band, "One of the things I've always been the most suspicious of is answers that make really good sense and lead you to nice, pat, coherent conclusions." She probes him further—"you're also saying that you don't really believe in the existence of free will"—and Hunt replies, "I don't." He ties up free will in a complex net with his musical practice, responsibility and ethics, sociocul-tural context and value, and what he regards as the outdated eigh-teenth-century idea of time and space. He says:

> As long as there's this conception of, in the grid of time and space I can act as a free agent and I can make initia-tive and spontaneous choice, you think that means that in fact, if we all just work hard enough we could fix all of these bad things [problems in the world] and it's because we're bad that we don't do it, we're evil, we're not as evil as those people who are doing those really bad things.[30]

Earlier in the conversation, Hunt expounds on questions about whether the reason we do what we do is determined by what we are *designed* to do—because of the design of our nervous systems or the social roles we are designed to carry out. Later, he asks, "I mean, is there a chemical foundation for our morality? Is there a basic cellu-lar foundation for an ethical sense?" It comes out that he believed it to be illusory and risky to regard things as special in a way that isolates them: "It seems to me that free will is a very dangerous kind of thing because it continues to reinforce the notion of the extraordinary moment."

Do we regard Hunt's scores, then, as producing extraordinary moments, or simply as agents acting among many in a vast, ongo-ing, evolving cultural ecology? A Buddhist view might remove the

---

30 Jerry Hunt, interview by Ellen Band.

tension around *extraordinary* without diminishing in any way the *appreciation* of these moments.

Shaman No Shaman

Hunt was often labeled a "shaman" for the character of his performances, but in Band's interview, he makes his feelings clear about this in several ways. She asks, "Were you the one who came up with the shamanistic label?" He responds, "No, I've never said it to anyone. I've never described my work that way."

This is partially foreseeable in the somewhat startling nature of Hunt's physical performance persona, combined with the inscrutable nature of his emergent musical systems. A Hunt performance could be imagined to be a ritual practice. Hunt clarifies, "I know everyone likes to connect the shamanistic part because they see the kind of semi-occult things. I think it has more to do with the way I address people in performance than anything else."

Hunt would have been mortified to be judged as a pseudo-shaman, especially given his described disdain for "repulsive" drone music on the grounds that it's "pseudoreligious."[31]

It is strange to me, though in retrospect I understand it, how this possible mislabeling viraled its way through the rumor mill and became the hip thing to say about Hunt. Again, in Band's interview he asserts, "A lot of the way that people react to what I do . . . it's definitely a product of their imagination." In my view, this is the audience's problem.

Unwarranted presumptions of shamanism expose a known flaw in the human species: the necessity to ascribe causality for things we don't understand to mystical or pseudoreligious origins. Dubbing someone a shaman because of their strange sticks and rattling objects that seem to trigger scary electronic manifestations that seem like physically challenging apparitions reveals naive cultural presumptions among the onlookers. In another place, someone wearing a strange and frightening headdress, who chants incantations of anxious wails and generates palpitations in crowds, simply must also be a shaman. Let alone someone in a narrow-lapelled brown suit appropriate for a Texas door-to-door vacuum cleaner salesman who challenges audiences to find meaning in spatially diffused, information-packed noises wrought from hidden sensors embedded all over the place, and who makes incomprehensible

31 "Stompin' and Beatin' and Screamin'," 231

movements in front of them with strange objects—of course, this must also be a shaman. That's human nature.

Do we really know what a shaman is anyway? I think it's doubtful.

Value

In all my experiences interacting with Jerry Hunt, in whatever context they may have spontaneously appeared, conversations and performances always led to questions and ideas one could spend a lifetime fruitfully contemplating. That's true inspiration. Questions to ponder included those about the appropriateness of making distinctions among ideas about performance, composition, technology, complexity, simplicity, and even the separation of art and life. In Band's interview, Hunt referred to the last matter in this way: "The reason I propose to people the idea of getting rid of art completely is because I don't think we'd miss it. But I mean if you think about it a little bit, getting rid of art, something would fill its place and I think that would be life." Perhaps in a utopian view, we could imagine a human society in which there isn't a necessary distinction between art and life.

Ultimately, all these things tie into questions about how we value what we do. Hunt continued, "If you say to me, how is it that your work is more valuable than a man sweeping the streets? I just can't come up with an answer for it." Mindful analysis of value systems, questioning the specialness of what we do, is fundamental in truly reflexive, critical artistic practice. A critical practice always questions itself through feedback processes that guide its evolution and adaptation. It was natural for Hunt to expose this conundrum in his own thinking as well.

In my mind, this can also be a driver guiding a practice toward open, adaptive, evolutionary models that acknowledge and learn to value the non-prestatable nature of outcomes. Value can be discovered in such a process, and I believe Hunt's work lies in this domain. Open systems like this inevitably confront and work with the way phenomena spread through mediums, including human cultures. Injecting carefully chosen work into these mediums, accompanied by critique of its effect and influence, can become an expression of value. Perhaps Hunt's grappling with these matters played a part in his being drawn into the turbulence of American culture clashes that rose up during the latter part of his life and that are raging even more today. Nevertheless, the value that can be gleaned from the insights, questions, sparks of enlightenment, and significant challenges contained in Hunt's work is, in my opinion, beyond refute.

Acknowledgements

Special thanks to composer–sound artist Ellen Band for transcribing her illuminating 1989 taped interview with Jerry Hunt in a timely manner so that I could learn from it, reference it in this article, and draw quotations from it.

This essay was first published in a 1991 issue of *Contemporary Music Review* (volume six, part one) and is divided into three parts: The first deals with the compositional systems Haramand Plane and Ground, detailing their relation to electronic systems of memory and the mechanism by which Hunt adapts such systems for performances. The second section addresses the occult influences on Hunt's construction of the memory retrieval systems used in his interactive installations *Birome (ZONE): Cube*, 1986; *Birome (ZONE): Plane*, 1986; and *BIROME (Zone): CUBE (Frame)*, 1988. The final section offers a general technical overview of all of the above work. It has been lightly edited for clarity.

(1) Since 1978 my work utilizing electronic systems has not been based upon an extension of the instrumentation of performance practice and the convention-systems of performance practice in which an electrical system supplants, emulates, or extends some mechanical instrumentation analog model. It has been based upon a model of the translation of the mechanism of core information processing and production, as memory context-content exercise.

(2) This translation model, core information processing and production, has been used to produce a series of works in which the electronic systems constitute globally an *implicit memory model*, invariant, associative, context-defined, locked.

(3) The core translation of the electronic system as the information ground agent of performance has a component and interdependent interactive feature, a core model of performance as a process and procedure of convention manipulation.

(4) The action of performance is a mimetic transactional exercise in a content-context sensitive string interactive array-arrangement: the mimetic component is a string of residual affective interactive gestures, produced as transactional exercises.

(5) The translation of these models (implicit system core, agent active transaction) constitutes a convention ground for the exchange and interaction of two global contexts: *other*: self-referent, closed, invariant, coherent, stable; and *present*: multiply referent (quaquaversal), open (within the convention field), variant, not coherent (not contained through direct field limited invariance), unstable (a multiple-source arrangement is available through the social field groupings of the performance convention): heaven-earth.

(6) The *mechanism of memory* is a construction-arrangement, in all sense-states, of the electronic retrieval mechanism and the artifact array markers of gesture sight-sound in performance, and the mechanisms of derivation, extraction, and translation which produce the reflexive interaction between the layers of system as a procedure of retrieval and reassociation within a context-defined, hierarchically interpenetrative system of *layers, strings*, and *masks*.

[*absolute memory: repeatable behavior: invariant response: invariant coherent other*]

(*The performance transaction is peripherally self-referent by personal affective overlay; the reference strings and the hierarchical interpenetrations of strings [and/or layers] remain invariant [remote source].*)

(7a) Personal performance action is a special string of activity associated with an ensemble work group, a task-list, a history of material and components: each system of activity is associated through a group of hierarchical relations, but the context and available task-list references are uniquely defined by that system area: work for recording-playback by individuals and work for use, independently, by individuals (recording, installation systems), are directly related to the personal performance work and the affective overlays of this work, but occupy a technical and social group of guidelines that are specifically defined for that medium, as performance or as recording playback. As a consequence of the division, I have produced no recordings as documents of performances, or provided installation work as performance.

(7b) The definitions of personal performance involve the specification of a context of personal interaction, a context of individual and social occasional and situation responsibilities (fulfillment as convention), and an isolation of the context of performance activity as performance-compositional material: work for performance is produced as a transactional mimetic exercise: no direct performance action is defined as evocation: through this approach the system component becomes a plane of available response groups (image-sound, remote, local), which through some isolated specialized mechanism is made available at once as narrative succession for performance continuation, and as narrative succession of interaction (flags, markers of task-list) of each interdependent exchange feature of the direct and immediate *other*.

(8) The *system other* is proposed as an absolute, limited, invariant and self-referent retrieval mechanism. The self-referent and limited invariant string limits produce the narrative string which creates the content, direction, and succession of events as an extraction of strategy.

(9) *Layers, strings, and masks are separated components grouped through code definitions. Layers* define groups of parallel association or extension events which are accessed as variant isolates of string; *strings* define subcomponent continuous and contiguous streams of narrative (narrative as sequence and order binding strings, locked into a succession pattern of time and sound-sight); *masks* define groups of control string sets which act as determinative grids, with markers which scan layer-string codes to define the points of interassociative action.

(10) The core affective gesture of a performance action is the initiation of selection by isolation; continuation is sustained through the reflexive mechanism of the memory core translations. Gesture (the multiple value sound-sight-context: artifact array-core

implicit model and associative mechanism) is translated consistently and systematically.

(11) The *ground-model* for a work consists of groups of exercise strategies: one component of the strategy is embedded in the context or association definitions of the system itself, which in my use is defined as not only electronic system, alone, isolated, but the system in context of performance, in which the presentation is a gestural translation and transactional exercise of exchange and reflexive translation between *present/this, that/other, local/remote*: the layers present in the translations for performance consist of several levels of these subordinate models, resulting in parallel and interpenetrative layers of narrative sequences: the sequences are locked interdependently to the retrieval mechanism (electronic) and the intermediate reflexive component of the confrontation, as exercise, with the viewer-participant, audience, performer, system/performer, and artifact arrays/sensors (these are all reflexive interdependent layers).

(12) *The context-ground of convention manipulation specifies the exercise of strings of hierarchically grouped narratives* (serial scenario/narrative, plot strings functional at the convention level of performer, audience, the system, and the interaction mechanisms between these: these are conditionally parallel, and operate by their own strategic definition assignments): the mechanism of interaction is invariant within the defined context of any given performance: inherently, the interactions of performer/audience, performer isolation (against, toward, with), and system retrieval (response mechanism by mask, pattern, relief) operate by discrete separate systems: *hear-see* isolation, core-based in mutually assured and reinforced presence (present-other).

(13) A *performance* consists of the exercise of these layers with *targets* (the targets implicit in the memory strings, code associations, etc. of the reflexive memory retrieval mechanisms and the performance memory exercise, which always functions as context sensitive scanning, isolating, focusing, or masking), *masks* (for control and modulation), *arrays* (the artifact assemblies, or the retrieval layer contents and the mechanism of code and target association to these layers).

(14) The mechanisms to produce the requirements for the organization of a work, the continuous reserve sources of *memory, code, mask, target, artifact-array*, or *artifact array derivative*, remain invariant within the context of each system. There is no predictive or random development-goal or instant-spontaneous selective, additive choice (will) mechanism.

(15a) The context definitions are hierarchically related through arbitrary but invariant target demands: fixed, still.

(15b) Parameter isolation and reorganization are not utilized as mechanisms of variation: variation becomes, in this mechanism, an extractive isolate of translation, the shift between layer-levels of parallel fixtures and serial-string intersection or interjection of bursts or stills.

(16) The electronic mechanism is an exchange retrieval within the *invariant convention definition* of continuous selection: the convention manipulation procedure is *context limited memory retrieval*: the immediate, local mechanism of retrieval is a derivative of design (system formulation), change (input-output variables), and alternation (global orientation). There is *no* developmental additive strategy utilized in the specification and implementation of these operative mechanisms, which, as still reserves, in translation and transaction, involve a nonvolitional (selection), nonpurposive (strategy), and nonspontaneous (instant) mechanism in all modes of delivery or reflexive engagement.

(17) The memory and memory exercise reserves are conditionally grouped for implementation into categories related to access, persistence, and mechanism: long-term memory is encoded as a global system configuration and exists directly in the decisional strategies; short-term memory operates within the pattern and layer mask strategies. These reserves are translated as an unconditionally emergent floor-ground, the gesture components as ingressive and egressive, evoked and invoked.

(18) The system layer hierarchy is a *derivative* result of accumulative history models (everything done until then, everything arranged until then, everything available from the history of string events until that moment but predicted by rule always by that string and its selected *mask*). The system of artifacts comprises both concrete object-arrays and task-list object-array sequences, strategies, and procedures (transactional mimetic exercise in an *object array field*) which serve as *code markers* of the *narrative strings*.

Above and overleaf: Hunt's studio in his mother's home near Canton, Texas, ca. 1990.

II. System ground of Birome (ZONE): Cube, Birome (ZONE): Plane, and Birome (ZONE): Cube [frame]

(1) The performance-installation object-array proposes an interchange of content between a system physical presence as object and an information presence as object: both specifications are transparent and content-neutral.

(2) The arrangement subsumes the distances of content-object: no separation is imposed upon the participant/user/exerciser: the appearance is defined as a substantive embodiment of the whole.

(3) The presence of the object-array as an exercise object, without utilities, produces a directed interaction as slave-master with a byproduct of ethical discrimination (a sequence of distinction-exercises of reward-penalty and fulfillment-denial).

(4) The structure is implicit: the object-array arrangements are derivatives of the structure as object extensions of presence configured in such a way as not to identify the extensions as essences of *fulfillment* of the presence but to identify the extensions as *emanations* of the presence.

(5) The continuity, presence, and direction content-reserves specified for an object-array are equivalent information exchange targets: the artifact array of a performance-installation object presents systems of associations which are in themselves extensions.

(6) The distributed time-place appearance of features is a structural fulfillment, at once, of system global derivatives (implicit) and item-specific derivatives of some narrative goals (evoked and interactively engaged as skyring residue).

(7) The number-elements of the pattern components are transparently formatted by translation of frames of series of these number-elements into table-strings in correspondence with the mechanisms of the *Tarot* (a system of numbered playing card multiple level divination patterning), *Cabala* (a system of number-letter code correspondences), and *Enochian Watchtowers* (a system of number tables produced through angelic names devised through the skyring operations of John Dee with Edward Kelley).

The *Tarot* and the system of *Cabala* references are interpenetrated with the Dee *Watchtowers* through exchanged interlocks: the *Tarot* represents a system of "soft" divination mechanism. The *Cabala* employs a system of number significances and resultant paths produced by connecting correspondences related to the *Tree of Life* as subordinate number connections: these are used transparently as coherent and systematic codes for the arrangement of disposition of the content derivatives. The *Watchtowers* are number-sign systems arranged in rectangular tables: systematic movements in the tables produce series of angelic names and geometric configurations: movements of the names (letters, numbers) produce geometric configurations, or sigils of the magical names.

The interdependent and multiple-layer structure significances, the number translations, and the composite number systems are all used to produce an interlayered, multiple-plane interdependent system of significances translated as codes: the codes are used systematically and coherently as significant string groups in such a way as to produce a coherent language of information exchange: the surface-derivative features of the cards (their principal and prime number significances, the symbol and representational codes, including the historical and dramatic, narrative, or scenario content apparatus supporting each card) are used as *content-neutral* organizing mechanisms.

The sight-sound reserves, direct (present-local: not generated, not regenerated) and indirect (distant-remote: generated, regenerated), use derivative key-representations of many of these ensemble-patterns in deep reduction: the coding, sequence and arrangement of the surfaces of the incident-key components (sigil, *Tarot* content reduction derivative, *Watchtower* significance, or historical detail of the development of one of these traditional methods) are ultimately derived from the *Watchtower* table mechanisms: coding series are represented as connected systems in a manner similar to the sigil production in the *Watchtower* table arrangements in which geometric transformations of the sigils (by translation and/or rotation) produce derivative variations of the code series.

The content strings (sound, image) are categorized in such a way as to produce a continuous, ongoing reserve stream, each component of this stream defined by some characterizing feature and coded using the number-sigil mechanism: the interactive procedures (short-term memory exercises of comparison and mapping with feature detection) scan the codes through masks for retrieval pattern targets.

The memory system exercise extends in time: long- and short-term history monitor strings result in a delay and delay-variance action with respect to current participation: memory and retrieval in operation by this mechanism reinforce the sense of separation of categories: present: other-action: reaction (as dissociate and distinct categories, interlocked through the code mechanisms) – known: unknown – present: (local – immediate) – remote (distant

– delayed): the separation is organized as a continuous variation of threshold between remote and local systems.

Some derivative distinctions are coded to systematically index appropriate layers to the serial image stream. The code ranges are grouped as core-reserves, serving as object goals for the production of other layers of derivatives: each sound-image procedure is devised as a unique fulfillment of a code layer type or level of derivative of another code type: the table matrices (*Tarot*, *Watchtowers*, sigil operators translated to game strategies of *Rosicrucian chess*, a multilevel variation of conventional chess) provide index classifications (interdependent layer significances through number, position, orientation): the arrangement of layers is configured at the time of generation: the retrieval mechanism then operates on the index identifier transparently; subsequent or successive type derivatives can be introduced, modified, or extended: the mechanism of retrieval and the flood of attention points (the retrieval pattern and stream orientation) are content-transparent: the content ground and narrative string resultant are articulated globally by isolates of the string material which serve as flags of retrieval patterns and interaction (signal-semaphore).

The object representations (sound-sight) are all defined as derivatives of a common ground in which each object representation is a reductive gesture, at once reflective of a personal idiosyncratic history and a propositional object core for the provocation of participant-viewer-user (each sight-sound gesture is devised as an attention and memory exercise point, continuously occurring as a flood steam). The object and concrete object narratives occur as skyring streams available only as correlation and layers strings; they are not subject to personal identification and reorganization within their characterizing features by a participant-viewer-user (system-other [heaven:earth]).

III.   Interaction System Procedure: general technical description

(1) The sight-sound strings are arranged as a continuous sequence; a single frame entry-exit marker separates and defines subcomponents of the sequences. The material is arranged across at least two retrieval mechanisms in such a way as to allow search within one range of codes while another retrieval source is used for output. The subcomponents are layer and sequence priority coded. The codes are based on standard *SMPTE* timecode format. The layer and sequence arrangements are reconfigurable for each performance or use by reorganization of the codes (to accommodate

various performance sources, different system configurations of monitor and retrieval devices, etc.).

(2) The content strings are manipulated by translation of a group of monitor signals which generate continuously updated pattern masks from the history of activity of a performance action. The performance action is monitored by detectors: several detection configurations are used: differential sound detection (microphones or contact tremor-velocity detectors are used in pairs, the differences are used as monitor sources [swept filter peak sample detection]); video input (the scanned scene is analyzed at a group of points and successive frames produce a pattern of average movement and movement direction [video field peak white samples]); infrared or microwave scanning (rate of change detectors produce a series of values related to the average sample to sample movement and direction [peak rate of change detection]).

(3) The results of the detection are arranged as maps of values which represent the state changes through adjacently compiled pairs of sample moments taken during a performance: the maps are continuously updated and compared at a rate which is controlled by the rate of average activity (the sample rate adapts to the bandwidth): the differences produce the activity monitor sequences.

(4) The activity monitor sequences are used as control signals: the signals are formatted in such a way as to provide one of a pair of control statements to a decisional convention. This convention is based upon game strategies (*Rosicrucian chess, Tarot*). The game mechanisms are unchanged throughout a performance. The current layer-string code (*SMPTE* timecode location) is sampled and formatted (as a variable rate, continuously updated history string) in the same way as the activity monitor sequences are used for the other control string input to the decisional game mechanism. Results of the game strategy employed are formatted to produce a sequence of search codes for the audio-video strings.

(5) The retrieval mechanism is variably time dependent: the action of each retrieval or search produces a delay which depends upon the storage medium, the search strategy, and monitor code string. A system of variable thresholds for addresses of various layers is generated by comparing the immediate location with the request location; remote layers have higher thresholds, local layers have lower thresholds. As the request string of search and output actions is continuous, some layers are deleted from the output and search strings.

(6) The search-output code requests which have been serviced are accumulated and compared against the current lists of requests:

previously executed code string ranges are selectively deleted from the current string of requests. The rate of update of the request string is variable and depends upon the average rate of change of the retrieval-output and monitor string samples (faster successive requests produce faster successive updates).

(7) All the principal system action states have direct control inputs available (a specific address or monitor state can be directly and independently inserted or requested), including a set of basic global commands (start, reset, stop, impose search or output control range limits, impose global or local time limits).

THE FINLEY/HUNT REPORT
Karen Finley

Jerry Hunt and Karen Finley met at a new music festival in Rotterdam in December 1988. The following year, they embarked on a series of performances and collaborations, most notably *The Finley/Hunt Report* and an unrealized television opera based on the life of Lyndon B. Johnson that was cut short by Hunt's passing in 1993. *The Finley/Hunt Report* premiered at the Kitchen in New York in 1992 and was loosely based on NBC's *The Huntley-Brinkley Report*, an evening news program featuring two news anchors that aired from 1956 until 1970. Over the course of their collaboration, Finley famously became embroiled in a censorship scandal with the National Endowment for the Arts. The agency, then under siege by the Republican party and culturally conservative religious groups for its acceptance of sexually explicit art, cited Finley's frequent use of nudity as grounds for denying her a grant. The fact that Hunt sat on the NEA panel that had approved the grant only exacerbated the controversy. This final section of the book collects material related to collaboration between the two artists, including a proposal for their LBJ opera, photographs and ephemera from *The Finley/Hunt Report*, Hunt's letter to the NEA in response to agency chairman John Frohnmayer's conflict of interest allegations against the panels, and a new interview with Karen Finley about her creative relationship with Hunt. The interview is accompanied by two new paintings from Finley.

Karen Finley, *Free to Love*, 2021, mixed media on music notebook, 9 × 12 in.

Karen Finley, *Even Birds Giggle*, 2021, mixed media on music notebook, 9 × 12 in.

SPIRIT DRAWING — JERRY HUNT

Tell me how you are?
Are you fond of cats,
the kitties and bitties?
Say hello to Stephen who I
love and adore — adoration
his calm, sense of humor
and sex appeal
Tell me where you are in
your art & being —
I never want for a piece of bread
but a thistle whistle
will thrill me to the end.
Mom & Dad are here
with me — the kids and
even birds giggle
If my life had meaning
it was to be free to love.

—Karen Finley

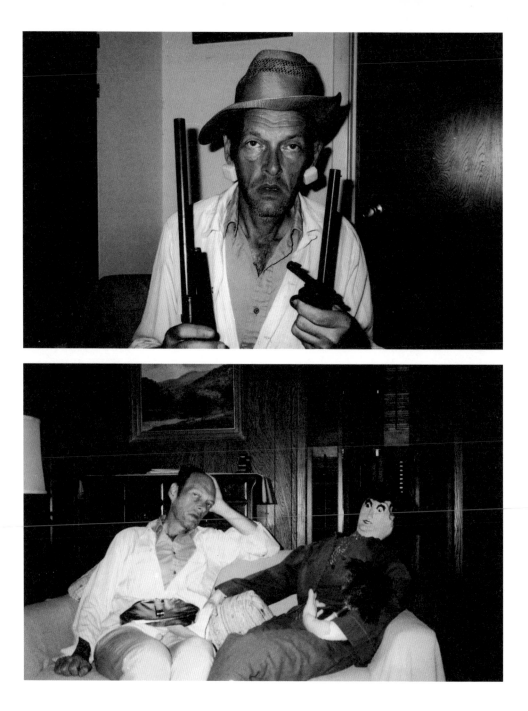

Hunt posing with guns and a doll, ca. 1990–91. Photographer unknown.

LAWRENCE KUMPF

Can you describe your first encounter with Hunt, or his first encounter with you, in 1988 at a new music festival in Rotterdam where you both performed? What attracted you to each other's work and how would you describe your practice in relation to his?

KAREN FINLEY

That's a really interesting question. I met Jerry first in Rotterdam, as you said, at a new music festival, where there were many different people. I think that it was just meeting each other. When we met each other, even before we were performing, we liked each other. We had an instant attraction to each other. We both had wry senses of humor, we took things seriously but not *seriously*. And I think that I reminded him of one of his friends from when he was growing up, too. I reminded him of someone.

He was also interested in expanding his work, and he knew that I was also working within music. I had recorded some work with Mark Kamins, dance-beaty music, you know, techno music. That interested him. We had conversations about that, about music—it was in those conversations. It wasn't something like this immediate light bulb goes on. It's just, we liked each other. And people would do that, and still do that: you meet someone, you think about how you can continue being in connection with the person. I think that was behind it as well.

TYLER MAXIN

And so who initiated the collaboration, or how did it come about?

KF To tell you the truth, there wasn't something like *all of a sudden*—it isn't a contract like that. It was more that we were talking, thinking, and things happened together. It was sort of a mutual situation. Also, we were always being invited to places to perform. Somehow, then, the first place where we were going to be performing was New Music America. I can't even remember if I was invited or he was, but somehow that came together. Then later we went to the Kitchen, where we did *The Finley/Hunt Report*.

TM Your first performance with Hunt, at Merkin Concert Hall in New York, was part of New Music America [on November 12, 1989] on an evening billed as a "computer music extravaganza." Kyle Gann, in the *Village Voice*, called the collaboration "inspired" and described the performance as each of you doing what you do separately, but together. Can you describe these performances from your perspective?

KF   These performances, basically, [involved] musical texts that I had already created. They're texts from performances—poems and verses. We were working on them, he would be accompanying and also doing solos. We were sometimes constructing it almost like in jazz, where each person would take a turn doing some of the work. So, it was an experiment. It was an improvisation as well, even though we had worked on it. That piece wasn't an evening-length work, it was a shorter performance.

LK   Sure, the program was on a bill with Leah Singer and Elliott Sharp, Steve Coleman, Paul Lansky, Mark Waldrep, and Todd Winkler. The works performed were titled "Why the Veal Calf Can't Walk?" and "Babalon (String)"—were these two separate pieces? Was the former the title of the piece you were performing and the latter the title of Jerry's composition?

KF   Yes. Oh, but see, it wasn't always like that, in that way. He would be accompanying me with things, and then maybe I would be accompanying him, too. But we didn't really look at it as accompanying, we looked at it as, maybe they're happening simultaneously. But, as well, we felt that there was a sense of humor in it, because we were parodying the idea of accompaniment. Jerry was a trained, classical pianist, but he also had, in his earlier career, accompanied singers or vocalists.

We found it rather humorous that the kind of text we were making was innovating on, being experimental with, the idea of performing these classic traditions in musical . . . or pop tropes. We were kind of deconstructing that, and that interested us very much. That was very important to Jerry, because of his training, in that he was breaking out and rebelling from those traditions or standards. That he was trying to—I wouldn't say break out of—but he was trying to contribute to that form. We were more like scientists in a laboratory, but we both were in on the joke, even though the subject matter we were dealing with was serious.

LK You've described working in a burlesque house in college and how that impacted your own performance practice. And of course Jerry, as a teenager, worked as the pianist in strip clubs in Dallas. Your description of the way the performers could generate so much attention around an elbow, or other seemingly inconsequential parts of the body, and dramatize that, somehow reminded us of Hunt's use of wands and gestures to attract attention or create a momentary collective focus during the course of his fairly abstract performances. Hunt was certainly interested in charismatic figures. I'm wondering if you could talk about your relationship with night-life and popular art forms as they relate to your practice?

KF Jerry had worked as a piano player in burlesque houses, and he in fact did work with Jack Ruby, who was his boss. We had that interest—we both had worked in other kinds of performance, for economics. And it was *economy*—I mean, I worked at Danceteria and Area because I needed a job. And then sometimes one's work in those areas, those clubs within the art world, influenced the art-making, too.

LK In a 1988 interview with Richard Schechner, you described your process then as being "medium"-like, often built off intensive bouts of associative writing, and said that you had been interested in a "psychic type of work." Hunt was also interested in using spiritual and intuitive, "automatic" processes. Did this come up in your conversations? Did you share particular reference points in that area?

KF Yes, all the time.

LK Could you describe any particular shared points of reference in that area?

KF I think it was just that we had a mutual interest there, and we didn't have to prove or justify or validate it. And that I didn't see him as being an eccentric person. I found him normal. And I think he felt that way with me, so there's a comfort in our way, that we weren't the exceptions, we didn't really have to be proving the ways that we created.

TM   How did the project at the Kitchen come about? Can you talk about the development of *The Finley/Hunt Report* [June 11–14, 1992]?

KF   Well, at that time, there was a lot that was going on in my life from . . . well, we applied for this grant, first, and that grant then also had difficulties, you see, because of the NEA issue.[1] But we were interested in taking some of these texts and creating a musical score for them, and I think it's because we were using this as kind of a case study that eventually we were interested in making an opera, or some type of musical. So we started with this format: I would be presenting texts, we would go over the texts and the music, and then we would create. A lot of it was over the phone. I went over to Texas and worked with him, too, and I think he even came to New York, too. That's how we collaborated.

TM   And so the work is based around parodies of television talk shows, and you were also—

KF   I wouldn't say that. That was sort of like our joke. You have to write something, you know, it was a parody because at that time, talk shows . . . but it wasn't a parody. We thought that it would be funny if we could imagine that this was the kind of show you would be having—that we could be the band for David Letterman, for example—or if we were to have our own show. We were looking into the future of what entertainment could look like. But it wasn't a parody in this *Saturday Night Live* way. It was a conceptual process, or conceptual leaning towards people to end that divide of popular entertainment. That's what we were doing. That was the claim in calling it

1   For more on the NEA controversy, see Lawrence Kumpf and Tyler Maxin, "Transmissions from the Pleroma," on page 60 of this volume; for a detailed, first-person account from the artist, see Karen Finley, *A Different Kind of Intimacy: The Collected Writings of Karen Finley* (New York: Thunder's Mouth Press, 2000), 102–5.

LETTER TO THE NEA

Jerry Hunt
Rt. 1, Box 240
Canton, Texas 75103
(214)-848-4324

August 1990

As one of the panel members invited to serve on the most recent Inter-Arts: New Forms panel of the NEA, the events surrounding the denial of several selected Inter-Arts: New Forms grants have become a matter of personal injury and misrepresentation, since these efforts have taken the form of an indirect assault on the artists, using false allegation and allusion about the panel, the panel members, and the panel process. This is insulting to me personally, and to many other panel members as well. In response to my letters to the National Endowment staff and director requesting some explanation of why these charges by allusion and innuendo have not been challenged and refuted by the NEA and the director of the NEA, John Frohnmayer, I have received only a recounting of the same vague implications and allusions about the Inter-Arts panel and panel members, some selected artists and institutions, and a short statement thanking me for my valuable contribution to the NEA panel process. There has not been any evidence presented to support any accusation, only implication and suggestion by association. The copies of press material compiled by the NEA and sent to me recently by Loris Bradley, a senior specialist at the NEA Inter-Arts program, eloquently document the irresponsible program of charges and accusations conducted to malign the panel members indirectly or directly.

All of the various allegations do not change or counter the actual facts of the Inter-Arts selection process: the panel for the Inter-Arts: New Forms category was called and assembled according to the protocols and standards set up by the NEA, and all of the decisions were made in a manner which completely followed the procedures of the NEA designed to eliminate any possible conflict of interest in decision, discussion, or voting. When I was invited to serve on this panel, I called the Inter-Arts staff and specifically questioned my selection because of the possible appearance of my name as a collaborator on three proposals which I thought might be submitted to the New Forms Category. (I had discussed submitting three collaborations with three different artists during the previous year.) I was told the NEA staff had reviewed one proposal, a collaboration with Karen Finley, submitted by the Kitchen—a presenting organization in New York City—in which my name appeared, that this proposal in no way disqualified me from service on the panel, and that if all panel members who were similarly involved in a proposal were disqualified, it would be impossible to assemble representative peer review panels.

I saw the procedures for eliminating conflict of interest followed in every detail. Every aspect of every possible conflict in each proposal was eliminated by computer editing, materials selection, and panel assignment; every aspect of discussion and voting was transcribed by audio recording and written record; panelists were absent during all discussion or voting on any aspect of any proposal in which they were associated in any way, directly or indirectly. I never received any information about the status of the Kitchen proposal during or after the panel meetings, either from NEA staff or other panel members. Suddenly, weeks later, after the refusal of funding for grants to a group of four artists recommended by a separate panel in another separate category, proposals involving work of several of these same artists which had been approved by the Inter-Arts selection were countered by arbitrarily contrived after-the-fact allegations and innuendo about the selection process.

It was wrong, and remains wrong, to arbitrarily put a group of grants into suspicion after the fact, using only vague allegations of conflict as a justification for targeting these specific grants. No one should have the right to bring charges about the process of any public institution in this manner: if procedural difficulties exist, either unintentionally or as a matter of policy in the NEA, then these are difficulties which should affect all of the grants, both those whose funding was recommended by the panel and those whose funding was denied: the same process affected all of the proposals in the same manner, using the same procedures.

It is deeply troubling that John Frohnmayer has not defended the procedures of review that the NEA has found acceptable over a period of years. If real procedural difficulties can be documented at some level of the NEA review, then all grant funding should be suspended and the entire process evaluated by an independently appointed group of investigators. If the procedures of the NEA are flawed or "perceived" as flawed, there are legal, proper, and publicly accountable mechanisms available for the investigation and correction of these flaws. It seems clear to me and many other observers that no decision on the part of the recent Inter-Arts panel could justify either this attack on the artists whose projects were denied, or the campaign of allusion to a suddenly discovered conflict of interest which has been selectively focused on and targeted to a tiny number of grants. Any of the Inter-Arts: New Forms panel members could be held up to public suspicion on the same arbitrary charges of "perceived" conflict of interest about any of the other grants which have not received selective attention or funding.

Rather than providing evidence or documentation of the mechanisms of conflict of interest which the existing policies of the NEA could allow or perhaps promote, this program of after-the-fact attack, using implication and allusion without addressing any factual supporting evidence, has exposed and/or created the suspicion of special interest manipulation of the NEA for the apparent purpose of the imposition of some idiosyncratic political agenda or temporary fantasy invention of some individuals, groups, or politicians who wish to impose their vision of moral, social, or political purity on the arts.

The actions of the NEA and the National Council have been and continue to be inexcusable: I am bound by a sense of personal integrity to counter this sprinkling of attacks by direct or indirect association throughout the accounts of these matters, and will continue to refuse to be used as a tool in the agenda of attack on the artists and institutions targeted for this selective abuse. It is no consolation to me to have incidental personal assurances of faith in my personal integrity tucked by officials of the NEA and the National Council into statements of distrust of the institution I was asked to serve and served in good faith. The actions of the NEA and the National Council make me a liar and/or a tool of political manipulation. I am not the first and won't participate as the latter.

Jerry Hunt
Canton, Texas
August 1990

Program for *The Finley/Hunt Report* at the Kitchen, New York, June 11–14, 1992.

Contact sheet of Hunt and Finley performing *The Finley/Hunt Report* at the Kitchen, New York, June 11–14, 1992. Photos: Dona Ann McAdams.

Hunt and Finley performing *The Finley/Hunt Report* at the Kitchen, New York, June 11–14, 1992. Photo: Dona Ann McAdams.

Stills from video components used on the set of *The Finley/Hunt Report*, 1992.

a talk show. We thought that was very funny. Jerry always had different levels of conversation going on, his own world going on. So, we would have our own kind of jokes or our own kind of narrative about it, because we just thought it was very, very funny.

LK   Jerry also had an interest in television as a means of distributing his work. In the '70s he created abstract video works with David Dowe for public television, and your unrealized collaborative opera on LBJ was meant to be broadcast on TV like Robert Ashley's *Perfect Lives* (1977–83). Did the fact that you were also appearing on talk shows at the time influence *The Hunt/Finley Report*? Was there a shared interest in mass media that informed this project?

KF   Not exactly. I mean, if one's own life and experience go into something, yes—but it wasn't something clinical, saying, "Oh, I did this work in the '70s, and I did this experiment. I'm going to bring that into this." I think that as artists you bring your life's knowledge and experience into your practice and your collaborations. So I trusted whatever he had. I'm sure he brought that with him. I had a TV show that I was a host of, *Bad Music Videos* (1986). Doing things with artists' video, and with artists working within music and in media, was part of our work. We had an awareness of it, but it wasn't as if there was some moment where there's a realization. It was just that we knew that both of us had a lot of different experiences, and that's also what interested us in working together.

LK   I'm curious about the LBJ project you had been working on at the time of his death. Jerry writes about it as an "opera for home viewing." Did you go down to Canton to work on that as well?

KF   Well, we had started to work on it and we had the outline. When I visited him we went to the Sixth Floor Museum at Dealey Plaza together. I had an interest in—and later I did the work on—Jackie Kennedy. I think I might have even brought up other artists' work that had worked with [JFK] . . . because [Hunt] had known Jack Ruby.
    [The trip focused on] things we would be working on next. But also this idea of taking formats and kind of deconstructing

LBJ PROPOSAL
Karen Finley and Jerry Hunt

This proposed work, *LBJ*, is a new television form, a documentary opera: the work is conceived as a ninety-minute program directly created as a video documentary opera to be presented for home viewing.

Through the plastic transformational characteristics of current video presentation and editing, the work will attempt to produce a composite form of new musical theater, fundamentally transforming the usual separations between operatic music theater presentation time, documentary narrative time, and commentary-document narrative time: the conceptual goal of the work is to produce, through the cross-coupling of the convention formalities of presentation in documentary, entertainment, and commentary television presentation, a specialized and transparent translational form of hearing/viewing experience which will share characterizing qualities of television presentation as information display, graphics, action, song animation, and immediate information source screens. Narrative episodes from the life experience of LBJ will be formally constructed using three forms of episodes: aria, tableaux, and commentary/document. Each episode form will use a dedicated technical, musical, and presentational component associated both formally and historically with the episode characteristics. The approximately seventeen episodes are roughly divided among a sequence of historical source periods: 1) birth/early days 2) Texas/life/career 3) Washington experience 4) assassination 5) war years 6) retirement/Texas 7) death. All of the event moments will be based in actual historical records, documentary video or film, photographs, diaries, and biographical and autobiographical material. All production work will be done in Texas to take full advantage of the materials and sources available, including ranch, Texas Hill Country, and LBJ Library location recording.

The source material of the work treats LBJ as an objective historical figure whose life experiences reflect the current complex of American social and moral values, mythologies, and aspirations. A systematic and structural program of source material will be presented in the three episode varieties consisting of period-based transformations of images, sound, and text. Each characterization will carry a unique affective and effective content sign, consolidated in the arias, each of which will be framed as a high relief focus element against one or more contiguous or overlapping tableaux (represented through video animation documentary source material) or commentary/documentary material (represented through audio/video composite assembly). The characterization development will use two principals (song/speech/action roles) appearing in role-transformation as paired, focused, and contrasted characteristics: the unifying characterization of LBJ will be displayed in a sound-vision high-relief setting of contrasts built around a conversational approach to selected historical situations (using singer/speaker/actor pairs as representatives) of LBJ and the important formative and career personalities of his public and private life: the narrative material will use, as a content-unifying force, available histories and records for Rebekah Baines Johnson and Lady Bird Johnson, presented theatrically as active and responsive agents.

The production and performance group for this work will consist of individuals who have had extensive experience in contemporary performance, music, theater, television, and electronic sound and vision production.

them, whether it was the TV or the opera. At first, we were going to be doing something with Nixon, then it was going to be LBJ and I was going to be playing his wife, Lady Bird. But we were going to do things where we would be reversing roles, too. We had scenes we were thinking about in the opera—we would have sets with wildflowers, there was going to be video, things like that. But it was just really in the beginning stages.

LK   One of the things that's interesting about the project is that it highlights Hunt's "offstage" persona, the way his friends knew him, in a way that he had not done in his own performances. We've done so many interviews where his friends and collaborators say, "I had no idea what he was doing on stage." Part of the project of this book and exhibition is to unpack a little more of his creative process as an artist. I'm wondering if you can offer any thoughts or reflections on Jerry, onstage and off?

KF   Well, I think Jerry knew what he was doing, and it actually kind of annoyed me when I . . . I mean, I didn't know him for all that long, just a very few years. But in our friendship we weren't always talking about music and about art, we were talking about daily life things, whether it's food or his cats or just the world and politics. It was just being together. And that's really important for artists to do, too.

I was annoyed sometimes when I would see the followers, the Jerry-followers, who thought, *oh, they couldn't understand it, he was so wonderful.* I didn't really see him in that way, as being eccentric. I felt he was creating this system with computers and his work. I thought he was very organized. He was very prepared. He knew what he was trying to do—to contribute to the form of experimental music and performance. And that he really wanted to be—and I know that you didn't want to be using this word—a shaman, having this spiritual way of leading the music going into this space. And he wanted to have chance be part of his work, too.

I think he also wanted to disorient the idea of the male within music. Looking at the male on the stage, whether it would be in musical groups—at the time most musicians would be male, in the way that you looked at them and their body, whether it be a sex symbol or within the groups—it was kind of an organization. He wanted to play with that. I felt that that was something that he was really trying to do as a form of a rebellion, also in terms of gender, or even in terms of expectations of desire or performativity. To me, it wasn't something that was so mysterious, but that he had an intention to do.

In his work, he was very strong. He was a very strong person. I learned so much from him, in the way that he protected his art and that he worked for it. And he was very loyal to the people that he loved. He had such a loyalty, and such a commitment. I was so moved by his commitment to the form, the experimental practice he was doing. He was so disciplined with his practice and all he strove to be—thinking of new forms of innovation. I still am moved. And then he was so gentle. He was a very, very, very, very gentle person, with such a wicked sense of humor.

PARTNERS
Stephen Housewright

The following text is an excerpt from Stephen Housewright's *Partners*, a memoir originally self-published in 1995 and reprinted by Blank Forms Editions in 2021. This final section of the book details the couple's final days together, recounting Hunt's illness, his "last performance," his cancer diagnosis, and, obliquely, his suicide.

As Jerry frequently pointed out, I've always been adept at seeing what I want to see. This "selective inattention" may have served us well during Jerry's illness: he sometimes had to prove to me he couldn't do what I thought he could, and, on occasion, he happily failed. After his hospital stay in Kaufman, I began to see more clearly, more honestly, how sick he was, and the way other people reacted to his appearance helped me—forced me—to bring his condition into focus.

The visiting nurse came four or five times to monitor Jerry's vital signs and listen to his chest. He was eager for her visits, and she always managed to allay some of his anxiety by reminding him that recuperating from pneumonia takes a long time, especially for people with COPD. Each time she came, she said she thought he was moving air more efficiently in his lungs.

Her calls would begin with my telling her, as we walked to the house from her car, how anxious and despondent Jerry was, and her visits would end along the same route, with my thanking her for her encouragement and concern and for how generous she had been with her time (she always had to telephone her next client to tell them she'd be a little late). I couldn't help notice, however, on these trips to the driveway, that she wasn't as encouraging to me as she had been to Jerry. She later told me that she knew he was dying the first time she came.

Jerry made a trip to the library with me one Sunday afternoon. We had taken full advantage of the medical research materials there over the years: the physicians' drug manuals and the accompanying CDs, which included articles from medical journals and reference sources, had helped us learn about the side effects of some of the medicine Jerry was taking. We also gained a fuller understanding of the nature and likely course of Jerry's disease.

I don't know everything Jerry investigated that day, but he did read extensively about antibiotics. Several times during the afternoon, he came to my floor to have some coffee and rest at the table in the staff area. As always, my colleagues and friends got a kick out of seeing him; they'd all told me again and again that they'd never met anyone like him. Even as ill as he was, he was outrageous, ranting on about doing his own bronchoscopy and about having Dr. Jack Kevorkian (notorious at the time for having helped terminally ill patients commit suicide) as his "personal physician." When he came out to the service desk area, he would so command all our attention that the library patrons just had to stand and wait their turn.

After the hilarity would come the questions: Is he serious? Is he getting better? Everyone was obviously concerned, and I look back now on a year filled with the kindnesses of every type that they showed me, from volunteering on short notice to work in my place when I had to be with Jerry to knowing just when to ask about him and when not to.

One expression of thoughtfulness especially touched me. Yolanda was on her way to work one day and spotted a chair on wheels someone had left on the side of the road. She had her husband pull over, and they loaded it into their pickup and brought it in to offer to me. I had been talking about how hard it was to find a chair for Jerry that was both comfortable and would allow him, without getting up, to roll from the computer or the synthesizer to his desk and back. Our needs were on her mind.

The Humanities Division gave me a surprise birthday party: a complete lunch and a birthday cake, all beautifully served on two large tables. Shortly after we'd sat down to eat, Jerry called from Canton to tell me that he had unexpectedly run out of the medicine he used in his breathing machine and that he was going to Canton (seven miles from our house) to get the prescription refilled. He would call me again, he said, when he got back, so I would know he'd made the trip all right. I begged him to call our neighbor, Garland, who I assured him would be glad to run the errand for him. *No*, he insisted; he'd be careful, he'd take his time. I was extremely upset. Jerry hadn't driven alone in weeks. In addition to his shortness of breath and overall weakness, he was taking powerful antibiotics and an array of analgesics.

My panic was such that I don't remember how much, if anything, I told my friends about the nature of the call, although everyone knew it had been from Jerry. Brian had devised a birthday scavenger hunt for me, and I went off to follow his witty clues from book to book until I located the treasure: a box of Indian sweets that Tarlika had brought. Shortly after I returned, Jerry called to tell me that he was home and had made the trip fine; he had only gone off the road once. Whether or not I had been able to disguise my anxiety, I am sure I made no attempt to conceal my giddy relief.

Having Judy here was a joy and a comfort, although it hurt to see how shocked she was when she saw Jerry. She fell into our simple routine, helping with chores in such unobtrusive ways that I only realized all she had done much later. The best thing was the three of us to sit and visit, reminiscing about the adolescence we shared while watching *The X-Files*, *Mad About You*, and the British sitcoms that gave Jerry some diversion during the last weeks. Judy listened to what Jerry had to say about his illness and what it was stealing from his life and his future, and she offered her loving sympathy without a trace of false optimism. She knew then as I do now that he often told her things in order for me to hear them.

As our joint birthday party approached, Jerry began to doubt that he would be up to attending. Certainly, everyone would understand if he were not able to make it, but I pressured him a little because I believed going would be good for his spirits. It was to be a happy evening, a celebration—almost twenty longtime friends would be there.

Weeks earlier, I had written the poet Mark Doty to ask if he would record his poem "The Wings" from *My Alexandria* (1993) so that I could play it at the party as my gift to Jerry. He agreed, and he sent me a tape of a reading of the poem in Provincetown—a reading he dedicated to Jerry and me. Before the tape arrived, however, I had decided not to use it that night. As I watched Jerry grow worse, I began to feel that the poem would be too wrenching for an occasion that I wanted, above all, to be a joyous one. I did read the poem to Jerry myself one night after Judy had left, and I listened to Mark's tape, alone, on Jerry's birthday.

Dressing and leaving the house had become very difficult for Jerry; he wore robes around the clock unless he had to go out. I could see we were going to be late for the party, so I called ahead. As soon as we entered Paul and Oz's home, Jerry was led into the living room and seated beside Judy, and Oz asked me to accompany her to the dining room to assign places at the long table. I shuffled the name cards she'd made and placed them in such a way as to separate couples while she followed along behind me and made a reference list to post at the door. As I worked, I became aware of how quiet the living room had grown as everyone took in the change they'd seen in Jerry and strained to hear him.

Jerry and I were seated at the head of the table, in front of the beveled windows that I'd looked through for so many years—they were behind the piano that had been moved in for the Sunday afternoon concerts. The Lebanese food was delicious: thyme pie, baba ghanoush, falafel, and various meat dishes with white wine. My matchmaking must have been successful because everyone seemed to be engaged in lively conversation.

When we'd all just about finished eating, Jerry began to speak to the group. (He himself hadn't eaten much, and even I was too nervous, too distracted, to be able to concentrate on the food.) He talked a little about what a good life we'd had, how lucky we'd been in one another (in spite of my "meanness"), and in our friends. And then, he made his way around the table, addressing remarks first to one person and then another, recalling events from years back or mentioning special traits that he had always appreciated about the individual. He regretted that Houston and Jill weren't with us. It was as though, in his steady gaze at each guest, he shone a light on the uniqueness—and value to him—of each relationship. Because his voice was so weak and his breathing difficulty forced him to speak so slowly, we all hushed any table noises to be able to hear.

There was a moment of relief and laughter when Jerry described a certain period of time and happened to mention lava lamps. "Jerry—wait just a minute," Paul interrupted, jumping up from his seat and rushing out of the room. And he returned with one, a gift for us from Oz and him and David and Norma McManaway.

When I talked with some of these friends later about the monologue Jerry delivered that night, several of them characterized it as a "piece," as Jerry's last performance. It had been extraordinary, the way it wove together sentiments, ideas, and personalities in the most unpredictable and yet exactly right manner. As I listened to him, looking into the beams of his eyes and stealing occasional glimpses at their targets down the table, I felt again that familiar excitement that had always come from the way he could heighten my perception of the world, enthralling me by his extraordinary way of seeing it. Just as he'd done this for me for thirty-five years, from that day on the blacktop outside the junior high school cafeteria when he demanded to know the secret the green door was keeping, so had he done it for almost as long for most of those people listening to him now.

There could have been no better celebration—and no more fitting memorial—because Jerry himself led it.

Dessert was served in the game room, but Jerry soon came up to me to say that he had begun to feel bad and that he thought we should leave. Oz packed some food for us to take along, and Judy and others gathered up the gifts we'd received and loaded the car out front. We got Jerry settled in the front seat, and I noticed Toni standing on the front lawn staring at Jerry with tears in her eyes. I went over to her and told her something I had wanted to tell her for years: that Jerry had told me her appreciation of his talent and her support of his work at SMU, almost thirty years ago, had helped his parents accept the fact that they had a homosexual son because they saw from the way she regarded him that his sexual orientation would not be an obstacle to success.

* * *

We had reached our second goal, but just barely. Jerry continued to feel worse as the evening wore on, and around midnight he asked me to take him to the emergency room of the Kaufman hospital. We supposed that the antibiotics he was taking for the pneumonia weren't working, and the young doctor on duty that night agreed that that might be the case. After examining Jerry's records, however, he talked very frankly with Jerry about the possibility that there was more making him feel bad than just pneumonia. He changed the prescription for antibiotics and released Jerry to return home shortly after daybreak.

I began to see a change in Jerry's emotional state after the party. Where he had been despondent, even depressed before, he was now often agitated and sometimes desperate. He could not sleep in the bed at all, and he got what little rest he did by putting his head down on his desk. The nights were long for him, and he seemed to want to keep me with him late. The last few mornings Judy was here, he called me on the intercom at dawn to ask me to come over. After she left, I set up a cot in the living room of the brick house and slept there to be close to him, leaving the bed available to him whenever he might feel like trying to lie down.

He wanted me to take him to Dr. Harris's office the day before Judy's departure, and she repeated what the resident at Kaufman had told him. Jerry had been taking antibiotics so long that he had developed a bad case of thrush, and he was feeling worse and worse in spite of all the medication. Dr. Harris asked him if he would let her set up an appointment with a pulmonary specialist in Mesquite to discuss a bronchoscopy, and Jerry agreed. He had to know now, he said, if he had cancer.

I took Judy to the airport the next day. She had done so much for us during the week she was here, and I was able to work a day or two more than I would otherwise have been because she offered to stay with Jerry. I know it meant a lot to him to see how concerned she was for me and how close we are. And it was good for me to see the two of them renew their friendship as they sat talking or watching TV—just as they had when we were all teenagers, and I left them to spend a couple of weeks with my aunt in Kilgore. I waited for Judy in the car while she told Jerry goodbye. When she got in, she said, "Well, that was hard."

We saw Dr. Zevallos the next week, on the day before Thanksgiving. He told us pretty much what the other two specialists had, but he admitted that what he saw on the X-rays did look like a tumor. Jerry asked if it were cancer, what could be done. Dr. Zevallos told us that there was some chance that the tumor (or tumors) might respond to radiation and chemotherapy—we could talk about that after the bronchoscopy—but that such treatments wouldn't make Jerry feel better and might not even prolong his life by much.

Jerry was very frank with Dr. Zevallos, as he had been with all the other doctors he had seen. He was interested in the quality of life—merely adding days was without meaning if his life was without meaning. "We've had a wonderful life together," I said. To avoid a long delay from the upcoming holidays, the bronchoscopy was scheduled and performed that afternoon. Dr. Zevallos came to the waiting room and told me that yes, it was cancer. He said it was in both lungs as well as in the esophagus, and there was some involvement with the vocal cords. "Well, that's it, then," I said. He mentioned again that some radiation might help, but I got the feeling that he didn't really believe it would.

When they let me into Jerry's room, he was sitting up straight in his paisley hospital gown, the color good in his cheeks and his eyes unusually wide open and bright. The nurse asked him if he wanted a soft drink, and he replied he'd split a Coke with me. "It wasn't so bad. Actually, I don't remember much about it," he said. It was a pleasure sitting there with him, drinking our drink, and enjoying the illusion the drugs loaned us that everything was OK.

It wasn't until we were halfway home that he asked me what the doctor had said. I told him everything.

We had an ice storm that night, and the lights were off for eight hours. Jerry was frantic, even though I had brought over a large kerosene stove from the barn house, and we had plenty of kerosene lamps, candles, and flashlights. He had me call the electric cooperative every hour or so, and I was told each time that all their crews were out and working as fast as they could.

On Thanksgiving Day, he dictated a letter to Steve Peters, the producer of the Nonsequitur album. He went over with me the notes he had made earlier about how to edit the audiotapes for that CD as well as the videotape for the *Hemisphere* laser disc. I helped him set up two mics in the bedroom, and we put an assortment of sound-making devices on a card table at the foot of the bed: bells, rattles, metal and plastic objects, and sticks to beat them with. While I monitored the audio levels in the study, Jerry created one of the soundtracks for *Haramand Plane*. Later that afternoon, he showed me a list he'd made of the composers and performers he believed would promote his work. That night, we called Judy and her family and told them about the results of the bronchoscopy. I heard Jerry tell my older niece, Jenny, that he only had a few more days and that they should all help me because I'd need them for the next few months. (Jamie later offered to come back to live with me.)

We decided it was time to call Bob, and we asked him to come up the next day. He had a hard time believing the bronchoscopy results; he didn't think Jerry was that sick. But when he arrived Friday afternoon and saw Jerry, he was convinced. The three of us talked a long time Friday night, sitting in the living room and looking over at the TV from time to time. "These last few days, Stephen's been like steel," Jerry said.

Saturday morning, Jerry needed more oxygen, so Bob and I made a quick trip to Athens to get a full cylinder. When we got back, we found him anxious—worried because we'd been gone so long. For lunch, I fixed a Mexican cheese omelet, and Jerry ate well.

After lunch, we talked a while. At one point, Jerry caught me staring at him, and he smirked. Then he got up to get dressed. He called me, needing help. I guided the belt around his waist, loop through the loop, my arms encircling him—and then I lost control: "If you ever needed proof how much I love you, this is it," I cried, kneeling before him with the side of my face against the front of his trousers.

"I never needed any proof," he replied. I noticed that he was steadying himself by holding onto the edge of the lavatory. "Stephen," he said quietly, "this sentimentality leads nowhere."

I stood up to help him finish the job. Bob and I were going to Walmart to return some slippers I had bought for Jerry that turned out to be too small. Jerry walked with us out to Bob's car.

"Bye-bye, Stephen," I heard Jerry say.

I turned around and looked him in the eye.

"Bye-bye, Jerry," I replied.

Then Bob drove me away.

Hunt and Stephen Housewright in the Netherlands, 1993. Photographer unknown.

EDITORS

LAWRENCE KUMPF is the founder and Artistic Director of Blank Forms. He has curated exhibitions such as "Henning Christiansen: Freedom Is Around the Corner" (2018) at 55 Walker Street, New York; "Catherine Christer Hennix: Traversée du Fantasme" (2018) at Stedelijk Museum, Amsterdam; and "Open Plan: Cecil Taylor" (with Jay Sanders) at the Whitney Museum of American Art, New York (2016). He is the editor of the Blank Forms journal and of *Catherine Christer Hennix: Poësy Matters and Other Matters* (Blank Forms Editions, 2019).

TYLER MAXIN is the Communications and Special Projects Associate at Electronic Arts Intermix (EAI), New York. His writing has appeared in publications including *Artforum*, *BOMB*, and *Film Comment*.

CONTRIBUTORS

KRIS PAULSEN is an associate professor of the history of art and film studies at Ohio State University. She is the author of *Here/There: Telepresence, Touch, and Art at the Interface* (MIT Press, 2017) in addition to many articles and essays about early video, experimental television, and new media art.

GEORGE E. LEWIS is the Edwin H. Case Professor of American Music at Columbia University, New York. His compositions are performed worldwide and he is the author of *A Power Stronger Than Itself: The AACM and American Experimental Music* (University of Chicago Press, 2008) and co-editor, with Benjamin Piekut, of the two-volume *Oxford Handbook of Critical Improvisation Studies* (Oxford University Press, 2016). Lewis is a Fellow of the American Academy of Arts and Sciences and the American Academy of Arts and Letters, a Corresponding Fellow of the British Academy, a MacArthur Fellow (2002), and a Doris Duke Artist (2019), and he has received fellowships from the John Simon Guggenheim Memorial Foundation (2015) and others.

GORDON MONAHAN is a composer and sound artist living in Meaford, Ontario. He creates works for piano, loudspeakers, video, kinetic sculpture, and computer-controlled sound environments that span genres and format from avant-garde concert music to multimedia installation. His commissions have been presented by many institutions, including DAAD Inventionen Festival, Berlin; the Kitchen, New York; and London Contemporary Orchestra, UK; and most recently include a series of collaborative performance works with the dancer Bill Coleman.

GUY DE BIÈVRE is a composer, musician, theorist, and teacher from Brussels. He holds a PhD from the School of Arts at Brunel University London and has curated sound art shows across Belgium and the Netherlands. He is currently working on an authorized biography of composer and filmmaker Phill Niblock.

DAVID ROSENBOOM is a post-genre composer-performer-interdisciplinary artist whose wide ranging practices span solo performance, large ensembles, and immersive installations, among other emergent musical forms. He holds the Roy E. Disney Family Chair in Musical Composition at the California Institute of the Arts in Santa Clarita, where he was a dean for three decades, and he previously taught at York University in Toronto and Mills College in Oakland, California. His work uses interactive technologies, multicultural collaborations, artscience, and neuromusic, and has been presented internationally, including in major retrospectives at the Whitney Museum of American Art, New York; Centre Pompidou-Metz, France; and Tokyo Opera City.

KAREN FINLEY is an interdiscipliary artist and educator who performs, exhibits, and lectures worldwide. She holds an MFA from the San Francisco Art Institute and is the author of eight books, most recently *Grabbing Pussy* (OR Books, 2018). Finley is a professor in Art and Public Policy at Tisch School of the Arts, New York University.

Edited by Lawrence Kumpf and
  Tyler Maxin
Managing Editor: Ciarán Finlayson
Assistant Editors: Joe Bucciero,
  Lucy Flint
Copyeditors: Heather Holmes,
  Dana Kopel
Design: Alec Mapes-Frances
Interns: Parker Allen, Clarice Lee,
  Camila Santos Escamez, Guy Weltchek

Blank Forms Editions is supported by
the Andy Warhol Foundation for the
Visual Arts, the Robert Rauschenberg
Foundation, and Agnes Gund.

Blank Forms is a nonprofit
organization supporting emerging and
historically significant artists who
produce work across disciplines, often
rooted in traditions of experimental
and creative music. We aim to establish
new frameworks to preserve, nurture,
and present these artists' work and
to build platforms for practices
underrepresented in art's commercial,
institutional, and historical fields.
Blank Forms collaborates with
artists on commissions, exhibitions,
publications as well as archival and
estate projects within contemporary
cultural ecosystems and in perpetuity.
In presenting and documenting this
work, Blank Forms seeks to foster an
artistic community founded upon
engaged and equitable conversations
across continents, media, and
generations.

ISSN 2642-7052
ISBN 978-1-953691-09-5 (hardcover)
ISBN 978-1-953691-05-7 (paperback)

Unless otherwise noted, all images are
from the Jerry Hunt archive, courtesy
Stephen Housewright.

Printed by Ofset Yapımevi in Turkey

Blank Forms
468 Grand Avenue #3D
Brooklyn, NY 11238
blankforms.org